GUIDE TO FOOD STORAGE

Follow this guide for food storage, and you can be sure that what's in your freezer, refrigerator, and pantry is fresh-tasting and ready to use in recipes.

In the Freezer (at -10° to 0° F)

Dairy and Eggs

Cheese, hard	6 months
Cheese, soft	6 months
Egg substitute, unopened	1 year
Egg whites	1 year
Egg yolks	1 year
Ice cream, sherbet	1 month

Fruits and Vegetables

Commercially frozen fruits	1 year
Commercially frozen vegetables	8 to 12 months

Meats, Poultry, and Seafood

Beef, Lamb, Pork, and Veal

Chops, uncooked	4 to 6 months
Ground and stew meat, uncooked	3 to 4 months
Ham, fully cooked, half	1 to 2 months
Roasts, uncooked	4 to 12 months
Steaks, uncooked	6 to 12 months

Poultry

All cuts, cooked	4 months
Boneless or bone-in pieces, uncooked	9 months

Seafood

Fish, fatty, uncooked	2 to 3 months
Fish, lean, uncooked	6 months

In the Refrigerator (at 34° to 40° F)

Dairy and Eggs

Butter	1 to 3 months
Buttermilk	1 to 2 weeks
Cheese, hard, wedge, opened	6 months
Cheese, semihard, block, opened	3 to 4 weeks
Cream cheese, fat-free, light, and ⅓-less-fat	2 weeks
Egg substitute, opened	3 days
Fresh eggs in shell	3 to 5 weeks

Meats, Poultry, and Seafood

Beef, Lamb, Pork, and Veal

Ground and stew meat, uncooked	1 to 2 days
Roasts, uncooked	3 to 5 days
Steaks and chops, uncooked	3 to 5 days

Chicken, Turkey, and Seafood

All cuts, uncooked	1 to 2 days

Fruits and Vegetables

Apples, beets, cabbage, carrots, celery, citrus fruits, eggplant, and parsnips	2 to 3 weeks
Apricots, asparagus, berries, cauliflower, cucumbers, mushrooms, okra, peaches, pears, peas, peppers, plums, salad greens, and summer squash	2 to 4 days
Corn, husked	1 day

In the Pantry (keep these at room temperature for 6 to 12 months)

Baking and Cooking Staples

Baking powder
Biscuit and baking mixes
Broth, canned
Cooking spray
Honey
Mayonnaise, fat-free, low-fat, and light (unopened)
Milk, canned evaporated fat-free
Milk, nonfat dry powder
Mustard, prepared (unopened)
Oils, olive and vegetable
Pasta, dried
Peanut butter
Rice, instant and regular
Salad dressings, bottled (unopened)
Seasoning sauces, bottled
Tuna, canned

Fruits, Legumes, and Vegetables

Fruits, canned
Legumes (beans, lentils, peas), dried or canned
Tomato products, canned
Vegetables, canned

©2009 by Oxmoor House, Inc.
Book Division of Southern Progress Corporation
P. O. Box 2262, Birmingham, Alabama 35201-2262

ISBN-13: 978-0-8487-3284-4
ISBN-10: 0-8487-3284-7
ISSN: 1526-1565
Printed in the United States of America
First Printing 2009

Be sure to check with your health-care provider before making any changes in your diet.
Weight Watchers and **POINTS** are registered trademarks of Weight Watchers International, Inc., and are used under license by Oxmoor House, Inc.

OXMOOR HOUSE, INC.
VP, Publishing Director: Jim Childs
Editorial Director: Susan Payne Dobbs
Brand Manager: Victoria Alfonso
Managing Editor: L. Amanda Owens

WEIGHT WATCHERS® ANNUAL RECIPES FOR SUCCESS 2010
Editors: Rachel Quinlivan, R.D.; Elizabeth J. Taliaferro
Project Editor: Diane Rose
Assistant Project Editor: Emily Chappell
Senior Designer: Emily Albright Parrish
Director, Test Kitchens: Elizabeth Tyler Austin
Assistant Director, Test Kitchens: Julie Christopher
Test Kitchens Professionals: Kathleen Royal Phillips, Catherine Crowell Steele,
    Ashley T. Strickland
Photography Director: Jim Bathie
Senior Photo Stylist: Kay E. Clarke
Associate Photo Stylist: Katherine Eckert Coyne
Production Manager: Theresa Beste-Farley

CONTRIBUTORS
Designer and Compositor: Carol O. Loria
Copy Editor: Dolores Hydock
Proofreader: Carmine Loper
Indexer: Mary Ann Laurens
Interns: Christine Taylor, Angela Valente
Menu Planner Editor: Carolyn Land Williams, M.Ed., R.D.
Recipe Development: Gretchen Feldtman Brown, R.D.; Jaime Harder Caldwell, M.A., R.D.; Maureen Callahan, R.D.;
    Nancy Hughes; Karen Levin; Alison Lewis; Deborah Snyder; Katherine Younger
Test Kitchens Professionals: Jane Chambliss Drennan, Deborah Wise
Nutritional Analyses: Kate Wheeler
Food Stylist: Ana Price Kelly
Photographer: Lee Harrelson

Cover: Rocky Road Brownie Sandwiches, page 48

WeightWatchers®
ANNUAL RECIPES *for* SUCCESS
2010

Oxmoor
House®

contents

Blender Gazpacho, *page 146*

Seared Scallops with Soy-Ginger Sauce, *page 72*

Coconut-Oat Cookies, *page 42*

Weight Watchers®
Annual Recipes for Success 2010

This new cookbook empowers you to make the right food choices every day. There's never been a better time to make a positive change for your health, and you can do it while still enjoying the foods you love. This book offers:

- An introduction to the Weight Watchers® Momentum™ program
- Nine truly inspiring weight-loss Success Stories from people just like you
- Over 275 great-tasting recipes that bring pleasure back to mealtime
- A **POINTS**® value per serving for every recipe
- Nutritional analysis with every recipe (see "About Our Recipes" on page 192)
- More than 35 color photographs of delicious recipes
- Step-by-step recipe instructions, prep and cook times, and secrets from our Test Kitchens
- Five Seasonal Menus, each with a Game Plan for preparing the meal to help you enjoy the fruits of each season
- Four weeks of 7-Day Menu Planners that incorporate many recipes from the cookbook plus some new ones, too

Our Favorite Recipes **All of our recipes** are rigorously tested to ensure ease of preparation and excellent taste. But some are a cut above the rest. Here are our favorites from this year. We hope you enjoy them just as much.

Turkey-Sausage Meatloaf, **POINTS** value per serving: 4 (page 98). A blend of Italian turkey sausage and turkey breast paired with pasta sauce ensures a satisfying weeknight meal.

Golden Onion and Dried-Fruit Crostini, **POINTS** value per serving: 2 (page 23). Melted Brie adds a hint of nuttiness to the savory-sweet layer atop crispy bread in this unique appetizer.

Orange Biscuits, **POINTS** value per serving: 4 (page 29). Fresh orange rind is used in both the biscuits and the sweet frosting to infuse these treats with a refreshing citrus taste.

Grouper with Pan-Roasted Tomatoes, *POINTS* value per serving: 4 *(page 66)*. The fresh, spicy zest of garlic and herbs and the sweetness of roasted cherry tomatoes enliven the grouper, creating a quick summer entrée.

Greek Steak Salad, *POINTS* value per serving: 4 *(page 109)*. This entrée highlights some of summer's freshest flavors, including tomatoes, cucumber, and mint. Thinly sliced flank steak lends itself nicely to this main-dish salad.

Salmon Burgers, *POINTS* value per serving: 7 *(page 113)*. A spicy combination of onions, hot sauce, kosher salt, and pepper added enough dynamic flavor to these substantially sized fresh salmon burgers to earn our Test Kitchens' highest rating.

Sweet Lime Summer Fruits, *POINTS* value per serving: 1 *(page 102)*. Refreshing lime and white grape juices add a breezy element to this pretty fruit salad. It works perfectly as a cool ending to a warm-weather lunch.

Butternut Squash and Leek Risotto, *POINTS* value per serving: 7 *(page 82)*. Aromatic leeks, warm butternut squash, and creamy Arborio rice come together in an extraordinary one-dish meal.

Apricot and Wasabi–Sauced Pork Tenderloin, *POINTS* value per serving: 4 *(page 90)*. Pungent Japanese horse-radish and sweet apricot preserves combine in a simple sauce that's drizzled over pork tenderloin for a memorable entrée.

Strawberry Frozen Yogurt, *POINTS* value per serving: 1 *(page 47)*. Fresh thyme sprigs contribute a whisper of lemon-mint that delights the taste buds in this distinctive dinner finale.

Poblano-Chicken Chowder, *POINTS* value per serving: 5 *(page 153)*. Chicken, potato, and mild poblano peppers are the base for this hearty chowder. A handful of cilantro added at the very end brightens the flavor.

Baked Apples with Toffee and Almonds, *POINTS* value per serving: 6 *(page 36)*. A buttery toffee-chocolate center is a surprise filling in this warm apple dessert. Cool whipped topping adds a creamy finish.

Weight Watchers® momentum™

One of the keys to successfully losing weight and keeping it off is a plan that is healthy, doesn't leave you feeling hungry or deprived, and is sustainable for a long time. That's why Weight Watchers introduced the Momentum™ program.

The Momentum™ program combines the latest in scientific research with successful aspects of previous Weight Watchers food plans. It teaches a more satisfying way of eating by guiding people toward healthy foods that help them feel satisfied longer so they can build the skills to achieve their goals and live healthier.

THE MOMENTUM™ PROGRAM HELPS YOU:

- Learn how to make smarter eating choices and stay satisfied longer with Filling Foods.
- Learn the benefits of tracking what you eat and drink in order to learn portion sizes and be in better control. Tracking what you eat is scientifically proven to be an effective tool to help weight loss.
    - Research shows that people tend to underestimate how much they eat. Tracking builds awareness, which helps reduce mindless eating.
    - You'll learn to use your body's signals to recognize satisfaction so that you know when to stop eating.
- Learn how to avoid emotional eating by listening to your body's hunger signals and assessing whether you're really hungry.
- Learn about the flexibility of the Weight Watchers **POINTS**® Weight-Loss System.

WHAT ARE FILLING FOODS?

Filling Foods are foods that have been scientifically proven to help keep you feeling satisfied longer. They are a central component of the Momentum™ program.

- They are lower in calories but contain a high percentage of water, fiber, and sometimes air.
- Members are encouraged to choose Filling Foods as part of their daily **POINTS** Target to keep hunger at bay. Examples of Filling Foods include:
    - Whole wheat pasta, brown rice, potatoes, and grains
    - Vegetables and fruits
    - Whole-grain cereals—without added sugar, nuts, or dried fruit
    - Lean meats, poultry, fish, eggs, beans, and meat substitutes such as tofu
    - Fat-free milk and milk products
    - Soups made with Filling Foods

If you're looking to achieve a healthy lifestyle, you can do it with the Momentum™ program—whether it's in the meeting room or online.

WEIGHT WATCHERS® MEETINGS

Support can be an important part of weight-loss success. Weight Watchers weekly meetings offer guidance and tools to help you stay motivated and achieve your weight-loss goals using the Momentum™ program. Meeting Leaders and other successful Weight Watchers members provide encouragement in a personal way. Members can share tips and tricks, and Leaders, who have already lost weight with Weight Watchers, share strategies on how to maintain a healthy lifestyle.

WEIGHT WATCHERS ONLINE

Weight Watchers also offers an effective online-only option at **www.weightwatchers.com**. Online subscribers have access to interactive weight-loss tools and expert tips as well as meal ideas, recipes, and other helpful strategies that are the cornerstone of the Momentum™ program.

KEY STATS AND FACTS

The new Weight Watchers Momentum™ program stays true to Weight Watchers core value: providing people with a scientifically proven, healthy, doable, livable way to lose weight. The Momentum™ program addresses member needs so they will stay satisfied while achieving a safe, healthy weight loss[1] with sustainable results.

- People who attend Weight Watchers meetings lose three times more weight than those who try to do it on their own.[II]

- Regular meeting attendance with Weight Watchers was significantly correlated with both weight loss and weight-loss maintenance.[III]
- Weight Watchers members who follow a plan that focuses on eating low-energy-density foods or one that emphasizes portion control show comparable significant decreases in caloric intake, along with significant improvements in body mass index and waist circumference.[IV]
- Keeping track of food intake can boost weight-loss success.[V]

[I] With Weight Watchers, members can expect to have a safe rate of weight loss—up to two pounds a week after the first three weeks (during which you could lose more).

[II] S Heshka, F Greenway, JW Anderson, RL Atkinson, FL Greenway, JO Hill, S Phinney, RL Kolotkin, K Miller-Kovach, X. Pi-Sunyer. "Weight Loss with Self-help Compared with a Structured Commercial program: a randomized controlled trial," *Journal of the American Medical Association* 2003; 289 (14): 1792-1798.

[III] S Heshka, F Greenway, JW Anderson, RL Atkinson, JO Hill, S Phinney, K Miller-Kovach, X. Pi-Sunyer. "Self-Help Weight Loss Versus a Structured Commercial program after 26 Weeks: a randomized controlled study," *Obesity Research* 1999; 7(S1): 19S.

[IV] V Nguyen, et al. "Evaluation of Weight-loss Diets on Glycemic Index, Glycemic Load, Body Mass Index and Insulin Resistance," *The FASEB Journal* 2007; 21(5): A694.

[V] Boutelle KN, Kirschenbaum DS. "Further support for consistent self-monitoring as a vital component of successful weight control." *Obes. Res.* 1998 May; 6(3): 219-24.

Too Much of a Good Thing

"Too much of anything is too much—even 'good,' healthy stuff!"

I had lost weight many times, only to regain it—and more. At my heaviest, I joined Weight Watchers® with my best friend and started following the *POINTS*® Weight-Loss System. I needed to lose almost 50 pounds and was certain I never would.

THE GOOD STUFF   I hadn't gained weight with "bad" foods; my portion sizes of "good" foods had been out of whack. It was life changing to realize that too much of anything is too much.

I began focusing on small, attainable weight-loss goals and enjoying those successes. Suddenly the weight loss was adding up.

PLATEAU CITY   Then I hit a major plateau. My weight stayed the same, no matter what. I changed what I ate, when I ate, and the exercise I did—and feared I would never reach my goal. Luckily, around that time, my sister also joined Weight Watchers, and her involvement remotivated me. I looked forward to sharing stories from the weekly meetings with her.

REACHING HER DESTINATION   When a fellow member committed to continuing to attend meetings, I decided these meetings would also continue to be a part of my life—regardless. At that moment, I stopped stressing and accepted. After that the weight seemed to fly off!

Now at my goal weight, it is a thrill as a tall woman to feel "tiny."

Catherine

AGE **26**   HEIGHT **5'9"**

WAS **210.8 lbs**   LOST **49.2 lbs***

WEIGHT **161.6 lbs**

AS OF **3/7/2009**

*Results Not Typical

When Catherine joined Weight Watchers, little did she know it would end her weight battle for good.

CATHERINE'S TIPS

- Familiarize yourself with the food options in the back of the Week 1 booklet.
- Get in a little exercise each day.
- Remember, it isn't about perfection; it's about persistence.

I'm an Inspiration!

*"Daily movement is the key
to maintaining weight loss."*

Susan

AGE **49**   HEIGHT **5'7"**

WAS **198.2 lbs**   LOST **42.8 lbs***

WEIGHT **155.4 lbs**

AS OF **4/15/2009**

*Results Not Typical

Susan used to think of the people in Weight Watchers success stories as everyday heroes—now she's one, too!

In my 30s and 40s, I was frustrated with my weight, spending a small fortune on diets and eating plans. Every New Year's resolution was to lose weight. Finally, at 45, I wanted to spend the second half of my life healthy and fit.

DAILY DILIGENCE   I joined Weight Watchers meetings and started following the ***POINTS***® Weight-Loss System. I kept a food journal and stuck to the plan. I chose healthier restaurants and watched my portions.

I now attend a body sculpting class three times a week, which really helps define my body. Daily movement is the key to maintaining weight loss, but it's no longer my excuse to eat anything I want.

I DESERVE IT!   I've always enjoyed WeightWatchers.com for the Success Stories. My heroes tend to be ordinary people who have done extraordinary things, and many can be found on the site. When I was asked to do a photo shoot in New York City, I felt so pampered and special.

A SHINING MOMENT   I have done so many things in my life that I'm proud of—getting married, having my son, earning bachelor's and master's degrees—but one of my proudest achievements was receiving my Weight Watchers gold key for Lifetime Membership. It was a moment I'll never forget!

SUSAN'S TIPS

- Do "mini" workouts throughout the day: stretching, parking far from stores, taking the stairs, etc.
- Enjoy treats in moderation.
- If you go off the plan, don't give up. Attend a meeting, weigh in, and start over!

Tomorrow Is Different

"Every day is still a challenge, but I have the tools to get through."

I never felt in control of my eating or comfortable with my body. Every day I vowed to get my eating under control. When I failed, I knew I needed help creating a healthier relationship with food.

JUMPING IN I joined Weight Watchers® and started following the **POINTS**® Weight-Loss System. I jumped right in and was fortunate to have endless support from friends and family.

I cruised to my initial 10-percent goal—then hit a plateau. Hovering for months within a five-pound range, I felt discouraged and embarrassed.

LETTING GO I tapped into three resources for success: commitment, belief, and patience. And my plateau forced me to make healthy adjustments. I consistently got the Good Health Guidelines into my meal plans. I hired a personal trainer who helped me add more strength training and really push myself.

MOVING AGAIN The scale began moving again! I encountered many challenges: I moved, got a new job and apartment, started a relationship, went on vacation, and enjoyed many family celebrations.

At goal, every day is still a challenge, but I have the tools to get through. With help from Weight Watchers, my tomorrow will be different!

Randi

AGE **36**   HEIGHT **5'4"**

WAS **175 lbs**   LOST **34 lbs***

WEIGHT **141 lbs**

AS OF **2/14/2009**

*Results Not Typical

This member turned a plateau into opportunity.

RANDI'S TIPS

- Wait 15 minutes to eat something you think you want. If you want it after that time, it's not a passing urge.
- When dining out, portions are huge, so make a habit of giving food away for people to taste.
- Use the Web site for inspiration and rely on the Community for helpful tips and great advice.

Coming Clean with Myself

"The hardest part of losing weight was learning how to manage special events successfully."

I was thin in my teens, so I didn't watch what I ate. Later, I gained weight because of poor eating habits and not exercising. Then I used pregnancy as an excuse to eat fast food, fried foods, and sweets—and gained 40-plus pounds with each pregnancy.

MAKING THE CHANGE After that, I was too busy to pay attention to what I ate. Eventually, I went over the mark I swore I'd never hit outside of pregnancy. I had to get under control.

Then a coworker told me I needed to join Weight Watchers with her, which jolted me into reality. I joined and started following the **POINTS**® Weight-Loss System.

The hardest part was learning how to manage special events successfully. I learned to plan, start with a big salad, and stop when I was comfortable but not full. I also started to play volleyball with the kids at family barbecues.

EVERYDAY STRATEGIES One past weakness was free food at the office. To take away temptation, I'd tell myself, "I don't know how long that's been out." That made it seem less appetizing!

I'm very competitive and wanted to beat that scale. So I'd say, "I'm not accepting any excuse—that thing is going down!" and set my goal to lose two pounds every week.

When my sister handed me a size 6 to try on, I swore it wouldn't fit—but it did! It was wonderful to finally reach my goal.

Sandra

AGE **45**   HEIGHT **5'8"**

WAS **211.8 lbs**   LOST **57.8 lbs***

WEIGHT **154 lbs**

AS OF **3/5/2009**

*Results Not Typical

Passing up free food and navigating celebrations got Sandra to goal.

TAKE-AWAY: SOCIALIZING ISN'T JUST ABOUT THE FOOD.

Focus on the social aspects of gatherings to become less caught up in mindless eating.

The Reluctant Dieter

"The new me is
way more energetic."

I had just lost my husband and was adjusting to raising two kids alone. So when a Weight Watchers meeting started up in my office, I paid no attention. But when coworkers joined, I reluctantly agreed to tag along.

MAKING UP FOR LOST TIME I started following the **POINTS**® Weight-Loss System, subscribing to Weight Watchers® eTools, and exercising. Within two months, I lost enough weight to keep me hooked.

I track my **POINTS** values and keep WeightWatchers.com up on my computer. I substitute lower-calorie versions of favorite foods or settle for smaller portions. If I really want something, I eat it and then work it off on the treadmill. Even restaurants aren't a challenge: I just zoom in on healthier menu items.

NEW ENERGY, NEW REWARDS The new me is way more energetic. But the best reward came with the make-over and photo shoot. Being treated like a model, dressing in great clothes, and meeting others who accomplished the same goal was like the greatest congratulations hug.

JUST ONE REGRET My only regret is that I didn't learn the value of healthy eating while my husband was alive. My consolation is that our kids will grow into strong and fit adults.

Audrey

AGE **39**   HEIGHT **5'7"**

WAS **263.8 lbs**   LOST **72.4 lbs***

WEIGHT **191.4 lbs**

AS OF **1/24/2009**

*Results Not Typical

This single mom thought she was happy at size 20. Now almost 75 pounds lighter,* she has only one regret: that she didn't change her ways while her husband was still alive.

AUDREY'S TIPS

- Portion control can be the hardest adjustment, but it's essential.
- Don't worry about the cost: You save enough by brown-bagging to more than offset the meeting fees.
- Sample tiny tastes of must-have foods to satisfy cravings.

Making a Difference

"I learned, and now help others learn, that it is possible to manage difficult situations."

As a child in Mexico, I was overweight and tormented. At 27, I settled in California, where the weight gain continued. Only after my doctor said I was obese did I get serious about losing weight. My husband told me about the Weight Watchers program. He knew it was the healthiest option for me.

SPEAKING OUT I started following the ***POINTS***® Weight-Loss System and lost weight. After becoming a Leader, members asked me to conduct meetings in Spanish—to address the needs of the community.

TAKING A CHANCE Uncertain whether we would have a following or not, my manager supported conducting meetings completely in Spanish. We started with 15 members. The following week there were 23—and now I lead five overflowing meetings per week.

For me and others who share my Mexican heritage, refusing calorie-laden dishes, like chiles rellenos, isn't just rejecting food; it's rejecting our culture. I learned, and now help others learn, that it is possible to manage difficult situations—and that portion control can go a long way in weight management.

I feel more attractive and have more energy than ever! Being overweight overshadowed many accomplishments in my life. With the weight off, I'm living life to my fullest potential.

Claudia

AGE **40** HEIGHT **5'5"**

WAS **192 lbs** LOST **58.6 lbs***

WEIGHT **133.4 lbs**

AS OF **2/10/2009**

*Results Not Typical

This dynamic Leader started Spanish-speaking meetings across the country.

CLAUDIA'S TIPS

- Exercise first thing in the morning or as soon as you get home.
- Take advantage of the support offered at the meetings and stay focused on your weight-loss goals.
- List the reasons you want to maintain a healthy weight and review them daily.

Lisa "Lite"

*"If I gain even five pounds,
I get back on track."*

Lisa

AGE **49**   HEIGHT **5'10"**

WAS **339.6 lbs**   LOST **160.6 lbs***

WEIGHT **179 lbs**

AS OF **5/16/2009**

*Results Not Typical

Since learning about portion control, Lisa no longer struggles with overeating.

At around age 10, I gained weight rapidly because I loved to eat—especially junk food. Being athletic helped me keep obesity at bay even as I got heavier. As an adolescent, I began years of yo-yo dieting.

WAITING FOR AN ANSWER   As my weight continued to increase, it took a toll on my body: I developed weak knees and an aching back. In 1997 as I listened to a sermon about having faith, I knew my prayer to be healthy would be answered. Then when my grandson was born, I wanted to be able to run, play ball, and ride bikes with him.

A NEIGHBOR'S NUDGE   I started walking with a neighbor and noticed that she was losing weight. She said she was going to a Weight Watchers® meeting nearby. She encouraged me to check WeightWatchers.com for a meeting near my office. I joined and started following the **POINTS**® Weight-Loss System.

DISCIPLINE, NOT DEPRIVATION   I learned how to control portions. I don't allow myself to feel deprived; if I really want something, I have it. I count **POINTS** values, write down what I eat, and stay on the plan.

If I gain even five pounds, I get back on track. I never want to have to worry about losing 160 pounds* again!

LISA'S TIPS

- The key to satisfying snacking is variety. Try combinations of fruits, nuts, and vegetables.
- Talk to other members about their journeys and struggles.
- Dining out shouldn't be impossible, as long as you're committed to making healthy choices.

Reaping the Rewards

"I'm grateful for the weekly meetings that encourage us to love and respect ourselves more, celebrate achievements, and find rewards other than food."

As a kid, I was larger than other children and teased incessantly. But if I wanted something to eat, my mom would get it; whatever she cooked was served in big portions.

THE BACKGROUND STORY From college on, I was the jolly fat guy of the group: entertaining, energetic, and able to drink large quantities of alcohol. But inside, I was confined to a private world in which I felt undesirable.

WAKE-UP CALL When I had to wear size 56 corduroy pants to a wedding reception, I knew I was large—even for me. I joined Weight Watchers the next day and started following the **POINTS**® Weight-Loss System. When the scale said 413.4 pounds, I practically cried.

I knew most weight-loss programs don't work because people don't stick to them. So I'm grateful for the weekly meetings that encourage us to love and respect ourselves, celebrate achievements, and find rewards other than food.

NEW MAN I changed my lifestyle and am happy with my progress and what I've accomplished. I still have 40 pounds or so to get to my goal, but I'll have doctors make sure the number on the scale is right for me. If it is, I'll stop there; if not, I'll go until I'm definitely healthy.

William

AGE **33** HEIGHT **6'1"**

WAS **413.4 lbs** LOST **176.4 lbs***

WEIGHT **237 lbs**

AS OF **5/28/2009**

*Results Not Typical

William is taking time to enjoy things he only dreamed of doing.

WILLIAM'S TIPS

- Eat veggies and fruit; avoid refined foods.
- If a sweet tooth flares up, eat fruit or a low-calorie fudge bar.
- Chart your progress along the way.

From Husky to Marathon Runner

"I used to come home every night and sit and watch TV—and eat."

As a kid, I'd "snack" in front of the TV after school. I hated shopping for clothes because none of the pants in the kids' section fit. After college, I tried to lose weight—but it never lasted.

HEALTH CONCERN   In 2005, I discovered I had high blood pressure, high cholesterol, and the onset of adult diabetes. Before prescribing medication, my doctor wanted me to lose weight. I lost 25 pounds, but it wasn't enough. I told a friend I was depressed about having to take pills for all my health problems. He said his mom was encouraging him to join Weight Watchers®—so we went together.

I started focusing on better food choices. Now I keep fruit on the counter, veggies in the fridge, low-fat crackers in my car, and healthy snacks at my office. Instead of watching TV, my partner and I walk after dinner.

NEW BEGINNING   I started power walking, lifting light weights, and doing Pilates and other muscle-toning exercises. I counted my steps, aiming for 10,000 a day. I ran and walked 15 minutes daily on the treadmill—and, gradually, went longer. Eventually, I ran all 26.2 miles of the Miami Marathon!

After my last physical, the doctor said there was no evidence of high blood pressure, high cholesterol, adult-onset diabetes—nothing! I never saw myself as an athlete before—now I do.

Carlos

AGE **40**   HEIGHT **5'7"**

WAS **228 lbs**   LOST **56.8 lbs***

WEIGHT **171.2 lbs**

AS OF **8/27/2009**

*Results Not Typical

Carlos overcame emotional eating habits and went on to run the Miami Marathon.

TAKE-AWAY: PUSH OUT OF YOUR COMFORT ZONE.

Try new activities you wouldn't have attempted when heavier. Discovering how much you enjoy new experiences will bolster your resolve.

appetizers & beverages

Texas Caviar, *page 19*

PB AND HONEY DIP

POINTS value: 2

PREP: 5 minutes

Silken tofu is the secret ingredient that adds creaminess and soy protein to this tasty dip. Serve with apple wedges or as a spread for bagels or toast.

- ½ cup natural-style creamy peanut butter (such as Smucker's)
- ½ cup silken tofu (about 4½ ounces)
- 3 tablespoons honey
- 1 tablespoon fresh lime juice
- ⅛ teaspoon ground cinnamon

1. Place all ingredients in a blender; process until smooth. Refrigerate in an airtight container for up to 1 week. YIELD: 16 SERVINGS (SERVING SIZE: 1 TABLESPOON).

PER SERVING: CAL 70 (54% from fat); FAT 4.2g (sat 0.7g); PRO 2.6g; CARB 5.1g; FIB 0.5g; CHOL 0mg; IRON 0.1mg; SOD 33mg; CALC 3mg

NATURAL PEANUT BUTTER

Natural peanut butter has a layer of oil on top that needs to be stirred back into the peanut butter before using. Although not as creamy as regular peanut butter, natural peanut butter is a healthier option because it doesn't contain trans fat, and it's high in monounsaturated fat.

ROASTED RED PEPPER AND SUN-DRIED TOMATO DIP

POINTS value: 1

PREP: 8 minutes

Pat the sun-dried tomatoes well with paper towels to remove excess oil before chopping. Serve this creamy dip with baked pita chips or raw vegetables.

- 1 cup bottled roasted red bell peppers
- 1 cup chopped drained oil-packed sun-dried tomatoes
- 1 (8-ounce) block fat-free cream cheese
- ⅓ cup (1¼ ounces) crumbled feta cheese
- 2 tablespoons light mayonnaise
- 1 tablespoon chopped fresh parsley
- 2 garlic cloves, halved
- ½ teaspoon black pepper
- ¼ teaspoon salt

1. Place all ingredients in a food processor; process until blended and desired consistency. Refrigerate, covered, until ready to serve. YIELD: 17 SERVINGS (SERVING SIZE: 2 TABLESPOONS).

PER SERVING: CAL 39 (46% from fat); FAT 2g (sat 0.7g); PRO 2.7g; CARB 3.2g; FIB 0.4g; CHOL 4mg; IRON 0.2mg; SOD 206mg; CALC 43mg

MEDITERRANEAN SPREAD ON MELBA TOASTS

POINTS value: 2

PREP: 13 minutes ■ **OTHER:** 1 hour

You can prepare and refrigerate this spread up to 2 days in advance. Then, assemble the appetizers just before serving your guests.

- 1 cup (8 ounces) tub-style ⅓-less-fat cream cheese, softened
- ½ cup chopped bottled roasted red bell peppers
- ¼ cup chopped pitted kalamata olives
- ¼ cup chopped fresh basil
- ¼ cup (1 ounce) grated fresh Romano cheese
- 1 garlic clove, minced
- 28 whole-grain melba toasts

1. Combine first 6 ingredients in a medium bowl; stir well. Cover and chill at least 1 hour.
2. Spread 1 tablespoon cream cheese mixture over each toast. YIELD: 14 SERVINGS (SERVING SIZE: 2 TOASTS).

PER SERVING: CAL 94 (47% from fat); FAT 4.9g (sat 2.7g); PRO 3.7g; CARB 8.9g; FIB 0.8g; CHOL 13mg; IRON 0.5mg; SOD 239mg; CALC 37mg

STRAWBERRY-PEAR PICKLED GINGER SALSA

POINTS value: 0

PREP: 15 minutes

This colorful salsa pairs nicely with gingersnaps or cinnamon-sugar pita chips, and it also livens up grilled chicken, fish, or pork. A ¼-cup serving has a ***POINTS*** value of 1.

- 1½ cups finely chopped strawberries
- 1 cup finely chopped peeled pear (about 1 medium)
- 1 tablespoon "measures-like-sugar" calorie-free sweetener (such as Splenda)
- 3 tablespoons finely chopped red onion
- 2 tablespoons finely chopped pickled ginger
- 1½ teaspoons grated fresh orange rind

1. Combine all ingredients in a medium bowl. Serve immediately. **YIELD: 10 SERVINGS (SERVING SIZE: 2 TABLESPOONS).**

PER SERVING: CAL 23 (4% from fat); FAT 0.1g (sat 0g); PRO 0.3g; CARB 5.6g; FIB 1.2g; CHOL 0mg; IRON 0.2mg; SOD 21mg; CALC 8mg

TEXAS CAVIAR

POINTS value: 0   *pictured on page 49*

                              PREP: 9 minutes ■ OTHER: 2 hours

This recipe is a crowd pleaser that's perfect for game day. Serve with light tortilla scoops or red bell pepper wedges.

- 1 (14-ounce) can black-eyed peas, rinsed and drained
- ½ cup chopped red bell pepper
- ½ cup thinly sliced green onions
- ½ cup refrigerated fresh salsa
- ½ cup chopped fresh cilantro
- 1 garlic clove, minced
- 1 tablespoon fresh lime juice
- 1 teaspoon dried oregano

1. Combine all ingredients in a medium bowl; stir until well blended. Cover and chill at least 2 hours or up to 8 hours. **YIELD: 10 SERVINGS (SERVING SIZE: ¼ CUP).**

PER SERVING: CAL 28 (0% from fat); FAT 0g (sat 0g); PRO 1.1g; CARB 5.2g; FIB 1.2g; CHOL 0mg; IRON 0.5mg; SOD 110mg; CALC 12mg

ITALIAN CRISPS

POINTS value: 1

                              PREP: 7 minutes ■ COOK: 9 minutes

This crunchy appetizer comes together in minutes and is simple enough to assemble while friends gather in the kitchen.

- 12 wonton wrappers
- Cooking spray
- ¼ cup commercial pesto
- 2 plum tomatoes, diced
- ⅓ cup (1¼ ounces) grated fresh Parmesan cheese

1. Preheat oven to 400°.
2. Cut wonton wrappers in half diagonally to form triangles. Place in a single layer on a baking sheet coated with cooking spray. Spray triangles with cooking spray. Bake at 400° for 6 minutes or until lightly browned.

3. Brush pesto evenly over crisps. Top evenly with tomato and cheese. Bake an additional 3 minutes or until cheese melts. Serve immediately. **YIELD: 24 SERVINGS (SERVING SIZE: 1 CRISP).**

PER SERVING: CAL 32 (48% from fat); FAT 1.7g (sat 0.4g); PRO 1.4g; CARB 2.8g; FIB 0.2g; CHOL 2mg; IRON 0.2mg; SOD 74mg; CALC 31mg

MASALA PUMPKIN SEEDS

POINTS value: 2

                              PREP: 1 minute ■ COOK: 5 minutes

This snack is made in a skillet using an Indian spice blend similar to curry powder called garam masala. The seeds double as a spicy garnish for simple salads or soups.

- ½ teaspoon canola oil
- 1 cup raw pumpkin seeds (such as Woodstock Farms)
- ¾ teaspoon salt-free garam masala (such as Frontier)
- ¼ teaspoon kosher salt
- ¼ teaspoon ground cumin
- Dash of ground red pepper

1. Heat a cast-iron skillet over medium heat until hot; add oil. Stir in pumpkin seeds.
2. Cook 4 minutes or until seeds are golden and begin to pop, stirring frequently. Cook, stirring constantly, 1 to 2 minutes or until most of the seeds are lightly browned. Remove from heat; stir in garam masala and remaining ingredients. **YIELD: 16 SERVINGS (SERVING SIZE: 1 TABLESPOON).**

PER SERVING: CAL 65 (76% from fat); FAT 5.5g (sat 0.9g); PRO 2.7g; CARB 1.4g; FIB 0.4g; CHOL 0mg; IRON 0.9mg; SOD 31mg; CALC 1mg

GARAM MASALA

Garam masala is a popular Indian spice blend that literally means "hot spice." Instead of being "hot" like chiles, this blend deepens the overall flavor profile of meats and vegetables. Unlike most spices, garam masala is usually added at the end of cooking to maintain its rich aroma. Store any unused garam masala in an airtight container in the freezer for up to 6 months.

WARM STUFFED DATES WITH PANCETTA

POINTS value: 3

PREP: 14 minutes ■ COOK: 5 minutes

Medjool dates are larger, softer, and sweeter than ordinary dates. Look for them in specialty grocery stores in the produce department or with other dried fruits at larger supermarkets.

  1 (3-ounce) goat cheese log
  1 teaspoon chopped fresh rosemary (optional)
 20 whole pitted Medjool dates
  1 ounce thinly sliced pancetta, cut into ¾-inch strips

1. Preheat broiler.
2. Combine goat cheese and rosemary, if desired. Spoon 1 rounded teaspoon of goat cheese mixture into each date. Wrap each date with a strip of pancetta.
3. Place wrapped dates on a baking sheet lined with foil; broil 5 minutes or until pancetta is crisp and cheese begins to melt. Serve warm or at room temperature. YIELD: 10 SERVINGS (SERVING SIZE: 2 STUFFED DATES).

PER SERVING: CAL 174 (18% from fat); FAT 3.5g (sat 2.2g); PRO 3.1g; CARB 36.2g; FIB 3.2g; CHOL 9mg; IRON 0.6mg; SOD 91mg; CALC 56mg

SWEET POTATO SQUARES WITH BOURBON-MAPLE GLAZE

POINTS value: 1

PREP: 24 minutes ■ COOK: 34 minutes

The unmistakable flavor created by quickly baking the sweet potatoes at a high temperature gives this appetizer a caramelized, salty, sweet flavor. The recipe received one of our highest ratings.

  2 large sweet potatoes (about 2 pounds)
  1 tablespoon olive oil
  ½ teaspoon black pepper
  ¼ teaspoon salt
  ½ cup maple syrup
  2 tablespoons brown sugar
  3 tablespoons bourbon
  ½ teaspoon ground ginger
  ½ teaspoon ground allspice
Cooking spray
  7 ounces smoked turkey sausage, cut into 32 slices

1. Preheat oven to 450°.
2. Peel sweet potatoes, and cut into 32 (1-inch) cubes. Discard any remaining sweet potato. Toss sweet potato cubes with oil, pepper, and salt in a broiler or roasting pan. Bake at 450° for 20 minutes, turning once after 10 minutes.
3. Combine syrup, brown sugar, and bourbon in a small saucepan; bring to a boil. Reduce heat, and simmer 6 minutes or until slightly thick. Remove from heat, and stir in ginger and allspice; cool slightly.
4. Heat a large nonstick skillet over medium-high heat. Coat pan with cooking spray. Add sausage, and cook 4 minutes on 1 side; turn slices, and cook 2 minutes or until lightly browned.
5. Place 1 sausage slice on top of 1 sweet potato cube; secure with a wooden pick. Repeat procedure with remaining sausage and sweet potato. Place skewers on a serving plate, and drizzle with maple glaze. YIELD: 32 SERVINGS (SERVING SIZE: 1 SAUSAGE SLICE, 1 SWEET POTATO CUBE, AND ABOUT ½ TEASPOON GLAZE).

PER SERVING: CAL 56 (11% from fat); FAT 0.7g (sat 0.2g); PRO 1.2g; CARB 10.3g; FIB 0.9g; CHOL 3mg; IRON 0.3mg; SOD 88mg; CALC 15mg

JERK FRENCH FRIES WITH PINEAPPLE AÏOLI

POINTS value: 3   *pictured on page 50*

PREP: 24 minutes ■ COOK: 30 minutes

These fries are crisp and spicy. A sweet pineapple aïoli made from purchased mayonnaise helps tame the heat.

 1¼ pounds baking potatoes (about 2 large)
  1 tablespoon olive oil
  1 teaspoon Caribbean jerk seasoning (such as McCormick)
  ½ teaspoon dried thyme
  ¼ teaspoon kosher salt
Cooking spray
  1 (8-ounce) can crushed pineapple, drained
  ⅓ cup light mayonnaise
  1 large garlic clove, minced

1. Preheat oven to 450°.
2. Wash potatoes and pat dry. Cut potatoes lengthwise into ¼-inch-thick slices. Stack slices, and cut lengthwise into ¼-inch strips. Place potato in a bowl, and drizzle with oil. Combine jerk seasoning, thyme, and salt; sprinkle over potato, tossing to coat.
3. Arrange potato in a single layer on a baking sheet coated with cooking spray. Bake at 450° for 20 minutes; stir gently, and bake an additional 10 minutes or until golden and crispy.

4. While potato bakes, combine crushed pineapple, mayonnaise, and garlic in a small bowl.

5. Remove fries from pan; serve with aïoli. YIELD: 6 SERVINGS (SERVING SIZE: ABOUT ¾ CUP FRIES AND ABOUT 2 TABLESPOONS AÏOLI).

Variation: If you prefer softer, thicker fries, cut them into ⅓-inch strips.

PER SERVING: CAL 156 (40% from fat); FAT 6.9g (sat 1.1g); PRO 2.3g; CARB 22.5g; FIB 1.6g; CHOL 5mg; IRON 1mg; SOD 239mg; CALC 23mg

JERK SEASONING

Jamaicans invented jerk seasoning for a practical reason: meat preservation. Today, however, this seasoning works well in adding a kick to any recipe, especially ones that include chicken and other meats. The basic ingredients of this traditional seasoning are allspice, Scotch bonnet peppers (one of the world's hottest peppers), and thyme.

CHIPOTLE SHRIMP AND OLIVE NACHOS

POINTS value: 2

PREP: 7 minutes ■ COOK: 3 minutes

If you'd like, use 1 cup chopped cooked chicken instead of the shrimp.

- ½ pound medium shrimp, cooked, peeled, and chopped
- ¼ cup sliced ripe olives
- 2 teaspoons chipotle hot pepper sauce
- 12 baked tortilla chips (such as Tostitos All-Natural)
- ¼ cup (1 ounce) preshredded reduced-fat 4-cheese Mexican blend cheese
- 2 tablespoons chopped fresh cilantro

1. Preheat oven to 400°.

2. Combine shrimp, olives, and pepper sauce in a small bowl. Arrange chips in a single layer on a baking sheet lined with foil. Spoon shrimp mixture evenly on chips; sprinkle evenly with cheese.

3. Bake at 400° for 3 to 4 minutes or until cheese melts. Sprinkle with cilantro just before serving. YIELD: 6 SERVINGS (SERVING SIZE: 2 NACHOS).

PER SERVING: CAL 89 (38% from fat); FAT 3.8g (sat 0.7g); PRO 7g; CARB 6.7g; FIB 0.4g; CHOL 48mg; IRON 0.8mg; SOD 206mg; CALC 48mg

CRAB AND HORSERADISH CUCUMBER CUPS

POINTS value: 1

PREP: 16 minutes ■ OTHER: 45 minutes

If your only option for purchasing lump crabmeat is a 16-ounce container, here is a simple idea to enjoy the 8 ounces not used in this recipe. Toss the excess crabmeat with avocado chunks, diced tomatoes, and minced green onions. Spoon the mixture onto a bed of greens; serve with bottled low-fat vinaigrette.

- 2 tablespoons light mayonnaise
- 2 tablespoons tub-style light cream cheese
- 1 tablespoon prepared horseradish
- 1 teaspoon fresh lemon juice
- ½ teaspoon salt
- ⅛ teaspoon ground red pepper
- ½ pound lump crabmeat, shell pieces removed
- 1 large English cucumber (about 1 pound)
- Paprika (optional)
- 2 tablespoons chopped fresh chives

1. Combine mayonnaise and next 5 ingredients in a medium bowl; gently stir in crabmeat. Cover and chill at least 30 minutes.

2. While crabmeat mixture chills, score cucumber lengthwise with tines of a fork. Cut crosswise into 24 (½-inch-thick) slices. Scoop out centers of cucumbers with a melon baller, being careful not to cut all the way through slice. Place cucumber slices, hollow sides down, on a paper towel; let stand 15 minutes.

3. Spoon crabmeat mixture into cucumber cups. Sprinkle with paprika, if desired, and top evenly with chives. YIELD: 12 SERVINGS (SERVING SIZE: 2 CUCUMBER CUPS).

PER SERVING: CAL 35 (39% from fat); FAT 1.5g (sat 0.5g); PRO 3.7g; CARB 1.6g; FIB 0.4g; CHOL 16mg; IRON 0.2mg; SOD 186mg; CALC 25mg

SUMMER SQUASH PIZZA

POINTS value: 2

PREP: 37 minutes ▪ COOK: 20 minutes
▪ OTHER: 1 hour and 5 minutes

1 package dry yeast (about 2¼ teaspoons)
1 teaspoon sugar
¾ cup warm water (100° to 110°)
2¼ cups all-purpose flour, divided
1 teaspoon salt, divided
Cooking spray
1½ cups shredded zucchini (1 medium)
1 cup shredded yellow squash (1 large)
¼ cup thinly sliced red onion
½ cup (2 ounces) grated fresh pecorino Romano cheese
¼ teaspoon freshly ground black pepper

1. Dissolve yeast and sugar in warm water in a large bowl; let stand 5 minutes.
2. Lightly spoon flour into dry measuring cups; level with a knife. Add 2 cups flour and ½ teaspoon salt to yeast mixture; beat with a mixer at medium speed until smooth. Turn dough out onto a floured surface. Knead until smooth and elastic (about 10 minutes); add enough of remaining ¼ cup flour, 1 tablespoon at a time, to prevent dough from sticking to hands (dough will feel sticky).
3. Place dough in a large bowl coated with cooking spray, turning to coat top. Cover and let rise in a warm place (85°), free from drafts, 1 hour or until doubled in size. (Gently press two fingers into dough. If indentation remains, dough has risen enough).
4. While dough rises, place zucchini and yellow squash in a colander; sprinkle with remaining ½ teaspoon salt. Toss well. Drain 1 hour.
5. Preheat oven to 450°.
6. Lightly coat hands with cooking spray. Gently press dough into a baking sheet coated with cooking spray. Bake dough at 450° for 8 minutes; remove from oven.
7. Squeeze excess liquid from zucchini and yellow squash. Sprinkle vegetable mixture and onion evenly over crust. Top with cheese; sprinkle evenly with pepper.
8. Bake at 450° for 12 minutes or until edges are browned. Cut into squares. YIELD: 16 SERVINGS (SERVING SIZE: 1 SQUARE).

Note: Substitute 1 (11-ounce) can refrigerated thin crust pizza dough for the homemade pizza dough, if desired. Follow package directions for prebaking dough.

PER SERVING: CAL 86 (12% from fat); FAT 1.1g (sat 0.7g); PRO 3.3g; CARB 15.2g; FIB 1g; CHOL 2mg; IRON 1mg; SOD 205mg; CALC 52mg

SMOKED SALMON–WRAPPED STUFFED OLIVES

POINTS value: 1

PREP: 20 minutes

⅓ cup (2½ ounces) tub-style light cream cheese, softened
2 teaspoons chopped fresh dill
¼ teaspoon freshly ground black pepper
14 super colossal–sized pitted ripe olives (such as Lindsay)
2 ounces sliced smoked salmon
14 decorative cocktail picks

1. Combine first 3 ingredients in a small bowl, stirring until smooth. Spoon cheese mixture into a heavy-duty zip-top plastic bag. Seal bag, removing as much air as possible. Snip a small hole in 1 corner of bag; squeeze filling evenly into olives.
2. Cut salmon slices into 3¼ x ½–inch strips. Wrap each olive with a salmon strip; secure with a cocktail pick. YIELD: 14 SERVINGS (SERVING SIZE: 1 STUFFED OLIVE).

PER SERVING: CAL 30 (66% from fat); FAT 2.2g (sat 0.8g); PRO 1.5g; CARB 1.3g; FIB 0.4g; CHOL 4mg; IRON 0.5mg; SOD 195mg; CALC 22mg

QUICK CRANBERRY AND GOAT CHEESE APPETIZERS

POINTS value: 2

PREP: 14 minutes ▪ COOK: 8 minutes
▪ OTHER: 40 minutes

1 cup fresh cranberries
1 small jalapeño pepper, seeded
½ cup currant jelly
⅛ teaspoon ground cloves
⅓ cup (1¼ ounces) crumbled goat cheese
⅓ cup (2½ ounces) tub-style light cream cheese
24 whole-grain melba toasts

1. Combine first 4 ingredients in a food processor; pulse 6 times or until finely chopped. Transfer mixture to a medium-sized heavy skillet. Bring to a boil over high heat; reduce heat, and simmer 6 minutes or until thick, stirring frequently. Remove from heat, and chill 40 minutes or to room temperature.

2. While cranberry mixture cools, combine goat cheese and cream cheese in a medium bowl; beat with a mixer at medium speed until smooth.

3. Spread about 1½ teaspoons cheese mixture onto each melba toast; top with 1½ teaspoons cranberry mixture. YIELD: 12 SERVINGS (SERVING SIZE: 2 TOASTS).

PER SERVING: CAL 107 (22% from fat); FAT 2.6g (sat 1.6g); PRO 3.3g; CARB 17.9g; FIB 1.1g; CHOL 7mg; IRON 0.6mg; SOD 138mg; CALC 27mg

KALAMATA AND HERB CHEESE MINI PHYLLOS

POINTS value: 3

PREP: 16 minutes

Tangy Greek kalamata olives and creamy herb-flavored cheese make an irresistible filling for prepared phyllo shells. Topped with fresh basil and tomatoes, these pretty mini appetizers received one of our Test Kitchens' highest ratings.

    15 pitted kalamata olives, divided
    ⅓ cup light garlic-and-herbs spreadable cheese (such as Alouette light)
    1 (2.1-ounce) package mini phyllo shells (such as Athens)
    3 tablespoons chopped fresh basil
    6 grape tomatoes, finely chopped

1. Cut 4 olives lengthwise into 4 wedges each; reserve 15 wedges. Finely chop remaining olive wedge and remaining 11 olives.

2. Combine chopped olives and cheese, stirring well. Spoon about 1 rounded teaspoon cheese mixture into each phyllo shell.

3. Top cheese mixture evenly with basil and tomato. Garnish stuffed shell with reserved olive wedges. YIELD: 5 SERVINGS (SERVING SIZE: 3 APPETIZERS).

PER SERVING: CAL 115 (64% from fat); FAT 8.2g (sat 2g); PRO 1.5g; CARB 8.6g; FIB 0.4g; CHOL 11mg; IRON 0.8mg; SOD 286mg; CALC 18mg

GOLDEN ONION, BRIE, AND DRIED-FRUIT CROSTINI

POINTS value: 2   pictured on page 51

PREP: 7 minutes ■ COOK: 31 minutes
■ OTHER: 30 minutes

    1 cup dried fruit bits (such as Sun-Maid)
    ½ cup apricot nectar
    ¼ cup golden raisins
    2 tablespoons honey
    2 tablespoons water
    5 ounces Brie cheese
    1 tablespoon olive oil
    2 cups coarsely chopped sweet onion (about 1 medium)
    2 tablespoons white balsamic vinegar
    20 (¼-inch-thick) slices diagonally cut French bread baguette
Chopped fresh chives (optional)

1. Combine fruit bits and next 4 ingredients in a small saucepan; bring to a boil. Reduce heat, and simmer 7 minutes. Cover, remove from heat, and let stand 30 minutes.

2. Place cheese in freezer for about 20 minutes or until firm. Cut cheese into ¼-inch cubes.

3. Heat olive oil in a large nonstick skillet over medium heat. Add onion, and cook 10 minutes or until onion is golden, stirring occasionally. Add vinegar, and cook 1 minute. Remove from heat, and cool completely.

4. Preheat oven to 400°.

5. Place baguette slices on a large baking sheet lined with foil. Bake at 400° for 10 minutes or until lightly toasted, turning after 5 minutes. Cool.

6. Add fruit mixture and cubed cheese to onion mixture; stir gently. Top each baguette slice evenly with fruit mixture. Bake at 400° for 3 minutes or until cheese melts. Sprinkle with chives, if desired. Serve immediately. YIELD: 20 APPETIZERS (SERVING SIZE: 1 BREAD SLICE AND ABOUT 1½ TABLESPOONS ONION MIXTURE).

PER SERVING: CAL 118 (28% from fat); FAT 3.7g (sat 1.6g); PRO 2.8g; CARB 19.1g; FIB 1.4g; CHOL 7mg; IRON 0.5mg; SOD 96mg; CALC 24mg

APRICOT NECTAR

Apricot nectar is a mix of apricot juice, sugar, and water. This sweet liquid contains a lot of sugar, but it also provides a large amount of vitamin A and, if you purchase the kind with added ascorbic acid, a very high level of vitamin C.

SMOKED TROUT–POTATO CANAPÉS

POINTS value: 1

PREP: 13 minutes

If you prefer, you can substitute smoked salmon or tuna in place of the trout.

- 4 ounces smoked trout, flaked
- 3 tablespoons fat-free sour cream
- 1 tablespoon prepared horseradish
- 3 tablespoons chopped fresh chives, divided
- 48 unsalted kettle-style potato chips (such as Kettle)

1. Combine trout, sour cream, horseradish, and 2 tablespoons chives in a small bowl. Spoon 1 teaspoon trout mixture onto each potato chip. Sprinkle evenly with remaining 1 tablespoon chives. Serve immediately. **YIELD: 24 SERVINGS (SERVING SIZE: 2 CANAPÉS).**

PER SERVING: CAL 34 (48% from fat); FAT 1.8g (sat 0.3g); PRO 1.7g; CARB 2.9g; FIB 0.3g; CHOL 4mg; IRON 0mg; SOD 4mg; CALC 4mg

SHRIMP-ARUGULA DUMPLINGS

POINTS value: 1

PREP: 20 minutes ■ **COOK:** 32 minutes

To make ahead, place assembled but uncooked dumplings in a single layer on a cornstarch-dusted platter, and cover with plastic wrap. Refrigerate up to 4 hours before cooking.

- ½ pound peeled medium shrimp
- 2 cups arugula or trimmed watercress
- 1 small shallot, peeled
- ¼ cup low-sodium soy sauce, divided
- 2 tablespoons rice vinegar, divided
- ¼ teaspoon black pepper
- ⅛ teaspoon salt
- 20 wonton wrappers
- 3 cups water
- Cooking spray
- 1 teaspoon grated peeled fresh ginger

1. Combine shrimp, arugula, shallot, 2 tablespoons soy sauce, 1½ tablespoons vinegar, pepper, and salt in a food processor; process 20 seconds or until smooth.
2. Working with 1 wonton wrapper at a time (cover remaining wrappers with a damp towel to keep them from drying), spoon 1 tablespoon shrimp mixture into center of wrapper. Moisten edges of wrapper with water; bring opposite corners to center, pinching points to seal. Bring remaining 2 corners to center,

pinching points to seal. Pinch 4 edges together to seal. Place wonton, seam side up, on a platter, and cover with plastic wrap. Repeat procedure with remaining wonton wrappers and shrimp mixture to form 20 wontons.
3. Bring 3 cups water to a boil in a 4-quart Dutch oven.
4. Place a collapsible steamer basket in pan; coat with cooking spray. Arrange enough wontons to form a single layer on steamer basket (do not stack wontons on top of each other). Coat wontons with cooking spray. Cover and steam 15 minutes.
5. Carefully remove steamer basket and wontons from pan. Place wontons on a serving platter, and cover. Keep wontons warm.
6. Add additional water to pan, if necessary. Repeat procedure with remaining wontons.
7. While wontons cook, stir together remaining 2 tablespoons soy sauce, 1½ teaspoons vinegar, and ginger. Serve with wontons. **YIELD: 10 SERVINGS (SERVING SIZE: 2 WONTONS AND ABOUT 1 TEASPOON DIPPING SAUCE).**

PER SERVING: CAL 70 (5% from fat); FAT 0.5g (sat 0.1g); PRO 5.7g; CARB 11g; FIB 0.4g; CHOL 35mg; IRON 1.3mg; SOD 374mg; CALC 24mg

TURKEY POT STICKERS

POINTS value: 2

PREP: 32 minutes ■ **COOK:** 16 minutes

Crisp, golden, and chewy, these pot stickers offer a deliciously satisfying textural contrast. They make a beautiful presentation served browned side up on a bed of shredded napa cabbage.

- 1 cup finely shredded napa (Chinese) cabbage
- ½ cup ground turkey
- ½ cup minced green onions
- 1½ tablespoons low-sodium soy sauce
- 2 teaspoons minced peeled fresh ginger
- 1 teaspoon dark sesame oil
- 2 garlic cloves, minced
- 28 wonton wrappers
- 1 tablespoon canola oil, divided
- 1 cup fat-free, less-sodium chicken broth, divided

1. Combine first 7 ingredients in a medium bowl.
2. Working with 1 wonton wrapper at a time (cover remaining wrappers with a damp towel to keep them from drying), spoon about 1 heaping teaspoon turkey mixture into center of wrapper. Moisten edges of wrapper with water; fold wonton in half, pinching edges together to seal. Flatten folded edge of pot sticker so it will sit flat. Holding pot sticker, flat side down, in the palm of one hand, form 3 to 4 pleats along the

seal with thumb and forefinger. Place pot sticker, pleated side up, on a platter. Cover with plastic wrap. Repeat procedure with remaining wrappers and turkey mixture to form 28 pot stickers.

3. Heat 1½ teaspoons canola oil in a large nonstick skillet over medium-high heat. Arrange 14 pot stickers in a single layer in pan; cook 1 minute or until browned on bottom. Add ½ cup chicken broth to pan; cover, reduce heat, and simmer 5 minutes. Uncover and cook 1 minute or until liquid almost evaporates.

4. Remove pot stickers to a serving platter; cover and keep warm. Repeat procedure with remaining 1½ teaspoons canola oil, 14 pot stickers, and ½ cup broth. Serve immediately. YIELD: 14 SERVINGS (SERVING SIZE: 2 POT STICKERS).

PER SERVING: CAL 74 (26% from fat); FAT 2.1g (sat 0.3g); PRO 3.6g; CARB 10g; FIB 0.5g; CHOL 6mg; IRON 0.8mg; SOD 196mg; CALC 14mg

SESAME SHRIMP SKEWERS

POINTS value: 2

PREP: 9 minutes ■ COOK: 5 minutes

Mirin and miso are ingredients that lend an authentic depth of flavor to the sauce. These ingredients can be found with the Asian products in most supermarkets.

> 2 tablespoons mirin (sweet rice wine)
> 1 tablespoon miso (soybean paste)
> 1 tablespoon low-sodium soy sauce
> 1 tablespoon peanut oil, divided
> 2 teaspoons fresh lime juice
> 1 teaspoon chili garlic sauce
> 1 green onion, thinly sliced
> ⅛ teaspoon garlic salt
> 1½ pounds large shrimp, peeled and deveined
> 1 tablespoon sesame seeds
> 1 tablespoon black sesame seeds

1. Combine mirin and miso in a small bowl, stirring with a whisk until smooth. Add soy sauce, 1 teaspoon peanut oil, lime juice, and chili garlic sauce, stirring until blended. Stir in green onions.

2. Sprinkle garlic salt on shrimp. Combine sesame seeds; sprinkle over shrimp, gently pressing with fingers to adhere. Thread shrimp onto each of 8 (6-inch) skewers.

3. Heat remaining 2 teaspoons oil in a large nonstick skillet over medium-high heat. Add skewers, and cook 3 minutes; turn and cook 2 minutes or just until shrimp turn pink. Arrange skewers on a serving platter and drizzle with half of sauce. Serve remaining half of sauce in a small bowl on the side for dipping. YIELD: 8 SERVINGS (SERVING SIZE: 1 SKEWER).

PER SERVING: CAL 95 (33% from fat); FAT 3.5g (sat 0.6g); PRO 12g; CARB 2.8g; FIB 0.3g; CHOL 105mg; IRON 2.1mg; SOD 270mg; CALC 44mg

RASPBERRY MILKSHAKES

POINTS value: 2

PREP: 5 minutes

> 1 cup fat-free milk
> 1 cup vanilla low-fat ice cream
> 1 cup frozen unsweetened raspberries
> 2 tablespoons seedless raspberry jam
> ½ teaspoon vanilla extract

1. Combine all ingredients in a blender; process until smooth. Serve immediately. YIELD: 4 SERVINGS (SERVING SIZE: ABOUT ⅔ CUP).

PER SERVING: CAL 105 (7% from fat); FAT 0.8g (sat 0.5g); PRO 4g; CARB 21.8g; FIB 1.9g; CHOL 4mg; IRON 0.1mg; SOD 60mg; CALC 126mg

TROPICAL GINGER FIZZ

POINTS value: 4

PREP: 6 minutes

Ginger beer gives this refreshing beverage the distinct flavors of ginger and lemon. Ordinary ginger ale would make a nice substitute. Consider serving it as a drinkable dessert at an outdoor barbecue.

> 1 cup pineapple juice
> ½ cup mango sorbet (such as Whole Fruit)
> ½ cup coconut sorbet (such as Ciao Bella)
> 1 (12-ounce) bottle ginger beer (such as Goya)
> 4 (4½-inch) slices fresh pineapple (about 5 ounces)

1. Combine pineapple juice and sorbets in a small pitcher; stir with a whisk until well combined. Gently stir in ginger beer. Pour into chilled glasses, and garnish with pineapple slices. Serve immediately. YIELD: 4 SERVINGS (SERVING SIZE: ¾ CUP).

PER SERVING: CAL 173 (12% from fat); FAT 2.4g (sat 2g); PRO 0.7g; CARB 34g; FIB 0.6g; CHOL 0mg; IRON 0.3mg; SOD 5mg; CALC 13mg

WATERMELON-LIMEADE COOLERS

POINTS value: 3

PREP: 3 minutes

Be sure to thoroughly chill the sparkling water and add it just before serving so it doesn't lose its fizz.

> 3 cups cubed seedless watermelon, chilled
> 1 (6-ounce) can frozen limeade concentrate, undiluted
> 1½ cups sparkling water, chilled
> 4 lime slices

1. Combine watermelon and limeade concentrate in a blender; process until smooth. Add sparkling water just before serving. Garnish with lime slices. YIELD: 4 SERVINGS (SERVING SIZE: 1 CUP).

PER SERVING: CAL 136 (0% from fat); FAT 0g (sat 0g); PRO 0.4g; CARB 37.1g; FIB 0.8g; CHOL 0mg; IRON 0.3mg; SOD 7mg; CALC 22mg

MINT JULEP SPRITZERS

POINTS value: 2

PREP: 7 minutes

This cocktail is lighter and more refreshing than the traditional Southern beverage. If you are not a bourbon fan, substitute white rum for the bourbon and add a squeeze of fresh lime for a mojito-like beverage with the same **POINTS** value.

> 24 small mint leaves
> 8 teaspoons superfine sugar
> ½ cup bourbon
> 4 cups crushed ice
> 2 cups sparkling water, chilled
> 4 mint sprigs (optional)

1. Place 6 mint leaves and 2 teaspoons sugar in each of 4 (12-ounce) glasses; stir gently with a wooden spoon to crush mint leaves (do not remove and discard mint). Add 2 tablespoons bourbon to each glass. Spoon 1 cup ice into each glass, and pour ½ cup sparkling water over ice. Garnish with mint sprigs, if desired. YIELD: 4 SERVINGS (SERVING SIZE: ABOUT 1 CUP).

PER SERVING: CAL 97 (0% from fat); FAT 0g (sat 0g); PRO 0g; CARB 8.4g; FIB 0g; CHOL 0mg; IRON 0mg; SOD 0mg; CALC 1mg

WHISKEY SOUR PUNCH

POINTS value: 4

PREP: 7 minutes

We think you will love this version of the classic cocktail as much as everyone in our Test Kitchens did. Sparkling water extends the volume and flavor without adding a single calorie.

> 1½ cups bourbon
> ½ (12-ounce) can frozen lemonade concentrate, thawed (about ¾ cup)
> 2 cups sparkling water
> 6 red maraschino cherries
> 6 thin lemon slices

1. Combine bourbon and lemonade concentrate in a pitcher, stirring until concentrate dissolves.
2. Fill 6 tall glasses with ice. Pour ⅓ cup bourbon mixture and ⅓ cup sparkling water into each glass; stir gently. Place a cherry and lemon slice in each glass. Serve immediately. YIELD: 6 SERVINGS (SERVING SIZE: ⅔ CUP).

PER SERVING: CAL 203 (0% from fat); FAT 0.1g (sat 0g); PRO 0.1g; CARB 19.4g; FIB 0.2g; CHOL 0mg; IRON 0.3mg; SOD 2mg; CALC 5mg

ORANGE ESSENCE HOT CHOCOLATE

POINTS value: 3

PREP: 5 minutes ■ **COOK:** 20 minutes

So rich and creamy, this makes a special treat on a cold winter night. If you have any left over, store it in the refrigerator, and reheat in the microwave.

> 1 cup fat-free milk
> 1 cup water
> 3 tablespoons brown sugar
> 1½ teaspoons grated fresh orange rind
> 2 teaspoons unsweetened cocoa
> 1 (3½-inch) cinnamon stick
> Dash of salt
> 1½ ounces bittersweet chocolate

1. Combine first 7 ingredients in a medium saucepan. Heat over medium heat, stirring until sugar dissolves and tiny bubbles form at edge of saucepan. Add chocolate, stirring constantly until chocolate melts. Strain hot chocolate through a sieve; discard solids. YIELD: 3 SERVINGS (SERVING SIZE: ABOUT ⅔ CUP).

PER SERVING: CAL 147 (30% from fat); FAT 4.9g (sat 3g); PRO 4.2g; CARB 22.2g; FIB 1.6g; CHOL 2mg; IRON 0.4mg; SOD 96mg; CALC 112mg

breads

Orange Biscuits, *page 29*

SWEET POTATO MUFFINS WITH BROWN SUGAR STREUSEL

POINTS value: 3

PREP: 15 minutes ■ **COOK:** 1 hour and 18 minutes
■ **OTHER:** 10 minutes

> 1 pound sweet potatoes (about 2 medium)
> 1 cup all-purpose flour
> ¾ cup toasted wheat germ
> ⅓ cup sugar
> 1 tablespoon baking powder
> 1 teaspoon ground cinnamon
> ½ teaspoon salt
> ½ teaspoon ground nutmeg
> ½ cup 1% low-fat milk
> 2 tablespoons canola oil
> 2 tablespoons orange juice
> 1 large egg
> 1 large egg white
> 1 teaspoon vanilla extract
> Cooking spray
> Brown Sugar Streusel

1. Preheat oven to 400°.

2. Wrap sweet potatoes in foil. Bake at 400° for 1 hour or until tender. Remove foil; cool 10 minutes or until cool enough to handle. Peel and mash sweet potatoes. Set aside 1 cup mashed sweet potato; reserve any remaining sweet potato for another use. Increase oven temperature to 450°.

3. Lightly spoon flour into a dry measuring cup; level with a knife. Combine flour and next 6 ingredients in a large bowl; stir well with a fork.

4. Combine reserved 1 cup mashed sweet potato, milk, and next 5 ingredients in a medium bowl, stirring with a whisk until smooth. Add sweet potato mixture to flour mixture, stirring just until moist.

5. Spoon batter evenly into 12 muffin cups coated with cooking spray. Top with Brown Sugar Streusel. Bake at 450° for 18 minutes or until a wooden pick inserted in center comes out clean. Remove muffins from pan immediately. Cool on a wire rack. YIELD: 12 SERVINGS (SERVING SIZE: 1 MUFFIN).

PER SERVING: CAL 163 (27% from fat); FAT 4.8g (sat 1g); PRO 4.9g; CARB 25.2g; FIB 2.8g; CHOL 21mg; IRON 1.6mg; SOD 275mg; CALC 96mg

Brown Sugar Streusel

POINTS value: 0

> 1 tablespoon all-purpose flour
> 1 tablespoon toasted wheat germ
> 1 tablespoon brown sugar
> ¼ teaspoon ground cinnamon
> ⅛ teaspoon salt
> 1 tablespoon butter

1. Combine all ingredients using your fingers until mixture resembles coarse meal. YIELD: ¼ CUP.

PER TEASPOON: CAL 18 (50% from fat); FAT 1g (sat 0.6g); PRO 0.3g; CARB 2g; FIB 0.2g; CHOL 3mg; IRON 0.1mg; SOD 32mg; CALC 2mg

SPICED PLUM MUFFINS

POINTS value: 4

PREP: 22 minutes ■ **COOK:** 20 minutes
■ **OTHER:** 10 minutes

Fresh plums add summer's sweet flavor and wonderful moistness to these delicious muffins. There's no need to peel the thin skin from the plums.

> 2¾ cups all-purpose flour
> ½ cup whole wheat flour
> 6 tablespoons sugar, divided
> 3 tablespoons baking powder
> 2½ teaspoons ground cinnamon, divided
> 1 teaspoon ground ginger
> ½ teaspoon salt
> ⅛ teaspoon freshly ground black pepper
> 2 large eggs
> 2 large egg whites
> 1½ cups plain fat-free yogurt
> ½ cup vegetable oil
> ⅓ cup honey
> 2 cups finely chopped ripe plums (about 1 pound)
> Cooking spray

1. Preheat oven to 350°.

2. Lightly spoon flours into dry measuring cups; level with a knife. Combine flours, ¼ cup sugar, baking powder, 2 teaspoons cinnamon, and next 3 ingredients in a large bowl; stir with a whisk. Make a well in center of mixture. Combine eggs and next 4 ingredients; add to flour mixture, stirring just until moist. Gently fold in plums.

3. Spoon batter evenly into 20 muffin cups coated with cooking spray. Combine remaining 2 tablespoons sugar and remaining ½ teaspoon cinnamon in a small bowl. Sprinkle sugar-cinnamon mixture over batter.

4. Bake at 350° for 20 minutes or until a wooden pick inserted in center comes out clean. Cool in pans 10 minutes on wire racks; remove from pans. **YIELD: 20 MUFFINS (SERVING SIZE: 1 MUFFIN).**

PER SERVING: CAL 180 (32% from fat); FAT 6.4g (sat 0.8g); PRO 4.1g; CARB 28.2g; FIB 1.3g; CHOL 22mg; IRON 1.4mg; SOD 301mg; CALC 155mg

CORN AND GREEN ONION MUFFINS WITH CHEDDAR

POINTS value: 2

PREP: 19 minutes ■ **COOK:** 23 minutes

These muffins are ideal with chili, stews, or chowders.

- ½ cup all-purpose flour
- ½ cup yellow cornmeal
- 1 tablespoon baking powder
- ½ teaspoon salt
- 6 tablespoons nonfat buttermilk
- ¼ cup plain fat-free yogurt
- 2 tablespoons butter, melted
- 1 large egg yolk
- 3 large egg whites
- 1½ tablespoons sugar
- ½ cup frozen whole-kernel corn, thawed
- ¼ cup (1 ounce) reduced-fat shredded Cheddar cheese
- 1 tablespoon chopped green onions
  Cooking spray

1. Preheat oven to 350°.

2. Lightly spoon flour and cornmeal into dry measuring cups; level with a knife. Combine flour, cornmeal, baking powder, and salt in a medium bowl; stir with a whisk. Combine buttermilk, yogurt, butter, and egg yolk in a large bowl; stir with a whisk. Add flour mixture to buttermilk mixture, stirring just until moist.

3. Beat egg whites with a mixer at medium speed until foamy. Gradually add sugar; beat until medium peaks form. Fold egg whites into batter. Gently fold corn, cheese, and onions into batter.

4. Spoon batter evenly into 10 muffin cups coated with cooking spray. Bake at 350° for 23 minutes or until muffins spring back when touched lightly in center. **YIELD: 10 MUFFINS (SERVING SIZE: 1 MUFFIN).**

PER SERVING: CAL 113 (29% from fat); FAT 3.6g (sat 2.1g); PRO 4.2g; CARB 16.4g; FIB 0.7g; CHOL 29mg; IRON 0.9mg; SOD 310mg; CALC 127mg

Note: If you prefer miniature muffins, spoon 1 tablespoon batter into 31 miniature muffin cups coated with cooking spray. Bake at 350° for 15 minutes or until muffins spring back when touched lightly in center. **YIELD: 31 MINIATURE MUFFINS (SERVING SIZE: 2 MINIATURE MUFFINS).**

PER SERVING: CAL 36 (30% from fat); FAT 1.2g (sat 0.7g); PRO 1.4g; CARB 5.3g; FIB 0.2g; CHOL 9mg; IRON 0.9mg; SOD 100mg; CALC 41mg

ORANGE BISCUITS

POINTS value: 4   *pictured on page 53*

PREP: 24 minutes ■ **COOK:** 14 minutes
■ **OTHER:** 5 minutes

These tender, citrus-glazed biscuits received our Test Kitchens' highest rating.

- 3 cups all-purpose flour
- 3 tablespoons granulated sugar
- 4 teaspoons baking powder
- 1 teaspoon baking soda
- ¾ teaspoon salt
- ⅓ cup chilled butter, cut into small pieces
- 1½ tablespoons grated fresh orange rind, divided
- 1⅓ cups low-fat buttermilk
- 3 tablespoons fresh orange juice, divided
  Cooking spray
- ¾ cup powdered sugar

1. Preheat oven to 425°.

2. Lightly spoon flour into dry measuring cups; level with a knife. Combine flour and next 4 ingredients in a large bowl; cut in butter with a pastry blender or 2 knives until mixture resembles coarse meal. Stir in 1 tablespoon orange rind.

3. Combine buttermilk and 2 tablespoons orange juice; add to flour mixture, stirring just until moist.

4. Turn dough out onto a lightly floured surface; knead lightly 4 times. Pat dough to ¾-inch thickness; cut with a 2½-inch biscuit cutter. Place biscuits on a baking sheet coated with cooking spray; lightly coat tops with cooking spray.

5. Bake at 425° for 14 minutes or until lightly browned.

6. While biscuits bake, combine powdered sugar, remaining 1½ teaspoons orange rind, and remaining 1 tablespoon orange juice. Let biscuits cool 5 minutes on a wire rack; drizzle icing evenly over biscuits. **YIELD: 13 SERVINGS (SERVING SIZE: 1 BISCUIT).**

PER SERVING: CAL 199 (24% from fat); FAT 5.2g (sat 3.2g); PRO 4g; CARB 34g; FIB 0.9g; CHOL 13.9mg; IRON 1.5mg; SOD 404mg; CALC 137mg

CURRANT SCONES

POINTS value: 3

PREP: 11 minutes ■ COOK: 17 minutes

Dried currants are tiny dried grapes. If you don't have any in your pantry, substitute an equal amount of chopped raisins.

  1 cup all-purpose flour
  2 tablespoons sugar
  1 teaspoon baking powder
  ½ teaspoon salt
  2 tablespoons chilled butter, cut into small pieces
  ¼ cup nonfat buttermilk
  1 large egg, lightly beaten
  1 teaspoon vanilla extract
  ½ cup dried currants or chopped raisins
  ⅓ cup regular oats
  Cooking spray
  1 teaspoon sugar

1. Preheat oven to 375°.
2. Lightly spoon flour into a dry measuring cup; level with a knife. Combine flour, 2 tablespoons sugar, baking powder, and salt in a bowl; cut in butter with a pastry blender or 2 knives until mixture resembles coarse meal.
3. Combine buttermilk, egg, and vanilla; add to flour mixture, stirring just until moist. Stir in currants and oats. Turn dough out onto a lightly floured surface; knead lightly 3 times with floured hands. Pat dough into an 8-inch circle on a baking sheet lined with parchment paper. Cut dough into 8 wedges, cutting into but not through dough. Coat top of scones with cooking spray; sprinkle with 1 teaspoon sugar.
4. Bake at 375° for 17 minutes or until golden. Serve warm. YIELD: 8 SERVINGS (SERVING SIZE: 1 WEDGE).

PER SERVING: CAL 147 (24% from fat); FAT 3.9g (sat 2.1g); PRO 3.4g; CARB 25.3g; FIB 1.2g; CHOL 34mg; IRON 1.3mg; SOD 243mg; CALC 61mg

ALL ABOUT CURRANTS

Currants, which are quite popular in the UK, offer a tangy, nutritional punch to the American dinner table. Fresh currants are part of the gooseberry family and are in season from June through August. Dried currants, however, are simply small, seedless grapes, though they taste more flavorful and tart than raisins. This small fruit offers high levels of vitamin C, iron, and potassium.

BANANA-HONEY BREAD

POINTS value: 3

PREP: 10 minutes ■ COOK: 50 minutes
■ OTHER: 10 minutes

For a fast, mess-free way to mash bananas, place them in a large zip-top plastic bag, and seal, removing as much air as possible. Gently squeeze the bag with your hands until the bananas are mashed. Snip a small hole in 1 corner of the bag, and squeeze out the bananas.

  2¼ cups all-purpose flour
  ¾ cup whole wheat flour
  1 tablespoon baking powder
  ½ teaspoon ground cinnamon
  ¼ teaspoon salt
  ¼ teaspoon baking soda
  ½ cup dried currants
  ¾ cup honey
  ¼ cup vegetable oil
  5 large bananas, mashed
  2 large eggs
  Cooking spray

1. Preheat oven to 350°.
2. Lightly spoon flours into dry measuring cups; level with a knife. Combine flours and next 4 ingredients in a large bowl, stirring with a whisk. Stir in currants.
3. Combine honey and next 3 ingredients in a medium bowl, stirring with a whisk. Add honey mixture to flour mixture, stirring with a whisk until dry ingredients are moist.
4. Pour batter into 2 (8 x 4–inch) loaf pans coated with cooking spray. Bake at 350° for 50 minutes or until a wooden pick inserted in center comes out clean. Cool in pans 10 minutes on a wire rack; remove from pans. Cool completely on wire rack. YIELD: 20 SERVINGS (SERVING SIZE: 1 SLICE).

PER SERVING: CAL 177 (18% from fat); FAT 3.6g (sat 0.5g); PRO 3.2g; CARB 35.2g; FIB 2.1g; CHOL 21mg; IRON 1.3mg; SOD 126mg; CALC 54mg

FUDGY CHOCOLATE-ZUCCHINI BREAD

POINTS value: 4

PREP: 26 minutes ■ **COOK:** 50 minutes
■ **OTHER:** 5 minutes

Lining loaf pans with wax paper in addition to coating them with cooking spray ensures that these extramoist loaves will come out successfully. To line a pan with wax paper, place the pan on a sheet of wax paper, trace around its bottom, and cut out the shape with scissors. Place the wax paper in the pan after spraying the paper with cooking spray. The paper will adhere and lie flat.

2½ cups all-purpose flour
1¾ cups sugar
½ cup unsweetened cocoa
1½ teaspoons baking soda
1 teaspoon salt
1 teaspoon ground cinnamon
½ cup vegetable oil
⅓ cup plain fat-free yogurt
1 large egg, lightly beaten
2 teaspoons grated fresh lemon rind
3 tablespoons fresh lemon juice
2½ cups shredded zucchini (about 2 medium)
1 cup semisweet chocolate chips
3 large egg whites
Cooking spray

1. Preheat oven to 350°.
2. Lightly spoon flour into dry measuring cups; level with a knife. Combine flour and next 5 ingredients in a large bowl, stirring with a whisk.
3. Combine oil and next 4 ingredients in a small bowl; add to flour mixture, stirring just until moist. Fold in zucchini and chocolate chips.
4. Beat egg whites with a mixer at high speed until stiff peaks form. Gently fold egg whites into the zucchini mixture.
5. Spoon batter into 2 (8½ x 4½–inch) loaf pans coated with cooking spray and lined with wax paper.
6. Bake at 350° for 50 minutes or until bread springs back when touched lightly in center. Let stand in pan 5 minutes. Remove from pan, and remove wax paper; cool completely on a wire rack. YIELD: 24 SERVINGS (SERVING SIZE: 1 SLICE).

PER SERVING: CAL 194 (34% from fat); FAT 7.3g (sat 1.8g); PRO 3g; CARB 31.1g; FIB 1.4g; CHOL 8.9mg; IRON 1.2mg; SOD 190mg; CALC 14mg

SMOKED CHEDDAR, PEPPER, AND BACON BISCOTTI

POINTS value: 2

PREP: 16 minutes ■ **COOK:** 54 minutes
■ **OTHER:** 5 minutes

This savory rendition of biscotti is perfect to serve alongside a hearty soup or main-dish salad.

2½ cups all-purpose flour
2 teaspoons baking powder
¾ teaspoon coarsely ground black pepper
¾ teaspoon salt
2 large eggs
1 large egg white
2 tablespoons fat-free milk
2 teaspoons olive oil
¾ cup (3 ounces) shredded smoked Cheddar cheese
4 center-cut bacon slices, cooked and crumbled
Cooking spray

1. Preheat oven to 350°.
2. Lightly spoon flour into dry measuring cups; level with a knife. Combine flour and next 3 ingredients in a bowl; stir with a whisk.
3. Combine eggs, egg white, milk, and olive oil in a large bowl, stirring well with a whisk. Add flour mixture, cheese, and bacon, stirring until well blended (dough will be crumbly). Turn dough out onto a lightly floured surface; knead lightly 7 times. Divide dough in half. Shape each portion into a 6 x 4–inch log; place logs 5 inches apart on a baking sheet coated with cooking spray.
4. Bake at 350° for 30 minutes or until golden brown. Remove logs from baking sheet; cool 5 minutes on a wire rack.
5. Reduce oven temperature to 325°. Cut each log diagonally into 12 (½-inch-thick) slices using a serrated knife. Place slices, cut sides up, on baking sheet; bake at 325° for 12 minutes. Turn slices over; bake an additional 12 minutes or until crisp. Remove from baking sheet; cool completely on a wire rack. YIELD: 24 SERVINGS (SERVING SIZE: 1 SLICE).

PER SERVING: CAL 75 (28% from fat); FAT 2.3g (sat 0.9g); PRO 3.3g; CARB 10.3g; FIB 0.4g; CHOL 22mg; IRON 0.7mg; SOD 159mg; CALC 54mg

CHEDDARY SKILLET CORN BREAD

POINTS value: 4

PREP: 10 minutes ■ COOK: 25 minutes

1½ cups cornmeal
½ cup all-purpose flour
1 teaspoon baking powder
1 teaspoon sugar
½ teaspoon baking soda
¼ teaspoon salt
¼ teaspoon ground red pepper
1¼ cups (5 ounces) reduced-fat shredded extrasharp
   Cheddar cheese, divided
1 tablespoon canola oil
1¼ cups low-fat buttermilk
¼ cup egg substitute
⅓ cup chopped onion
Butter-flavored cooking spray

1. Preheat oven to 425°.
2. Combine cornmeal and next 6 ingredients in a medium bowl; stir well with a whisk. Stir in ¾ cup cheese.
3. Heat oil in a 9-inch cast-iron skillet over medium heat until hot.
4. While oil heats, combine buttermilk, egg substitute, and onion; add to dry ingredients, stirring just until dry ingredients are moist. Stir in hot oil. Tilt pan to coat bottom with oil remaining in pan. Pour batter into prepared pan. Coat batter with cooking spray.
5. Bake at 425° for 20 minutes. Sprinkle top with remaining ½ cup cheese; bake an additional 5 minutes or until corn bread is golden and cheese melts. Cut into wedges to serve. YIELD: 10 SERVINGS (SERVING SIZE: 1 WEDGE).

PER SERVING: CAL 191 (29% from fat); FAT 6.1g (sat 0.4g); PRO 6.5g; CARB 27.6g; FIB 1.2g; CHOL 13mg; IRON 1.5mg; SOD 335mg; CALC 144mg

HOW TO MAKE PANCAKES

For fluffy pancakes, follow the golden rule: Always pour wet ingredients into dry ones. After you prepare the batter, pour only about ¼ cup of it into the center of the hot pan for ordinary-sized pancakes. (Flick a drop of water onto the pan. If it sizzles and evaporates, your pan is at the perfect temperature.) Let the batter spread naturally instead of pouring it in a circle. Next, wait for the edges to turn golden, and look for bubbles to appear. Slide a spatula underneath the pancake, and quickly flip it over. Let it cook for 2 or 3 more minutes, slip it onto a plate, and get ready to pour on some syrup.

CARROT CAKE PANCAKES WITH CREAM CHEESE SAUCE

POINTS value: 4   *pictured on page 52*

PREP: 13 minutes ■ COOK: 7 minutes per batch

Sprinkle these pancakes with additional cinnamon, and then serve with fresh fruit and coffee for an unforgettable breakfast.

1¼ cups all-purpose flour
2 teaspoons baking powder
1½ teaspoons ground cinnamon
½ teaspoon salt
¾ cup fat-free milk
⅓ cup packed brown sugar
1 tablespoon canola oil
2 large eggs
½ cup finely grated carrot (about 1 large)
⅓ cup flaked sweetened coconut
Cooking spray
Cream Cheese Sauce

1. Lightly spoon flour into dry measuring cups; level with a knife. Combine flour and next 3 ingredients in a large bowl, stirring with a whisk.
2. Combine milk and next 3 ingredients, and add to flour mixture, stirring until smooth. Stir in carrot and coconut.
3. Pour about ¼ cup batter per pancake onto a hot non-stick griddle or nonstick skillet coated with cooking spray. Cook 4 minutes or until tops are covered with bubbles and edges look cooked. Carefully turn pancakes over; cook 3 minutes or until bottoms are lightly browned. Serve with Cream Cheese Sauce. YIELD: 10 SERVINGS (SERVING SIZE: 1 PANCAKE AND ABOUT 1 TABLESPOON CREAM CHEESE SAUCE).

PER SERVING: CAL 176 (24% from fat); FAT 4.6g (sat 2g); PRO 4.3g; CARB 29.6g; FIB 0.9g; CHOL 45mg; IRON 1.3mg; SOD 254mg; CALC 118mg

Cream Cheese Sauce

POINTS value: 1

¾ cup powdered sugar
¼ cup (2 ounces) tub-style light cream cheese, softened
1 tablespoon fat-free milk
½ teaspoon vanilla extract

1. Combine all ingredients in a small bowl; stir with a whisk until smooth. YIELD: 9 TABLESPOONS.

PER TABLESPOON: CAL 54 (17% from fat); FAT 1g (sat 0.7g); PRO 0.7g; CARB 10.5g; FIB 0g; CHOL 3mg; IRON 0mg; SOD 31mg; CALC 10mg

RICOTTA PANCAKES WITH BING CHERRY COMPOTE

POINTS value: 4

PREP: 13 minutes ■ **COOK:** 4 minutes per batch

These airy pancakes are fluffy and light. Use a firm but gentle hand while folding, and stop as soon as the batter is blended.

    Bing Cherry Compote
    4 large egg whites
    2 tablespoons sugar
    ¾ cup all-purpose flour
    ¼ cup whole wheat flour
    1 teaspoon baking powder
    ¼ teaspoon salt
    1 large egg
    1 cup fat-free ricotta cheese
    ¾ cup fat-free milk
    Cooking spray

1. Prepare Bing Cherry Compote.
2. While compote simmers, place egg whites in a large bowl; beat with a mixer at high speed until soft peaks form. Gradually add sugar, 1 tablespoon at a time, beating until stiff peaks form.
3. Lightly spoon flours into dry measuring cups; level with a knife. Combine flours, baking powder, and salt in another large bowl; stir with a whisk. Combine egg, cheese, and milk in a medium bowl; beat with a mixer until blended. Add cheese mixture to flour mixture, stirring until smooth. Gently stir one-fourth of egg white mixture into batter; gently fold in remaining egg white mixture.
4. Pour 2 tablespoons batter per pancake onto a hot nonstick griddle or nonstick skillet coated with cooking spray. Cook 2 minutes or until tops have a few bubbles and edges look cooked. Carefully turn pancakes over; cook 2 minutes or until bottoms are lightly browned. Serve with Bing Cherry Compote. YIELD: 7 SERVINGS (SERVING SIZE: ABOUT 6 PANCAKES AND ABOUT 3½ TABLESPOONS COMPOTE).

PER SERVING: CAL 231 (4% from fat); FAT 1g (sat 0.3g); PRO 9.9g; CARB 46.2g; FIB 1.5g; CHOL 36mg; IRON 1.2mg; SOD 246mg; CALC 149mg

Bing Cherry Compote

POINTS value: 1

    4 cups frozen pitted dark sweet cherries
    ¼ cup sugar
    ¼ teaspoon ground cinnamon

1. Combine all ingredients in a large skillet. Cook over medium heat 12 minutes or until cherries are thoroughly heated, stirring often. YIELD: 1½ CUPS.

PER TABLESPOON: CAL 28 (0% from fat); FAT 0g (sat 0g); PRO 0.3g; CARB 7.2g; FIB 0.2g; CHOL 0mg; IRON 0.1mg; SOD 0mg; CALC 4mg

PECAN WAFFLES

POINTS value: 4

PREP: 10 minutes ■ **COOK:** 7 minutes per batch

To keep waffles warm and crisp after cooking, place them directly on the rack in a preheated 300° oven until time to serve.

    1¼ cups all-purpose flour, divided
    ¾ cup pecan halves
    1 tablespoon sugar
    1½ teaspoons baking powder
    ¼ teaspoon baking soda
    ¼ teaspoon salt
    1¾ cups nonfat buttermilk
    ¼ cup butter, melted
    1 large egg yolk
    3 large egg whites
    Butter-flavored cooking spray
    ¾ cup sugar-free maple-flavored syrup (such as Mrs. Butterworth's)

1. Lightly spoon flour into dry measuring cups; level with a knife. Process half of flour and pecans in a food processor 30 seconds or until pecans are finely ground.
2. Transfer flour mixture to a large bowl. Add remaining flour, sugar, and next 3 ingredients, stirring well with a whisk.
3. Combine buttermilk, butter, and egg yolk, stirring well with a whisk. Add to flour mixture, stirring well with a whisk.
4. Beat egg whites with a mixer at high speed until stiff peaks form (do not overbeat). Fold egg whites into batter.
5. Coat a waffle iron with cooking spray; preheat. Spoon about ⅓ cup batter per 4-inch waffle onto hot waffle iron, spreading batter to edges. Cook according to manufacturer's instructions until waffle iron stops steaming. Repeat procedure with remaining batter. Serve with syrup. YIELD: 12 (4-INCH) WAFFLES (SERVING SIZE: 1 WAFFLE AND 1 TABLESPOON SYRUP).

PER SERVING: CAL 163 (51% from fat); FAT 9.3g (sat 3g); PRO 4.5g; CARB 17.2g; FIB 1g; CHOL 27mg; IRON 1mg; SOD 236mg; CALC 88mg

SOFT PRETZELS

POINTS value: 2

PREP: 40 minutes ■ COOK: 27 minutes
■ OTHER: 45 minutes

Our Test Kitchens staff raved over the opportunity to sample these pretzels warm from the oven. To encourage portion control, we suggest freezing any extra in an airtight container. Thaw and reheat at 350° for about 10 minutes per pretzel to recreate that fresh-from-the-oven taste.

        1 tablespoon sugar
        1 package dry yeast (about 2¼ teaspoons)
        1 teaspoon salt
    1⅔ cups warm water (100° to 110°)
    2½ cups whole wheat flour
        2 cups all-purpose flour, divided
        1 tablespoon butter, melted
    Cooking spray
      12 cups water
      ⅔ cup baking soda
      ¼ cup egg substitute
        1 teaspoon kosher salt

1. Dissolve sugar, yeast, and salt in warm water in a large bowl; let stand 8 minutes.
2. While yeast stands, lightly spoon flours into dry measuring cups; level with a knife. Add whole wheat flour, 1¾ cups all-purpose flour, and butter to yeast mixture; beat with a mixer at medium speed 5 minutes or until smooth and elastic, adding enough of remaining ¼ cup all-purpose flour, 1 tablespoon at a time, to prevent dough from sticking to sides of bowl.
3. Place dough in a large bowl coated with cooking spray, turning to coat top. Cover and let rise in a warm place (85°), free from drafts, 45 minutes or until doubled in size. (Gently press two fingers into dough. If indentation remains, dough has risen enough.)
4. Preheat oven to 425°.
5. Combine 12 cups water and baking soda in a large Dutch oven; bring to a boil.
6. Turn dough out onto a lightly floured surface; divide into 16 equal portions. Roll each portion into a 14-inch long rope; twist into pretzel shape.
7. Carefully drop 3 to 4 pretzels at a time into boiling water. Pretzels will sink to bottom of pan. When pretzels float to top (in about 10 seconds), remove from pan with a slotted spoon, and place on a cooling rack to drain and slightly dry.

8. Place pretzels on baking sheets coated with cooking spray. Brush pretzels with egg substitute, and sprinkle evenly with kosher salt. Bake at 425° for 17 minutes or until browned. YIELD: 16 SERVINGS (SERVING SIZE: 1 PRETZEL).

PER SERVING: CAL 134 (9% from fat); FAT 1.4g (sat 0.6g); PRO 4.8g; CARB 26.5g; FIB 2.8g; CHOL 2mg; IRON 1.6mg; SOD 512mg; CALC 11mg

DO THE TWIST

Pretzels remain a go-to snack food for those watching their weight because pretzels are lower in fat and more filling than potato chips or cookies. Pretzels come in hard and soft varieties. The dough used to make both types usually consists of water, flour, sugar, yeast, and salt. Between shaping and baking, pretzels are given a quick dip in boiling water that includes a generous amount of baking soda. This step promotes the distinctive caramel color. The difference between a hard, crunchy pretzel and the soft, chewy version lies in the amount of baking time. Hard, crisp pretzels bake at a lower temperature (about 350°F) for a longer amount of time, whereas the dough for soft pretzels is baked at a higher temperature (between 425° and 450°F) for a shorter time.

Although pretzels come in many shapes and sizes, the traditional pretzel shape is the twist. To form a twist, roll a portion of dough into a rope, and bend it into a U-shape. Then twist the ends together, and fold the tips down into a traditional pretzel shape, pinching gently to seal.

Before pretzels are baked, both hard and soft varieties are brushed with an egg mixture or egg substitute to give the surfaces a shiny finish and to help any add-on ingredients adhere to the dough. Salt, herbs, seeds, hard cheeses, and sugar are the most common ingredients sprinkled onto pretzels.

desserts

Coconut-Oat Cookies, *page 42*

BAKED APPLES WITH TOFFEE AND ALMONDS

POINTS value: 6   *pictured on page 54*

PREP: 15 minutes ■ **COOK:** 1 hour and 35 minutes

Select lunchbox-sized apples (about 2½ to 3 inches in diameter) for this chocolaty apple dessert. The generous, individually portioned serving of this dessert will satisfy your sweet tooth.

> 6 small Fuji apples
> 3 (1.4-ounce) chocolate-covered toffee candy bars, coarsely chopped and divided
> Cooking spray
> 1½ cups apple cider
> ¼ cup packed brown sugar
> 2 tablespoons brandy
> 2 teaspoons butter
> ⅓ cup sliced almonds, toasted
> 6 tablespoons frozen reduced-calorie whipped topping, thawed

1. Preheat oven to 350°.
2. Core apples, starting at stem end, cutting to, but not through, opposite end. Peel top one-third of each apple, and enlarge cavity opening to 1½ inches. Divide 5 tablespoons chopped toffee candy bar evenly among apples. Place apples in an 11 x 7–inch baking dish coated with cooking spray.
3. Combine cider and next 3 ingredients in a small saucepan; bring to a boil. Reduce heat, and simmer 2 minutes. Pour cider mixture over and around apples.
4. Bake, uncovered, at 350° for 1 hour and 20 minutes or until apples are tender, basting apples occasionally with pan juices.
5. Transfer apples to individual dessert dishes. Pour pan juices into a small saucepan; bring to a boil. Boil 10 minutes or until mixture is reduced to ¾ cup. Spoon reduced sauce over apples; sprinkle with remaining chopped toffee candy bar and almonds. Top with whipped topping. YIELD: 6 SERVINGS (SERVING SIZE: 1 APPLE, 2 TABLESPOONS CIDER SAUCE, ABOUT 1 TABLESPOON CHOPPED TOFFEE CANDY BAR, ABOUT 1 TABLESPOON ALMONDS, AND 1 TABLESPOON WHIPPED TOPPING).

PER SERVING: CAL 298 (32% from fat); FAT 10.6g (sat 4g); PRO 2.2g; CARB 46.9g; FIB 3.7g; CHOL 8mg; IRON 0.5mg; SOD 82mg; CALC 38mg

APPLE CREPES WITH REDUCED CIDER SAUCE

POINTS value: 4

PREP: 13 minutes
■ **COOK:** 18 minutes plus 1 minute per batch

> 2 teaspoons butter
> 5 cups sliced peeled apple (about 3 medium)
> ¼ cup sugar, divided
> 1 tablespoon brandy
> ½ teaspoon ground cinnamon
> ⅛ teaspoon salt
> 1 cup apple cider
> 1 tablespoon grated fresh orange rind
> 1 (3-inch) cinnamon stick
> Easy Cornstarch Crepes

1. Melt butter in a large nonstick skillet over medium-high heat. Add apples, 2 tablespoons sugar, brandy, ground cinnamon, and salt; cook, uncovered, 18 minutes or until apples are tender. Keep warm.
2. While apples cook, combine cider, remaining 2 tablespoons sugar, orange rind, and cinnamon stick in a medium saucepan; bring to a boil. Reduce heat, and simmer, uncovered, 15 minutes or until reduced by half. Discard cinnamon stick. Keep cider mixture warm.
3. Fold crepes into fourths, and place on plates. Top evenly with apples and cider sauce. YIELD: 5 SERVINGS (SERVING SIZE: 1 CREPE, ABOUT ½ CUP APPLES, AND 1½ TABLESPOONS SAUCE).

PER SERVING: CAL 208 (20% from fat); FAT 4.6g (sat 2.6g); PRO 2.7g; CARB 39.3g; FIB 1.7g; CHOL 11mg; IRON 0.5mg; SOD 176mg; CALC 42mg

Easy Cornstarch Crepes
POINTS value: 2

Traditional crepe batter with all-purpose flour is made at least an hour ahead of cooking to promote tenderness and to ensure even cooking. These nontraditional cornstarch crepes are every bit as tender and delicious, and they blend up quickly at the last minute.

> ⅓ cup 1% low-fat milk
> ¼ cup cornstarch
> ¼ cup egg substitute
> 1 tablespoon butter, melted
> 1 teaspoon sugar
> 1 teaspoon vanilla extract
> 1 teaspoon brandy
> ⅛ teaspoon salt
> Cooking spray

1. Preheat oven to 225°.
2. Combine all ingredients except cooking spray in a blender; process until smooth.
3. Heat a 5-inch crepe pan or small nonstick skillet over medium-high heat. Coat pan with cooking spray. Remove pan from heat. Pour 3 tablespoons batter into pan; quickly tilt pan in all directions so batter covers pan with a thin film. Cook about 1 minute or until edges and bottom are lightly browned.
4. Loosen crepe with a spatula and slide onto a parchment paper–lined baking sheet. (Do not turn and cook crepe on other side.) Keep crepes warm in oven. Repeat procedure with remaining batter. YIELD: 5 (5-INCH) CREPES.

PER CREPE: CAL 70 (37% from fat); FAT 2.9g (sat 1.6g); PRO 2.1g; CARB 7.6g; FIB 0.1g; CHOL 7mg; IRON 0.3mg; SOD 105mg; CALC 28mg

GRILLED PINEAPPLE WITH HONEY-LIME SAUCE

POINTS value: 3   *pictured on page 58*

PREP: 5 minutes ■ COOK: 6 minutes

Coat your measuring spoon with cooking spray before adding the honey. The honey will slide out cleanly; then you can measure the lime juice without having to wash the spoon.

        2 tablespoons honey
        2 tablespoons fresh lime juice
        1 (2-pound) pineapple, peeled and cored
     Butter-flavored cooking spray
        2⅔ cups vanilla low-fat frozen yogurt

1. Prepare grill.
2. Combine honey and lime juice in a small bowl, stirring until blended. Set aside.
3. Cut pineapple into 8 even slices; pat slices dry. Coat pineapple slices with cooking spray. Place pineapple slices on grill rack. Grill slices 3 minutes on each side.
4. Divide pineapple slices evenly among 8 dessert dishes. Top with frozen yogurt; drizzle with honey-lime sauce. YIELD: 8 SERVINGS (SERVING SIZE: 1 SLICE PINEAPPLE, ⅓ CUP FROZEN YOGURT, AND ½ TABLESPOON SAUCE).

PER SERVING: CAL 158 (4% from fat); FAT 0.7g (sat 0g); PRO 4.9g; CARB 34.2g; FIB 0.9g; CHOL 2mg; IRON 0.2mg; SOD 35mg; CALC 161mg

HONEY-ROASTED APRICOTS WITH CRÈME FRAÎCHE

POINTS value: 2

PREP: 3 minutes ■ COOK: 12 minutes

Apricots are at their peak in June and July. Select plump, firm fruit that is orange-yellow with consistent skin color.

        6 medium apricots, halved and pitted
        2 tablespoons brown sugar
        1 tablespoon honey
        1 teaspoon fresh thyme leaves
        4 teaspoons crème fraîche

1. Preheat broiler.
2. Place apricot halves, cut sides up, in an ungreased 11 x 7–inch baking dish.
3. Combine brown sugar, honey, and thyme; drizzle over apricots. Broil 7 minutes; turn apricots, and broil 5 minutes or until edges are browned, basting with syrup.
4. Place 4 apricot halves, cut sides up, on each of 3 dishes; drizzle with any remaining syrup. Top with crème fraîche. YIELD: 3 SERVINGS (SERVING SIZE: 4 APRICOT HALVES AND 1 TEASPOON CRÈME FRAÎCHE).

PER SERVING: CAL 113 (21% from fat); FAT 2.6g (sat 1.5g); PRO 1.2g; CARB 22.6g; FIB 1.5g; CHOL 6mg; IRON 0.5mg; SOD 7mg; CALC 18mg

CRÈME FRAÎCHE

Crème fraîche, a deliciously rich cream developed by French cooks, is thicker and less tangy than sour cream. It adds a nutty flavor and luxurious texture to fresh fruit desserts and classics like crepes, warm puddings, and cobblers. Look for it near the gourmet cheeses in your supermarket.

CHOCOLATE PUDDING WITH BRÛLÉED BANANAS

POINTS value: 6

PREP: 10 minutes ■ **COOK:** 15 minutes
■ **OTHER:** 1 hour

Use high-quality cocoa powder in this rich and silky pudding for an intense chocolate experience.

1½ cups 1% low-fat milk
5 tablespoons sugar
2 tablespoons unsweetened cocoa
2 tablespoons cornstarch
⅛ teaspoon salt
1 large egg yolk
2 ounces bittersweet chocolate, coarsely chopped
1½ teaspoons vanilla extract
1 teaspoon unsalted butter
2 small firm ripe bananas
2 teaspoons sugar

1. Place first 5 ingredients in a medium saucepan, stirring with a whisk until blended. Bring milk mixture to a boil over medium-high heat, stirring constantly with a whisk.
2. Place egg yolk in a medium bowl; gradually add half of hot milk mixture, stirring constantly with a whisk. Add egg mixture to pan; bring to a boil, stirring constantly. Cook 1 minute or until thick. Remove from heat; add bittersweet chocolate, vanilla, and butter, stirring until chocolate melts and mixture cools.
3. Divide pudding evenly among 4 (4-ounce) dessert dishes; cover surface of pudding with plastic wrap. Chill 1 hour.
4. Cut each banana diagonally into 16 slices. Place slices on a foil-lined baking sheet. Sprinkle 2 teaspoons sugar evenly over banana slices.
5. Holding a kitchen blowtorch about 2 inches from top of each banana slice, heat sugar, moving torch back and forth, until sugar is completely melted and caramelized (about 10 seconds each). Arrange banana slices evenly on top of puddings. Serve immediately. **YIELD: 4 SERVINGS**
(SERVING SIZE: ABOUT ½ CUP PUDDING AND 8 BANANA SLICES).

PER SERVING: CAL 279 (27% from fat); FAT 8.3g (sat 4.8g); PRO 5.7g; CARB 47.2g; FIB 3.3g; CHOL 58mg; IRON 0.8mg; SOD 123mg; CALC 125mg

CLASSIC CHEESECAKE

POINTS value: 5

PREP: 25 minutes ■ **COOK:** 1 hour ■ **OTHER:** 9 hours

Overbeating incorporates excess air into cheesecake batter and will cause the cake to rise and fall, producing cracks. This lightened version is no exception. Beat the batter just until the ingredients are blended and the mixture is smooth.

8 low-fat graham cracker cookie sheets, crumbled
1 teaspoon sugar
1 tablespoon butter, melted
1 tablespoon water
Cooking spray
1 (8-ounce) package fat-free cream cheese, softened
1 cup sugar
2 (8-ounce) packages ⅓-less-fat cream cheese, softened
1 tablespoon grated fresh lemon rind
¼ cup fresh lemon juice
1 tablespoon vanilla extract
1 large egg
5 large egg whites
1 cup plain fat-free Greek yogurt (such as Fage)
Fresh berries (optional)

1. Preheat oven to 300°.
2. Combine cracker crumbs and 1 teaspoon sugar in a food processor; pulse 5 times or until finely ground. With processor on, pour butter and water through food chute; process until crumb mixture is moist.
3. Firmly press crumb mixture into bottom of a 9-inch springform pan coated with cooking spray. Coat crumbs with cooking spray. Set aside.
4. Beat fat-free cream cheese and 1 cup sugar with a mixer at medium speed until creamy. Add ⅓-less-fat cream cheese and next 3 ingredients; beat until blended, stopping to scrape sides of bowl as needed. Add egg and egg whites, 1 at a time, beating just until blended (do not overbeat). Add yogurt, beating at low speed just until blended. Pour batter over prepared crust.
5. Bake at 300° for 1 hour or until cheesecake center barely moves when pan is touched. Run a knife around outside edge of cake. Turn oven off. Let cheesecake stand in oven with door partially open for 1 hour. Remove from oven, and cool completely on a wire rack. Cover and chill 8 hours. Cut into wedges to serve. Garnish with fresh berries, if desired. **YIELD: 12 SERVINGS**
(SERVING SIZE: 1 WEDGE).

Note: Running a knife around the baked cheesecake releases it from the sides of the pan and also prevents cracks.

PER SERVING: CAL 261 (35% from fat); FAT 10.1g (sat 6.1g); PRO 11.2g; CARB 30.6g; FIB 0.5g; CHOL 50mg; IRON 0.5mg; SOD 376mg; CALC 154mg

CHOCOLATE–CARAMEL CRUNCH ROULADE

POINTS value: 5   *pictured on page 56*

PREP: 32 minutes ■ COOK: 18 minutes
■ OTHER: 2 hours

Sweet, crunchy caramel is a surprise in this tender roulade. In Step Five, dusting the dishtowel with powdered sugar is an important step for success. It prevents sticking and tearing when you unroll the cake.

Cooking spray
¾ cup cake flour
6 tablespoons unsweetened cocoa
½ teaspoon baking powder
¼ teaspoon baking soda
¼ teaspoon salt
¾ cup packed brown sugar
2 teaspoons vanilla extract
2 large eggs
1 large egg white
⅓ cup strong brewed coffee, at room temperature
2 tablespoons powdered sugar
6 tablespoons granulated sugar
1 teaspoon butter
¼ cup fat-free caramel topping
3 cups frozen reduced-calorie whipped topping, thawed
Fat-free caramel topping (optional)
1 tablespoon unsweetened cocoa or powdered sugar

1. Preheat oven to 375°.
2. Coat a 15 x 10–inch jelly-roll pan with cooking spray; line bottom with parchment paper. Coat parchment paper with cooking spray. Set aside.
3. Lightly spoon flour into dry measuring cups; level with a knife. Sift together flour and next 4 ingredients.
4. Place brown sugar and next 3 ingredients in a large bowl; beat with a mixer at high speed 3 minutes or until well blended. Add flour mixture and coffee; beat at low speed 30 seconds or just until combined.
5. Pour batter into prepared pan, spreading evenly. Bake at 375° for 9 minutes or until cake springs back when touched lightly in center. Loosen cake from sides of pan using a narrow metal spatula; turn out onto a dishtowel dusted with 2 tablespoons powdered sugar. Carefully peel off parchment paper; cool cake 1 minute. Starting with a long side, roll up cake and towel together. Place, seam side down, on a wire rack; cool completely (about 1 hour).
6. While cake cools, combine granulated sugar and butter in a small heavy saucepan. Cook over medium-high heat until sugar dissolves, stirring frequently. Continue cooking 5 minutes or until golden (do not stir). Immediately pour caramelized sugar onto a parchment paper–lined baking sheet. Cool completely (about 20 minutes).
7. Break cooled caramelized sugar into pieces. Place pieces in a food processor; process until coarsely ground. Measure and set aside about 3 tablespoons coarsely ground caramelized sugar for garnish.
8. To assemble, unroll cake carefully and remove towel. Place ¼ cup caramel topping in a medium bowl; gently fold in whipped topping. Spread mixture evenly over cake, leaving a ½-inch border around edges. Sprinkle evenly with ground caramel. Reroll cake, and place, seam side down, on a platter. Cover and chill 1 hour.
9. Just before serving, cut cake into 10 slices. Drizzle caramel topping over slices, if desired, and sprinkle with reserved coarsely ground caramelized sugar and 1 tablespoon unsweetened cocoa or powdered sugar.

YIELD: 10 SERVINGS (SERVING SIZE: 1 SLICE ROULADE AND ABOUT 1 TEASPOON COARSELY GROUND CARAMELIZED SUGAR).

PER SERVING: CAL 227 (16% from fat); FAT 4.1g (sat 2.9g); PRO 2.9g; CARB 47.2g; FIB 1.3g; CHOL 43mg; IRON 1.4mg; SOD 166mg; CALC 38mg

HOW TO LINE A JELLY-ROLL PAN

Begin by tracing around bottom edge of jelly-roll pan on a sheet of parchment or wax paper. Cut out rectangle using kitchen shears. Coat the inside of jelly-roll pan with cooking spray. Fit parchment rectangle in bottom of pan, pressing down to help paper adhere. Continue as directed in recipe.

HOT CHERRY SHORTCAKES

POINTS value: 6

PREP: 10 minutes ■ COOK: 24 minutes

  7 cups frozen pitted dark sweet cherries
 10 teaspoons sugar, divided
  2 teaspoons grated fresh lemon rind
  1 tablespoon fresh lemon juice
 ½ cup all-purpose flour
 ¾ teaspoon baking powder
 ¼ teaspoon ground cinnamon
 ⅛ teaspoon salt
  1 tablespoon butter
  3 tablespoons fat-free milk
Butter-flavored cooking spray
  2 cups vanilla light ice cream

1. Preheat oven to 450°.
2. Combine cherries, 8 teaspoons sugar, lemon rind, and lemon juice in a medium saucepan. Cook over medium heat until sugar dissolves, stirring occasionally. Cover and cook 8 minutes or until cherries are soft. Uncover and cook 3 to 4 minutes or until juice is syrupy. Remove from heat.
3. While cherries cook, lightly spoon flour into a dry measuring cup; level with a knife. Place flour and next 3 ingredients in a medium bowl; stir with a whisk. Cut in butter with a pastry blender. Add milk; stir just until moist.
4. Drop dough in 6 equal portions onto a baking sheet coated with cooking spray. Coat dough with cooking spray, and sprinkle with remaining 2 teaspoons sugar. Bake at 450° for 10 minutes or until golden.
5. To serve, spoon cherry sauce and ice cream into shallow bowls. Top with biscuits. YIELD: 6 SERVINGS (SERVING SIZE: ABOUT ⅔ CUP CHERRY SAUCE, ⅓ CUP ICE CREAM, AND 1 BISCUIT).

PER SERVING: CAL 299 (13% from fat); FAT 4.4g (sat 2.5g); PRO 5.8g; CARB 62.9g; FIB 1.7g; CHOL 17mg; IRON 1.1mg; SOD 160mg; CALC 142mg

STRAWBERRY SHORTCAKES

POINTS value: 4

PREP: 15 minutes ■ COOK: 15 minutes
■ OTHER: 45 minutes

Tossing the strawberries with brown sugar instead of granulated sugar gives this classic dessert an unexpected hint of molasses flavor.

  2 cups quartered strawberries
  2 tablespoons brown sugar
1¼ cups all-purpose flour
  1 tablespoon granulated sugar, divided
  2 teaspoons baking powder
 ½ teaspoon salt
  3 tablespoons chilled butter, cut into small pieces
  9 tablespoons nonfat buttermilk
Cooking spray
  6 tablespoons frozen reduced-calorie whipped topping, thawed

1. Preheat oven to 400°.
2. Toss strawberries with brown sugar. Let stand 30 minutes, stirring occasionally.
3. While strawberries stand, lightly spoon flour into dry measuring cups; level with a knife. Combine flour, 2 teaspoons granulated sugar, baking powder, and salt in a bowl; cut in butter with a pastry blender or 2 knives until mixture resembles coarse meal. Add buttermilk, stirring just until moist. Turn dough out onto a lightly floured surface; knead 3 times. Pat dough into a 6 x 4–inch rectangle; cut into 2-inch squares. Coat tops of biscuits with cooking spray; sprinkle with remaining 1 teaspoon sugar. Place on a baking sheet coated with cooking spray. Bake at 400° for 15 minutes or until golden. Remove from pan, and cool 15 minutes on a wire rack.
4. Cut biscuits in half, and place on serving plates. Top each with strawberry mixture and whipped topping. YIELD: 6 SERVINGS (SERVING SIZE: 1 BISCUIT, ⅓ CUP STRAW-BERRIES, AND 1 TABLESPOON WHIPPED TOPPING).

PER SERVING: CAL 191 (30% from fat); FAT 6.3g (sat 3.8g); PRO 3.9g; CARB 30.5g; FIB 1g; CHOL 15mg; IRON 1.6mg; SOD 421mg; CALC 133mg

PEACH-BLUEBERRY CRISP

POINTS value: 6

PREP: 16 minutes ■ **COOK:** 35 minutes
■ **OTHER:** 15 minutes

4 chopped peeled large peaches (about 2 pounds)
2½ cups blueberries
3 tablespoons brown sugar
1 tablespoon fresh lemon juice
2 teaspoons cornstarch
Cooking spray
½ cup all-purpose flour
½ cup packed brown sugar
¾ cup old-fashioned rolled oats
1 tablespoon vanilla extract
½ teaspoon salt
¼ teaspoon ground cinnamon
¼ cup butter, melted

1. Preheat oven to 350°.
2. Combine peaches, blueberries, 3 tablespoons brown sugar, lemon juice, and cornstarch in a large bowl; toss gently to combine. Spoon peach mixture into an 8-inch square baking dish coated with cooking spray.
3. Lightly spoon flour into a dry measuring cup; level with a knife. Combine flour, ½ cup brown sugar, oats, vanilla, salt, and cinnamon in a medium bowl. Add butter, and stir thoroughly until mixture resembles coarse meal.
4. Sprinkle oat mixture over fruit mixture. Bake at 350° for 35 minutes or until topping is lightly browned and fruit mixture is bubbly. Let stand 15 minutes before serving. **YIELD: 6 SERVINGS (SERVING SIZE: ABOUT 1 CUP).**

PER SERVING: CAL 325 (25% from fat); FAT 9g (sat 5g); PRO 4.2g; CARB 60g; FIB 4.7g; CHOL 20mg; IRON 1.9mg; SOD 258mg; CALC 41mg

MIXED BERRY SUMMER PUDDING

POINTS value: 3

PREP: 12 minutes ■ **COOK:** 15 minutes
■ **OTHER:** 8 hours

4 cups strawberries, halved
1⅓ cups raspberries
1⅓ cups blueberries
⅔ cup sugar
1 tablespoon grated fresh lemon rind
3 tablespoons fresh lemon juice
Dash of salt
12 slices 100% whole wheat bread
1 cup plain fat-free Greek yogurt (such as Fage)
2 tablespoons sugar
½ teaspoon vanilla extract

1. Combine first 7 ingredients in a large saucepan. Bring to a boil over medium heat, stirring constantly; cook 15 minutes or until berries begin to fall apart, stirring often. Remove from heat, and cool slightly.
2. Stack bread in 3 groups of 4 slices each. Trim crusts from stacks using a serrated knife. Discard crusts. Slice each stack into 3 equal strips, creating 36 strips.
3. Spread ½ cup warm fruit mixture evenly in bottom of a 9 x 5–inch loaf pan.
4. Place 9 bread strips in a single layer over fruit mixture, arranging as necessary to form a single layer. Top with 1 cup fruit mixture, spreading evenly over bread strips to cover completely. Repeat procedure twice, using 18 strips of bread and 2 additional cups of fruit mixture.
5. Layer remaining 9 strips of bread over fruit mixture, and top with remaining ½ cup of fruit mixture, spreading to cover bread. Cover pudding with plastic wrap. Weigh down pudding using 3 (14- to 16-ounce) unopened cans. Chill 8 hours.
6. Combine yogurt, 2 tablespoons sugar, and vanilla in a small bowl, stirring until blended.
7. Remove cans and plastic wrap from pudding. Spoon pudding evenly into dessert dishes; top evenly with yogurt mixture. **YIELD: 10 SERVINGS (SERVING SIZE: ABOUT ½ CUP PUDDING AND ABOUT 1 TABLESPOON YOGURT MIXTURE).**

PER SERVING: CAL 185 (11% from fat); FAT 2.2g (sat 0g); PRO 7.1g; CARB 37.8g; FIB 6.6g; CHOL 0mg; IRON 1.3mg; SOD 178mg; CALC 77mg

COCONUT-OAT COOKIES

POINTS value: 3   *pictured on page 55*

PREP: 11 minutes ■ COOK: 17 minutes
■ OTHER: 5 minutes

  1¼ cups all-purpose flour
    1 cup old-fashioned rolled oats
   ¾ cup packed dark brown sugar
    1 teaspoon baking soda
   ⅛ teaspoon salt
   ¼ cup chilled butter, cut into small pieces
   ¾ cup flaked sweetened coconut
   ¼ cup water
    2 tablespoons light corn syrup
Cooking spray

1. Preheat oven to 350°.
2. Lightly spoon flour into dry measuring cups; level with a knife. Combine flour and next 4 ingredients in a medium bowl. Cut in butter with a pastry blender or 2 knives until mixture resembles coarse meal. Stir in coconut. Add water and corn syrup; stir just until dry ingredients are moist.
3. Turn dough out onto a lightly floured surface; knead 2 or 3 times. Roll dough to ½-inch thickness; cut with a 2½-inch cookie cutter. Reroll trimmings to make additional cookies.
4. Place cookies on a baking sheet coated with cooking spray. Bake at 350° for 17 minutes or until lightly browned. Cool on pan 5 minutes. Transfer to a wire rack to cool completely. YIELD: 16 COOKIES (SERVING SIZE: 1 COOKIE).

PER SERVING: CAL 128 (30% from fat); FAT 4.3g (sat 2.8g); PRO 1.8g; CARB 21.2g; FIB 1.1g; CHOL 8mg; IRON 0.9mg; SOD 131mg; CALC 11mg

TROPICAL MACAROONS

POINTS value: 1

PREP: 24 minutes ■ COOK: 20 minutes
■ OTHER: 5 minutes

These chewy, chocolate-drizzled macaroons include candied pineapple, ginger, and cinnamon for some exotic flavor.

    1 cup flaked sweetened coconut
    1 tablespoon all-purpose flour
   ½ cup sugar
   ⅛ teaspoon ground ginger
   ⅛ teaspoon ground cinnamon
Dash of salt
    2 large egg whites
   ½ cup finely minced candied pineapple
   ⅛ teaspoon almond extract
   ¼ cup dark chocolate chips (such as Hershey's Special Dark)

1. Preheat oven to 325°.
2. Combine coconut and flour, tossing to coat.
3. Combine sugar and next 3 ingredients. Beat egg whites with a mixer until soft peaks form. Add sugar mixture, 1 tablespoon at a time, beating until stiff peaks form.
4. Fold coconut mixture, pineapple, and almond extract into beaten egg whites. Drop by heaping tablespoons 2 inches apart onto baking sheets lined with parchment paper.
5. Bake at 325° for 20 minutes or until edges begin to brown. Cool on pans 5 minutes; remove from pans, and cool completely on wire racks.
6. Place chips in a small heavy-duty zip-top plastic bag; microwave at HIGH 15 seconds or until soft. Knead bag until smooth. Snip a tiny hole in 1 corner of bag; drizzle chocolate over macaroons. YIELD: 24 SERVINGS (SERVING SIZE: 1 MACAROON).

PER SERVING: CAL 60 (27% from fat); FAT 1.8g (sat 1.4g); PRO 0.6g; CARB 11g; FIB 0.4g; CHOL 0mg; IRON 0.2mg; SOD 12mg; CALC 1mg

LAVENDER SHORTBREAD

POINTS value: 4

PREP: 5 minutes ■ **COOK:** 25 minutes

Fragrant lavender adds a special twist to this traditional cookie. Find it in the produce department in sealed plastic bags or on the baking aisle among dried herbs and spices.

  6 tablespoons unsalted butter, softened
  1 cup all-purpose flour
  ½ cup powdered sugar
  ¾ teaspoon dried lavender (such as Melissa's)
  ⅛ teaspoon salt
  1 tablespoon ice water
Cooking spray
  1 tablespoon granulated sugar

1. Preheat oven to 350°.
2. Place butter in a medium bowl; beat with a mixer at medium speed until light and fluffy.
3. Lightly spoon flour into a dry measuring cup; level with a knife. Combine flour and next 3 ingredients in a medium bowl; stir well with a whisk. Gradually add flour mixture to butter, beating until well blended. Add water; stir just until moist (do not overmix).
4. Press dough into an 8-inch round cake pan coated with cooking spray. Sprinkle top with granulated sugar.
5. Bake at 350° for 25 minutes or until golden brown. Score shortbread to form 8 wedges. Remove round of shortbread from pan; cool completely on a wire rack. Gently separate into individual wedges. YIELD: 8 SERVINGS (SERVING SIZE: 1 WEDGE).

PER SERVING: CAL 168 (47% from fat); FAT 8.7g (sat 5.4g); PRO 1.7g; CARB 21g; FIB 0.4g; CHOL 23mg; IRON 0.8mg; SOD 38mg; CALC 7mg

ABOUT LAVENDER

Lavender is a beautifully aromatic spice that comes from the mint family and adds a mysterious flavor to baked goods. As the spice dries, the aroma grows stronger, so dried lavender is stronger than the fresh variety. Since it is so pungent, be sure to use it only in small amounts.

CHOCOLATE CHIP BISCOTTI

POINTS value: 3

PREP: 28 minutes ■ **COOK:** 35 minutes
■ **OTHER:** 10 minutes

This version is softer than ordinary biscotti and is loaded with chocolate morsels, a hint of brandy, and vanilla. Substitute orange juice for the brandy, if you prefer.

  1¾ cups sugar
  ¼ cup chilled butter, cut into small pieces
  2 large eggs
  2 large egg whites
  3 tablespoons brandy
  1 tablespoon vanilla extract
  3½ cups all-purpose flour
  1 teaspoon baking soda
  1 teaspoon baking powder
  ½ teaspoon salt
  1¼ cups semisweet chocolate minichips

1. Preheat oven to 375°.
2. Place sugar and butter in a large bowl; beat with a mixer at medium speed until well blended. Add eggs and next 3 ingredients. Beat 2 minutes.
3. Lightly spoon flour into dry measuring cups; level with a knife. Combine flour and next 3 ingredients, stirring well with a whisk. Add flour mixture to butter mixture; beat just until combined. Stir in chocolate minichips.
4. Turn dough out onto a lightly floured surface; knead lightly 3 or 4 times (dough will be soft). Divide dough into 3 equal portions. Shape each portion into a 14-inch-long roll. Carefully place rolls on a large baking sheet lined with parchment paper; pat rolls to 1-inch thickness, keeping rolls 3 inches apart.
5. Bake at 375° for 25 minutes. Remove rolls from baking sheet; cool 10 minutes on a wire rack.
6. Cut each roll diagonally into 12 slices. Place, cut sides down, on parchment paper–lined baking sheets. Bake at 375° for 10 minutes or until edges are golden brown. Remove from baking sheets; cool completely on wire rack. YIELD: 36 SERVINGS (SERVING SIZE: 1 BISCOTTO).

PER SERVING: CAL 130 (24% from fat); FAT 3.4g (sat 1.9g); PRO 2.1g; CARB 22.8g; FIB 0.7g; CHOL 15mg; IRON 0.8mg; SOD 98mg; CALC 13mg

PISTACHIO ROCHERS

POINTS value: 1

PREP: 10 minutes ■ **COOK:** 1 hour and 30 minutes
■ **OTHER:** 1 hour

Rocher is French for "boulder" or "rock". These cookies are shaped like small rocks, but the salty-sweet, melt-in-your-mouth treats are light and crisp due to long, slow baking.

- 2 large egg whites
- ¼ teaspoon cream of tartar
- ½ teaspoon vanilla extract
- ½ cup sugar
- ½ cup shelled dry roasted, lightly salted pistachios

1. Preheat oven to 225°.
2. Cover a baking sheet with parchment paper. Draw 20 (2-inch) circles on paper. Turn paper over; secure with masking tape.
3. Place egg whites and cream of tartar in a large bowl; beat with a mixer at high speed until foamy. Beat in vanilla. Gradually add sugar, 1 tablespoon at a time, beating 3 minutes or until stiff peaks form (do not underbeat). Fold in pistachios. Drop mixture by heaping tablespoons among 20 drawn circles on prepared baking sheet; spread to fill the circles using the back of a spoon.
4. Bake at 225° for 1 hour and 30 minutes. Turn oven off; cool in closed oven for 1 hour. Cool completely on pan. Carefully remove rochers from paper. Store rochers in an airtight container up to 1 week. YIELD: 20 ROCHERS (SERVING SIZE: 1 ROCHER).

PER SERVING: CAL 40 (34% from fat); FAT 1.5g (sat 0.2g); PRO 1.1g; CARB 5.9g; FIB 0.3g; CHOL 0mg; IRON 0.1mg; SOD 19mg; CALC 4mg

THE STAGES OF BEATING EGG WHITES

When you beat egg whites, use room-temperature eggs to get the most volume. Both hand and stand mixers work well, but if you use a stand mixer, watch carefully because it's easy to overbeat. If you prefer a hand-held mixer, the whisk attachment is the best choice. The first stage of beating egg whites is the foamy stage. When beaten to this stage, the whites will look bubbly and foamy. Next is the soft peak stage, at which point the whites will mound but have no sharp peaks. To bring egg whites to the stiff peak stage, beat until sharp peaks form when the beaters are lifted. There is no restoring overbeaten egg whites, so be careful to stop beating just as you reach the stage your recipe requires.

BANANA CREAM PIE

POINTS value: 4

PREP: 20 minutes ■ **COOK:** 15 minutes

- 9 low-fat graham cracker cookie sheets, crumbled
- 1 teaspoon sugar
- 1 tablespoon light butter, melted
- 1 large egg white
- Cooking spray
- ⅓ cup sugar
- 3 tablespoons cornstarch
- ⅛ teaspoon salt
- 2½ cups fat-free milk
- ½ cup egg substitute
- 1½ teaspoons vanilla extract
- 1½ cups ripe banana slices (about 2 medium)
- 1 (8-ounce) container frozen reduced-calorie whipped topping, thawed

1. Preheat oven to 350°.
2. Place crumbled graham crackers and 1 teaspoon sugar in a food processor; process until crumbs form. Add butter and egg white; process until crumbs are moist. Press crumb mixture into bottom and up sides of a 9-inch pie plate coated with cooking spray. Bake at 350° for 12 minutes. Cool.
3. Combine ⅓ cup sugar, cornstarch, and salt in a medium saucepan; gradually add milk, stirring with a whisk. Cook over medium heat, whisking constantly, until mixture comes to a boil; cook 1 minute. Remove from heat.
4. Gradually whisk one-fourth of hot mixture into egg substitute; add to remaining hot mixture. Cook over medium-low heat 2 minutes or until mixture thickens, stirring constantly with a whisk. Remove from heat; stir in vanilla.
5. Arrange banana slices in bottom of prepared crust. Pour filling over bananas. Cover surface of filling with plastic wrap. Chill thoroughly.
6. Remove plastic wrap; spread whipped topping evenly over filling. YIELD: 10 SERVINGS (SERVING SIZE: 1 WEDGE).

PER SERVING: CAL 201 (19% from fat); FAT 4.3g (sat 3.1g); PRO 5.2g; CARB 36.4g; FIB 1g; CHOL 3mg; IRON 0.8mg; SOD 173mg; CALC 144mg

The Chinese discovered a gem when they began brewing green tea. Some scientists believe that green tea may fight heart disease and cancer, and the modest amount of caffeine it contains promotes alertness. One tea bag, which will make 1 (8-ounce) cup of tea, has 0 calories, 20 milligrams of potassium, 0 grams of sugar, and 45 milligrams of caffeine. It is more delicate than black tea, so when steeping, use very hot (rather than boiling) liquid. Store green tea bags in a cool, dark place. We recommend not using tea that's older than 6 months, as most of the flavor vanishes after that point.

GREEN TEA CRÉME BRÛLÉE

POINTS value: 5

PREP: 5 minutes ■ COOK: 1 hour and 8 minutes
■ OTHER: 8 hours and 20 minutes

2 cups 2% reduced-fat milk
¾ cup nonfat dry milk
3 green tea bags
1 vanilla bean, cut in half lengthwise
⅔ cup sugar, divided
4 large egg yolks
½ cup fresh raspberries (optional)

1. Heat first 4 ingredients over medium heat in a medium-sized heavy saucepan to 180° or until tiny bubbles form around edge of pan, stirring frequently (do not boil). Remove from heat; cover and let stand 20 minutes. Scrape seeds from vanilla bean into milk mixture; discard bean.
2. Preheat oven to 300°.
3. Combine ⅓ cup sugar and egg yolks in a medium bowl; beat with a whisk until thick and pale. Gradually add milk mixture to egg yolk mixture, stirring constantly with a whisk. Strain mixture through a sieve into a bowl; discard solids.
4. Divide mixture evenly among 5 (4-ounce) custard cups. Place custard cups in a 9-inch square baking pan; add hot water to pan to a depth of 1 inch.
5. Bake at 300° for 50 to 55 minutes or until a knife inserted in center comes out clean. Remove ramekins from pan; cool completely on a wire rack. Cover and chill at least 8 hours.
6. Place remaining ⅓ cup sugar in a small heavy saucepan; cook over medium heat 4 minutes or until sugar dissolves and is golden, shaking pan often. Immediately pour (do not spoon) a thin layer on top of custard

in ramekins, tipping each quickly until caramelized sugar coats custard. Garnish with raspberries, if desired.
YIELD: 5 SERVINGS (SERVING SIZE: 1 CUSTARD).

PER SERVING: CAL 238 (21% from fat); FAT 5.5g (sat 2.5g); PRO 9.6g; CARB 38g; FIB 0g; CHOL 173mg; IRON 0.4mg; SOD 121mg; CALC 294mg

CUSTARDS WITH MAPLE WALNUTS

POINTS value: 5

PREP: 5 minutes ■ COOK: 50 minutes
■ OTHER: 8 hours

Each spoonful of this silky custard includes liquid caramel from the bottom of the cup.

¾ cup sugar, divided
2 large eggs
2 cups 2% reduced-fat milk
½ teaspoon vanilla extract
⅛ teaspoon salt
6 tablespoons chopped walnuts
1 tablespoon maple syrup

1. Preheat oven to 350°.
2. Place ½ cup sugar in a medium-sized heavy skillet; cook over medium heat 5 minutes or until sugar dissolves, gently shaking pan as sugar melts. When bottom of sugar becomes liquid, stir slowly until golden. Immediately pour evenly into 6 (4-ounce) custard cups, tipping quickly to coat bottoms of cups.
3. Combine eggs and remaining ¼ cup sugar in a medium bowl, stirring with a whisk. Add milk, vanilla, and salt, stirring with a whisk until smooth. Divide mixture evenly among prepared custard cups. Place cups in a 13 x 9–inch baking pan; add hot water to pan to a depth of 1 inch. Bake at 350° for 45 minutes or until a knife inserted in center comes out clean. Remove cups from pan; cool completely on a wire rack. Cover and chill 8 hours.
4. While custards bake, combine walnuts and maple syrup in a medium-sized nonstick skillet. Cook over medium heat 8 minutes, stirring constantly, until nuts are fragrant, dry, and crystallized. Cool completely.
5. Top chilled custards evenly with maple walnuts.
YIELD: 6 SERVINGS (SERVING SIZE: 1 CUSTARD AND 1 TABLESPOON WALNUTS).

PER SERVING: CAL 219 (33% from fat); FAT 8g (sat 1.9g); PRO 5.9g; CARB 32.3g; FIB 0.5g; CHOL 77mg; IRON 0.6mg; SOD 113mg; CALC 117mg

DARK CHOCOLATE SOUFFLÉ WITH ORANGE CUSTARD SAUCE

POINTS value: 5

PREP: 16 minutes ■ **COOK:** 38 minutes

This decadent chocolate dessert will definitely impress your guests. For the best flavor, select a premium dark chocolate, such as Scharffen Berger.

Cooking spray
¾ cup sugar, divided
⅓ cup unsweetened cocoa
1 tablespoon cornstarch
⅛ teaspoon salt
¾ cup 1% low-fat milk
1 large egg yolk, lightly beaten
4 ounces dark chocolate, finely chopped
5 large egg whites
¼ teaspoon cream of tartar
1 cup packed vanilla light ice cream, thawed
1 tablespoon Grand Marnier (orange-flavored liqueur)

1. Preheat oven to 400°.
2. Coat a 1½-quart soufflé dish with cooking spray; sprinkle with 2 tablespoons sugar.
3. Combine ¼ cup sugar, cocoa, cornstarch, and salt in a small saucepan. Gradually add milk, stirring with a whisk until blended. Bring to a boil over medium heat; cook until thick (about 1 minute), stirring constantly. Remove from heat. Gradually stir in egg yolk. Add chocolate, stirring until chocolate melts.
4. Place egg whites in a large bowl; beat with a mixer at high speed until foamy. Add cream of tartar, beating until soft peaks form. Add remaining 6 tablespoons sugar, 1 tablespoon at a time, beating until stiff peaks form. Gently stir one-fourth of egg white mixture into chocolate mixture; gently fold chocolate mixture into remaining egg white mixture. Spoon into prepared soufflé dish.
5. Bake at 400° for 10 minutes; reduce oven temperature to 375°, and bake an additional 25 minutes or until puffy and set.
6. While soufflé bakes, combine ice cream and liqueur. Serve soufflé immediately from oven with ice cream mixture. YIELD: 8 SERVINGS (SERVING SIZE: ⅛ OF SOUFFLÉ AND 1½ TABLESPOONS SAUCE).

PER SERVING: CAL 217 (28% from fat); FAT 6.8g (sat 3.8g); PRO 5.6g; CARB 36.7g; FIB 1.9g; CHOL 31mg; IRON 1.2mg; SOD 97mg; CALC 66mg

Soufflé comes from a French word meaning "to inflate" or "to breathe," which perfectly describes the dessert's delicately light texture. Soufflés begin to deflate as soon as they leave the oven, so plan your dinner so that the soufflés finish baking just as it's time to serve them.

LEMON SOUFFLÉ

POINTS value: 3

PREP: 30 minutes ■ **COOK:** 14 minutes

These vibrant citrusy soufflés are perfect for entertaining because they can be prepared and refrigerated up to 1 hour ahead. Simply add a minute or two to the baking time to make certain they are set.

Cooking spray
3 tablespoons sugar
4 large egg yolks
⅔ cup sugar, divided
1 cup low-fat buttermilk
⅓ cup all-purpose flour
4 teaspoons butter, melted
1 tablespoon grated fresh lemon rind
5 tablespoons fresh lemon juice
4 large egg whites

1. Preheat oven to 375°.
2. Coat 10 (4-ounce) ramekins or custard cups with cooking spray; sprinkle evenly with 3 tablespoons sugar. Place prepared ramekins on a baking sheet.
3. Place egg yolks in a large bowl; beat with a mixer at high speed for 2 minutes. Gradually add ⅓ cup sugar, beating until thick and pale, about 2 minutes. Add buttermilk and next 4 ingredients, beating at low speed.
4. Place egg whites in a large bowl; beat with a mixer at high speed until foamy. Gradually add remaining ⅓ cup sugar, 1 tablespoon at a time, beating until stiff peaks form.
5. Gently stir one-third of egg white mixture into lemon mixture; gently fold in remaining egg white mixture. Spoon into prepared ramekins, leveling with a knife. Wipe ramekin rims clean with a paper towel.
6. Bake at 375° for 14 minutes or until puffy and set. Serve immediately. YIELD: 10 SERVINGS (SERVING SIZE: 1 SOUFFLÉ).

PER SERVING: CAL 136 (24% from fat); FAT 3.6g (sat 1.8g); PRO 3.9g; CARB 22.7g; FIB 0.2g; CHOL 87mg; IRON 0.4mg; SOD 63mg; CALC 37mg

PEACH ICE CREAM

POINTS value: 2

PREP: 14 minutes ■ **COOK:** 10 minutes
■ **OTHER:** 2 hours and 10 minutes

Fresh, midsummer peaches are ideal for making this old-fashioned favorite. If your peaches aren't perfectly ripe and soft, coarsely mash them in the food processor.

    2 cups 2% reduced-fat milk
    ¾ cup granulated sugar
    ⅛ teaspoon salt
    3 large egg yolks
    1 large egg
    3 cups mashed peeled peaches
    ⅓ cup packed brown sugar
    1 tablespoon fresh lime juice

1. Cook milk over medium-high heat in a heavy saucepan 6 minutes or until hot. Remove from heat.
2. Combine granulated sugar and next 3 ingredients in a medium bowl; beat with a mixer at high speed until thick and pale. Gradually add about one-fourth hot milk to egg mixture, stirring constantly with a whisk. Add to remaining hot milk, stirring constantly. Cook over medium heat 4 minutes or until mixture reaches 160°, stirring constantly with a whisk. Transfer mixture to a bowl. Cover and chill 30 minutes.
3. Combine peaches, brown sugar, and lime juice; add to chilled milk mixture. Pour mixture into the freezer can of a 4-quart ice-cream freezer, and freeze according to manufacturer's instructions. Spoon ice cream into a freezer-safe container. Cover and freeze 1 hour or until firm. YIELD: 18 SERVINGS (SERVING SIZE: ½ CUP).

PER SERVING: CAL 85 (17% from fat); FAT 1.6g (sat 0.7g); PRO 2g; CARB 16.5g; FIB 0.4g; CHOL 48mg; IRON 0.3mg; SOD 37mg; CALC 43mg

STRAWBERRY FROZEN YOGURT

POINTS value: 1

pictured on page 57

PREP: 24 minutes ■ **COOK:** 20 minutes
■ **OTHER:** 1 hour and 30 minutes

Fresh thyme may seem like an unusual ingredient in a dessert, but in this recipe, it adds a delicate herb flavor that complements the sweet strawberries.

    8 cups strawberries, halved
    ¼ cup packed brown sugar
    2 fresh thyme sprigs (optional)
    10 tablespoons granulated sugar
    ¼ cup water
    1 tablespoon fresh lemon juice
    Dash of salt
    1 (17.6-ounce) carton plain fat-free Greek yogurt
    1 tablespoon vanilla extract
    Fresh thyme sprigs (optional)

1. Place strawberries, brown sugar, and, if desired, thyme in a medium saucepan. Cook over medium–low heat 20 minutes or until strawberries begin to fall apart. Remove from heat; remove and discard thyme sprigs.
2. While strawberries cook, combine granulated sugar and next 3 ingredients in a small saucepan. Bring to a boil; boil 1 to 2 minutes or until sugar dissolves. Stir syrup into cooked strawberry mixture. Cool 1 hour.
3. Process half of strawberry mixture in batches in a blender until puréed. Pour puréed strawberry mixture into the freezer can of a 3-quart ice-cream freezer. Repeat procedure with remaining strawberry mixture. Add yogurt and vanilla to ice-cream freezer, stirring well with a whisk. Freeze according to manufacturer's instructions. Spoon into a freezer-safe container. Cover and freeze until firm. Garnish with thyme sprigs, if desired. YIELD: 16 SERVINGS (SERVING SIZE: ½ CUP).

PER SERVING: CAL 85 (2% from fat); FAT 0.2g (sat 0g); PRO 3.2g; CARB 18.1g; FIB 1.4g; CHOL 0mg; IRON 0.4mg; SOD 23mg; CALC 35mg

BLUEBERRY-POMEGRANATE SORBET

POINTS value: 2

PREP: 49 minutes ■ COOK: 3 minutes
■ OTHER: 3 hours

If fresh berries are out of season, frozen ones work just as well. To get the same delicious results with frozen blueberries, measure the frozen berries first, and then thaw them completely before proceeding.

    ¾ cup sugar
    ¼ cup water
    8 cups blueberries
Dash of salt
    1 cup blueberry-pomegranate juice
    1 tablespoon white rum (optional)

1. Combine sugar and water in a saucepan; bring to a boil. Cook, stirring constantly, until sugar dissolves. Cool completely.
2. Combine one-fourth of sugar mixture and 2 cups blueberries in a blender; process until smooth. Transfer mixture to a sieve over a large bowl. Repeat procedure with remaining sugar mixture and blueberries. Press blueberry mixture through sieve, reserving liquid in bowl; discard skins and seeds. Add salt, blueberry-pomegranate juice, and, if desired, rum.
3. Pour mixture into the freezer can of a 2- to 3-quart ice-cream freezer, and freeze according to manufacturer's instructions. Spoon sorbet into a freezer-safe container. Cover and freeze until firm. YIELD: 13 SERVINGS (SERVING SIZE: ½ CUP).

PER SERVING: CAL 107 (3% from fat); FAT 0.3g (sat 0g); PRO 0.7g; CARB 27.4g; FIB 2.2g; CHOL 0mg; IRON 0.3mg; SOD 14mg; CALC 7mg

FROZEN CHOCOLATE-CHERRY PIE

POINTS value: 6   *pictured on page 53*

PREP: 8 minutes ■ OTHER: 8 hours

    4 cups chocolate low-fat frozen yogurt, softened
    1½ cups red maraschino cherries, drained and chopped
    1 (6-ounce) chocolate cookie piecrust (such as Keebler)
    ½ cup frozen reduced-calorie whipped topping, thawed
    2 tablespoons grated bittersweet chocolate (optional)
    8 red maraschino cherries with stems (optional)

1. Combine frozen yogurt and cherries in a large bowl; fold gently to combine. Spoon yogurt mixture into piecrust. Cover and freeze 8 hours or until firm.

2. Cut into wedges, and top with whipped topping. Garnish with grated bittersweet chocolate and maraschino cherries with stems, if desired. Serve immediately. YIELD: 8 SERVINGS (SERVING SIZE: 1 WEDGE).

PER SERVING: CAL 275 (23% from fat); FAT 7.1g (sat 2.5g); PRO 5.1g; CARB 50.6g; FIB 1.1g; CHOL 5mg; IRON 0.1mg; SOD 178mg; CALC 168mg

ROCKY ROAD BROWNIE SANDWICHES

POINTS value: 5   *pictured on cover*

PREP: 15 minutes ■ COOK: 14 minutes
■ OTHER: 10 hours

Cooking spray
    ¾ cup all-purpose flour
    ½ cup unsweetened cocoa
    ½ teaspoon baking powder
    ⅛ teaspoon salt
    ¾ cup sugar
    ¼ cup canola oil
    1½ teaspoons vanilla extract
    2 large egg whites
    1 large egg
    2½ cups rocky road low-fat ice cream (such as Breyers)

1. Preheat oven to 350°.
2. Line 2 (8-inch) square baking pans with parchment paper, allowing 2 inches parchment paper to hang over the edge of each pan. Coat paper with cooking spray.
3. Lightly spoon flour into dry measuring cups; level with a knife. Combine flour and next 3 ingredients in a medium bowl. Combine sugar and next 4 ingredients in a medium bowl. Add sugar mixture to flour mixture, stirring until combined. Divide batter between prepared pans. Coat a spatula with cooking spray; spread batter evenly in each pan. Bake at 350° for 14 minutes or until a wooden pick inserted in center comes out clean. Cool brownies completely in pans on a wire rack.
4. Spread ice cream over 1 brownie in pan. Remove other brownie from pan, peel away parchment paper, and invert over ice cream layer. Press gently. Cover and freeze 8 hours or until firm. Remove from pan, and cut into 9 equal pieces. Serve immediately, or wrap individually and freeze up to 1 month. YIELD: 9 SERVINGS (SERVING SIZE: 1 SANDWICH).

PER SERVING: CAL 244 (42% from fat); FAT 11.4g (sat 3g); PRO 5.2g; CARB 35.2g; FIB 4.1g; CHOL 32mg; IRON 1.3mg; SOD 81mg; CALC 26mg

Texas Caviar, *page 19*

Jerk French Fries with
Pineapple Aïoli,
page 20

Golden Onion,
Brie, and Dried-Fruit
Crostini, *page 23*

Carrot Cake Pancakes with
Cream Cheese Sauce, *page 32*

Orange Biscuits, *page 29*

Frozen Chocolate-Cherry Pie,
page 48

Baked Apples with Toffee and Almonds, *page 36*

Coconut-Oat Cookies, *page 42*

Chocolate–Caramel Crunch
Roulade, *page 39*

Strawberry Frozen Yogurt, *page 47*

Grilled Pineapple with
Honey-Lime Sauce, *page 37*

Barbecued Salmon with
Maple-Lemon Glaze,
page 68

Seared Scallops with
Soy-Ginger Sauce,
page 72

Grilled Barbecue Shrimp, *page 73*

Spicy Fish Sticks with
Chipotle Ketchup, *page 68*

Grouper with Pan-Roasted Tomatoes,
page 66

Creole Vegetables on
Cheese Grits, *page 82*

Greek Frittata, *page 84*

Butternut Squash and Leek Risotto,
page 82

fish & shellfish

Grilled Barbecue Shrimp, *page 73*

FISH ESCOVITCH

POINTS value: 5

PREP: 14 minutes ■ **COOK:** 44 minutes

- 2 tablespoons olive oil, divided
- 2 cups thinly sliced onion
- 1 cup chopped carrot
- 1 cup sliced red bell pepper
- 1 cup sliced green bell pepper
- 1 cup thinly sliced zucchini
- ½ cup white vinegar
- 3 tablespoons fresh lemon juice
- 12 black peppercorns
- 1 bay leaf
- 4 (6-ounce) flounder or other firm white fish fillets
- ½ teaspoon salt
- ½ teaspoon freshly ground black pepper

1. Heat 2 teaspoons oil in a large nonstick skillet over medium–high heat. Add onion and carrot; cook 5 minutes or until tender, stirring often. Add bell peppers and zucchini; cook 3 minutes, stirring often. Add vinegar and next 3 ingredients; bring to a boil. Reduce heat; simmer, uncovered, 30 minutes or until liquid is almost absorbed, stirring often. Discard bay leaf.
2. Heat remaining 4 teaspoons oil in a large nonstick skillet over medium–high heat. Sprinkle fish with salt and pepper. Add fish to pan; cook 3 minutes on each side or until fish flakes easily when tested with a fork. Spoon vegetables evenly over fish. Serve hot or chilled. YIELD: 4 SERVINGS (SERVING SIZE: 1 FILLET AND ABOUT ¾ CUP VEGETABLES).

PER SERVING: CAL 250 (32% from fat); FAT 8.9g (sat 1.4g); PRO 30.3g; CARB 12.4g; FIB 3.3g; CHOL 80mg; IRON 1.1mg; SOD 444mg; CALC 54mg

ROASTED GROUPER WITH HERBED BREADCRUMBS

POINTS value: 6

PREP: 12 minutes ■ **COOK:** 14 minutes

Select grouper fillets that are as uniform in thickness as possible. If a fillet is uneven, loosely fold under the thin end to even out the thickness.

- 2 (1.5-ounce) slices firm white bread, torn into small pieces (such as Pepperidge Farm)
- ¼ cup chopped fresh chives
- 3 tablespoons chopped fresh parsley
- ½ cup nonfat buttermilk
- 4 (6-ounce) grouper or other firm white fish fillets
- ¼ teaspoon salt
- ¼ teaspoon freshly ground black pepper
- 2 tablespoons butter, melted

1. Preheat oven to 400°.
2. Place first 3 ingredients in a food processor; pulse until coarse crumbs form.
3. Pour buttermilk into a large bowl. Place breadcrumbs in a shallow dish.
4. Sprinkle fish with salt and pepper. Dip fish in buttermilk, and dredge in breadcrumb mixture, pressing firmly to coat. Place fish on a baking sheet lined with parchment paper. Drizzle butter over fish. Bake at 400° for 14 minutes or until fish flakes easily when tested with a fork. YIELD: 4 SERVINGS (SERVING SIZE: 1 FILLET).

PER SERVING: CAL 280 (26% from fat); FAT 8.2g (sat 4.3g); PRO 36.3g; CARB 13g; FIB 0.7g; CHOL 78mg; IRON 1.8mg; SOD 431mg; CALC 92mg

GROUPER WITH PAN-ROASTED TOMATOES

POINTS value: 4

pictured on page 61

PREP: 5 minutes ■ **COOK:** 12 minutes

- 2 teaspoons paprika
- 1 tablespoon olive oil, divided
- 1 teaspoon freshly ground black pepper
- ¼ teaspoon salt
- 4 (6-ounce) grouper or other firm white fish fillets
- Cooking spray
- 2 garlic cloves, minced
- ½ teaspoon crushed red pepper
- 1 cup grape or cherry tomatoes, halved
- 2 tablespoons fresh lemon juice
- ¼ cup chopped fresh parsley

1. Combine paprika, 2 teaspoons oil, pepper, and salt in a small bowl. Rub paprika mixture on both sides of each fillet. Set aside.

2. Heat a large nonstick skillet over medium-high heat; coat pan with cooking spray. Add fish, and cook 4 minutes on each side or until fish flakes easily when tested with a fork. Remove fish from pan, and keep warm.

3. Place remaining 1 teaspoon oil in pan over medium heat. Add garlic and crushed red pepper. Sauté until tender. Add tomatoes and lemon juice. Cook 2 minutes or until mixture is hot and tomatoes begin to burst. Spoon tomato mixture over fish, and sprinkle with parsley. YIELD: 4 SERVINGS (SERVING SIZE: 1 FILLET AND ¼ CUP TOMATOES).

PER SERVING: CAL 206 (24% from fat); FAT 5.6g (sat 0.9g); PRO 33.8g; CARB 4.1g; FIB 1.2g; CHOL 63mg; IRON 2.1mg; SOD 215mg; CALC 61mg

GRILLED HALIBUT WITH AVOCADO SALSA

POINTS value: 6

PREP: 12 minutes ■ COOK: 6 minutes

Any leftover Avocado Salsa makes a great snack with baked tortilla chips. One tablespoon has a **POINTS** value of 1.

    1 large avocado, peeled and chopped
    ⅓ cup chopped seeded tomato
    ¼ cup finely chopped red onion
    2 tablespoons chopped fresh cilantro
    1 tablespoon fresh lime juice
    2 teaspoons olive oil
    1 garlic clove, minced
    ½ teaspoon salt, divided
    4 (6-ounce) halibut fillets
    ¼ teaspoon freshly ground black pepper
  Cooking spray

1. Prepare grill.

2. Combine first 7 ingredients in a medium bowl. Stir in ¼ teaspoon salt. Cover and chill.

3. Sprinkle fish with pepper and remaining ¼ teaspoon salt. Coat fish with cooking spray. Place fish on grill rack coated with cooking spray; grill 4 minutes. Turn fish; grill 2 minutes or until fish flakes easily when tested with a fork. Serve fish with salsa. YIELD: 4 SERVINGS (SERVING SIZE: 1 FILLET AND ¼ CUP SALSA).

PER SERVING: CAL 276 (43% from fat); FAT 13.2g (sat 2.5g); PRO 36g; CARB 5.1g; FIB 2.4g; CHOL 122mg; IRON 1mg; SOD 430mg; CALC 45mg

MAHIMAHI TOSTADAS

POINTS value: 5

PREP: 18 minutes ■ COOK: 21 minutes

Grilled fish has become a popular choice in Mexican favorites like tostadas, tacos, and enchiladas. When purchasing raw frozen fish, make sure it's solidly frozen and tightly wrapped. To quick-thaw it, place the wrapped frozen fish in cold water, allowing about 45 minutes to thaw a 12-ounce package.

    4 (6-inch) corn tortillas
  Cooking spray
    ⅓ cup cream-style corn
    ¼ cup reduced-fat sour cream
    ½ teaspoon grated fresh lime rind
    1 (12-ounce) package frozen mahimahi or other firm white fish fillets, thawed
    ¼ teaspoon freshly ground black pepper
    ⅛ teaspoon salt
    1 (16-ounce) can refried beans
  1½ cups shredded lettuce
    1 cup chopped tomato
    2 tablespoons chopped fresh cilantro

1. Preheat oven to 425°.

2. Spray corn tortillas with cooking spray. Place on a baking sheet, and bake at 425° for 13 minutes or until crisp and golden.

3. Combine corn, sour cream, and lime rind in a bowl.

4. Prepare grill.

5. Sprinkle fish with pepper and salt. Place fish on grill rack coated with cooking spray; grill 4 to 5 minutes on each side or until fish flakes easily when tested with a fork. Separate fish fillets into large chunks.

6. Spread beans evenly on tortillas; layer tortillas with lettuce, tomato, fish, corn mixture, and cilantro. Serve immediately. YIELD: 4 SERVINGS (SERVING SIZE: 1 TOSTADA).

PER SERVING: CAL 272 (15% from fat); FAT 4.6g (sat 1.9g); PRO 24.7g; CARB 34.8g; FIB 8.3g; CHOL 79mg; IRON 3.2mg; SOD 566mg; CALC 100mg

SPICY FISH STICKS
WITH CHIPOTLE KETCHUP

POINTS value: 6

pictured on page 61

PREP: 7 minutes ■ **COOK:** 4 minutes

Adding a few full-flavored ingredients takes this family favorite from routine to robust. Look for chipotle chile powder and salt-free Cajun seasoning alongside dried herbs and spices in the supermarket.

- ½ cup ketchup
- ¼ teaspoon chipotle chile powder
- ¼ cup yellow cornmeal
- 3 tablespoons all-purpose flour
- 1½ teaspoons salt-free Cajun seasoning
- 1½ teaspoons dried parsley
- ½ teaspoon garlic salt, divided
- 4 (6-ounce) mahimahi fillets
- 2 tablespoons canola oil

1. Combine ketchup and chipotle chile powder in a small bowl. Set aside.

2. Combine cornmeal, flour, Cajun seasoning, parsley, and ¼ teaspoon garlic salt in a shallow dish. Cut each fillet in half lengthwise, then in half crosswise. Press fish between paper towels until barely moist; sprinkle with remaining ¼ teaspoon garlic salt, and dredge in cornmeal mixture.

3. Heat oil in a large nonstick skillet over medium-high heat. Add fish; cook 2 minutes on each side or until fish flakes easily when tested with a fork. Serve with ketchup mixture. **YIELD: 4 SERVINGS (SERVING SIZE: 4 FISH STICKS AND 2 TABLESPOONS KETCHUP MIXTURE).**

PER SERVING: CAL 265 (28% from fat); FAT 8.3g (sat 0.8g); PRO 32.7g; CARB 13.8g; FIB 0.3g; CHOL 124mg; IRON 2.4mg; SOD 610mg; CALC 32mg

CHIPOTLE CHILE POWDER

Don't confuse this smoky, sweet spice with regular chili powder. The latter is a general combination of ground chile peppers and various spices like garlic powder, oregano, and cumin, while the former is quite specific—a pure product of ground dried jalapeño chiles. It contributes a spicy heat to sauces, grilling rubs, and chilis.

BARBECUED SALMON
WITH MAPLE-LEMON GLAZE

POINTS value: 7

pictured on page 58

PREP: 8 minutes ■ **COOK:** 25 minutes

As a delicious alternative to steaks or chops during warm-weather months, try this salmon to anchor your cookout. It pairs well with traditional sides like corn on the cob, salad, or green beans.

- 1 tablespoon brown sugar
- 2 teaspoons chili powder
- 1 teaspoon grated fresh lemon rind
- ¼ teaspoon salt
- ¼ teaspoon ground cumin
- 4 (6-ounce) salmon fillets
- Cooking spray
- ⅓ cup low-sodium soy sauce
- ⅓ cup maple syrup
- ¼ cup fresh lemon juice
- 2 green onions, chopped
- 4 garlic cloves, halved
- 2 green onions, thinly sliced
- ½ teaspoon sesame seeds, toasted

1. Prepare grill.

2. Combine first 5 ingredients in a small bowl; rub mixture evenly over fillets. Coat both sides of each fillet with cooking spray. Let stand while preparing glaze.

3. Combine soy sauce and next 4 ingredients in a small saucepan; bring to a boil. Reduce heat, and simmer 10 minutes or until reduced to about ½ cup. Strain glaze through a sieve into a bowl; discard solids.

4. Place fish, skin sides down, on grill rack coated with cooking spray; brush salmon with glaze. Grill 13 minutes or until fish flakes easily when tested with a fork, basting occasionally with glaze. (Do not turn fillets.) Discard any remaining glaze. Sprinkle each fillet with sliced green onions and sesame seeds. **YIELD: 4 SERVINGS (SERVING SIZE: 1 FILLET).**

PER SERVING: CAL 304 (29% from fat); FAT 9.8g (sat 1.6g); PRO 39.3g; CARB 15.8g; FIB 0.6g; CHOL 99mg; IRON 1.6mg; SOD 622mg; CALC 37mg

GLAZED SALMON WITH PINEAPPLE-CRANBERRY SALSA

POINTS value: 7

PREP: 23 minutes ■ COOK: 12 minutes
■ OTHER: 2 hours

2 cups finely chopped fresh pineapple
1 cup sweetened dried cranberries
¼ cup chopped red bell pepper
¼ cup chopped fresh cilantro
2 tablespoons chopped red onion
1 tablespoon minced seeded jalapeño pepper
1 teaspoon grated fresh lime rind
1 tablespoon fresh lime juice
¼ teaspoon salt
Dash of ground white pepper
2 tablespoons honey
2 tablespoons hoisin sauce
8 (6-ounce) salmon fillets
Cooking spray

1. Preheat broiler.
2. Combine first 10 ingredients in a medium bowl; cover and chill 2 hours.
3. Combine honey and hoisin sauce in a small bowl. Place fish, skin sides down, on a baking sheet coated with cooking spray. Brush with 2 tablespoons hoisin mixture. Broil 5 minutes or until glaze begins to lightly brown.
4. Brush fish with remaining hoisin mixture, and broil an additional 7 to 9 minutes or until fish flakes easily when tested with a fork. Serve with salsa. YIELD: 8 SERVINGS (SERVING SIZE: 1 FILLET AND ABOUT ½ CUP SALSA).

PER SERVING: CAL 347 (27% from fat); FAT 10.5g (sat 1.7g); PRO 38.8g; CARB 27.2g; FIB 1.8g; CHOL 99mg; IRON 1.2mg; SOD 229mg; CALC 20mg

HOW TO CUT FRESH PINEAPPLE

Pineapple is grown in warm, tropical regions like Hawaii. Although it does not become sweeter after picking, it will soften if left at room temperature. The prickly exterior of this exotic fruit resembles a pinecone but is easy to trim if you don't want to buy the precut version.

1. First, cut off the plume (the top leaves) and the base while the pineapple lies on a cutting board.
2. Flip the fruit so that it's standing upright. Try to avoid removing excess flesh as you slice down the sides to get rid of the rind.
3. Eliminate the fibrous core by cutting downward while the pineapple is still upright. To core the fruit more easily, consider investing in a round corer.

CHIPOTLE SALMON

POINTS value: 6

PREP: 9 minutes ■ COOK: 13 minutes

To make the sauce needed for this sweet and spicy glaze, buy a can of chipotle chiles packed in adobo sauce. Look for it alongside other Mexican food staples in the supermarket. You can store the remaining chipotle chiles and adobo sauce in an airtight container in the refrigerator for up to 1 month.

3 tablespoons adobo sauce
2 tablespoons brown sugar
¼ teaspoon kosher salt
Cooking spray
4 (6-ounce) salmon fillets (1½ inches thick)
2 tablespoons chopped green onions

1. Preheat oven to 450°.
2. Combine first 3 ingredients in a small bowl. Line a baking sheet with foil; coat foil with cooking spray. Place fish, skin sides down, on foil; brush fish with adobo mixture.
3. Bake at 450° for 13 minutes or until fish flakes easily when tested with a fork. Sprinkle with onions before serving. YIELD: 4 SERVINGS (SERVING SIZE: 1 FILLET).

PER SERVING: CAL 271 (32% from fat); FAT 9.6g (sat 1.5g); PRO 38.4g; CARB 8.1g; FIB 1.1g; CHOL 99mg; IRON 1.3mg; SOD 341mg; CALC 15mg

ALFREDO PENNE WITH SALMON AND SPINACH

POINTS value: 7

PREP: 5 minutes ■ COOK: 15 minutes

For the best-tasting results, we found it worth the extra expense to purchase a premium smoked salmon and a name-brand light Alfredo sauce.

- 8 ounces uncooked whole wheat penne pasta
- 1 tablespoon olive oil
- ½ cup chopped onion
- ½ cup dry white wine
- 4 ounces premium smoked salmon, cut into thin strips
- ⅔ cup light Alfredo sauce (such as Buitoni)
- ⅛ teaspoon ground white pepper
- 2 cups fresh baby spinach
- 2 tablespoons grated fresh Parmesan cheese

1. Cook pasta according to package directions, omitting salt and fat. Drain.
2. While pasta cooks, heat oil in a large nonstick skillet over medium–high heat. Add onion; cook 4 minutes or until tender, stirring occasionally. Add wine, and bring to a boil. Reduce heat; simmer, uncovered, 4 minutes or until reduced by half. Stir in fish, Alfredo sauce, and white pepper; cook 1 minute or until thoroughly heated.
3. Place hot cooked pasta in a large bowl. Add salmon mixture and spinach; toss gently to coat. Top with cheese. Serve immediately. YIELD: 4 SERVINGS (SERVING SIZE: 1½ CUPS).

PER SERVING: CAL 349 (29% from fat); FAT 11.1g (sat 3.6g); PRO 17g; CARB 47.7g; FIB 6.6g; CHOL 22mg; IRON 2.4mg; SOD 540mg; CALC 154mg

GRILLED RED SNAPPER WITH TROPICAL SALSA

POINTS value: 4

PREP: 12 minutes ■ COOK: 12 minutes

Pineapple gives this salsa its distinctive island flavor. If you're short on time, substitute canned pineapple tidbits packed in juice.

- ¾ cup finely chopped fresh pineapple
- 2 tablespoons diced peeled mango
- 2 tablespoons diced peeled kiwi
- 2 tablespoons diced red onion
- 2 teaspoons lime juice
- 1 teaspoon chili garlic sauce (such as Hokan)
- ¼ teaspoon dried oregano
- ½ teaspoon salt, divided
- 4 (6-ounce) red snapper fillets
- 2 tablespoons fresh pineapple juice
- ¼ teaspoon freshly ground black pepper

1. Prepare grill.
2. Combine first 7 ingredients and ¼ teaspoon salt; toss well.

3. Brush fish with pineapple juice; sprinkle with remaining ¼ teaspoon salt and pepper. Grill 6 minutes on each side or until fish flakes easily when tested with a fork. Serve with salsa. YIELD: 4 SERVINGS (SERVING SIZE: 1 FILLET AND ¼ CUP SALSA).

PER SERVING: CAL 191 (11% from fat); FAT 2.3g (sat 0.5g); PRO 33.9g; CARB 7.3g; FIB 0.9g; CHOL 60mg; IRON 0.5mg; SOD 382mg; CALC 62mg

RED SNAPPER WITH WHITE BEANS OVER SPINACH

POINTS value: 5

PREP: 8 minutes ■ COOK: 18 minutes

We really liked the addition of tomatoes and beans to this dish. They add color and make the dish more filling.

  2 teaspoons olive oil, divided
Cooking spray
  4 cups fresh baby spinach
  2 garlic cloves, minced
  ¼ teaspoon kosher salt
  ¼ teaspoon crushed red pepper
  4 (6-ounce) red snapper fillets
  1 cup halved grape tomatoes
  1 cup fat-free, less-sodium chicken broth
  ½ cup dry white wine
  ½ cup canned cannellini beans, rinsed and drained

1. Heat 1 teaspoon oil in a large nonstick skillet coated with cooking spray over medium–high heat. Add spinach. Sauté 2 minutes or until spinach wilts. Set aside; keep warm.
2. Combine garlic, salt, and pepper in a small bowl. Rub garlic mixture on both sides of fish.
3. Heat remaining 1 teaspoon oil in pan. Add fish; cook 3 to 4 minutes. Turn fish; add tomatoes, broth, and wine. Bring to a boil; reduce heat, and simmer 5 minutes. Add wilted spinach and beans; cook 3 minutes or until thoroughly heated. Serve immediately. YIELD: 4 SERVINGS (SERVING SIZE: 1 FILLET AND ABOUT ½ CUP SPINACH MIXTURE).

PER SERVING: CAL 269 (17% from fat); FAT 5.2g (sat 0.9g); PRO 39.3g; CARB 10.1g; FIB 3.2g; CHOL 63mg; IRON 2.8mg; SOD 466mg; CALC 136mg

TROPICAL CURRY PARCHMENT-BAKED TILAPIA

POINTS value: 6

PREP: 18 minutes ■ COOK: 30 minutes

Cooking in parchment paper is a simple French technique guaranteed to impress guests. Individual portions of fish along with other ingredients are baked inside a sealed packet of parchment paper. As the food bakes and lets off steam, each parchment packet puffs up. Let each guest slit their parchment packet at the table to unveil the colorful meal.

  1 medium-sized sweet potato, peeled
  1 (6-ounce) bag fresh baby spinach
  4 (6-ounce) tilapia fillets
  2 teaspoons red curry powder
  ½ teaspoon kosher salt
  1 mango, peeled and diced
  1 lime, cut into 4 wedges
  ¼ cup flaked sweetened coconut, toasted

1. Preheat oven to 350°.
2. Cut 4 (18 x 15–inch) rectangles of parchment paper. Fold each rectangle in half; open each rectangle flat.
3. Cut sweet potato into thin strips using a vegetable peeler. Divide sweet potato strips and spinach evenly among parchment rectangles near the fold. Top each with a fillet; sprinkle evenly with curry powder and salt. Top with mango; squeeze lime wedges over mango. Fold parchment in half over fish and vegetables. Tightly seal edges with narrow folds. Place packets on baking sheets.
4. Bake at 350° for 30 to 35 minutes or until puffed and lightly brown.
5. Place packets on plates; let guests cut packets open and sprinkle with toasted coconut. YIELD: 4 SERVINGS (SERVING SIZE: 1 PACKET).

PER SERVING: CAL 304 (14% from fat); FAT 4.6g (sat 2.3g); PRO 36.6g; CARB 32.5g; FIB 5.7g; CHOL 85mg; IRON 3.1mg; SOD 434mg; CALC 75mg

EN PAPILLOTE

This cooking method is ideal for healthy eating because little extra fat is required. Fast and not fussy, cooking *en papillote* ("in parchment") helps all the flavors blend together because the food cooks in its own juices. Instead of parchment paper, you can cook the ingredients in aluminum foil, which is easier to fold and, like the parchment paper, doesn't detract from the food's flavor.

Buy fresh live mussels, choosing ones with closed shells or shells that snap shut when you tap them. At home, discard the packaging, wrap the mussels in a moist towel, and store them in the fridge. Plan to use them within a day, and avoid storing them in plastic because they won't be able to breathe.

STEAMED MUSSELS

POINTS value: 8

PREP: 7 minutes ■ COOK: 11 minutes

2 teaspoons olive oil
2 large shallots, minced
2 garlic cloves, minced
4 pounds mussels (about 112), scrubbed and debearded
3 plum tomatoes, seeded and minced
½ cup dry white wine
¼ cup chopped fresh parsley

1. Heat oil in a large Dutch oven over medium-high heat; add shallots and garlic. Cook 2 minutes or until tender, stirring frequently.
2. Add mussels, tomato, and wine to pan; cover, reduce heat, and simmer 8 minutes or until shells open. Remove from heat; discard any unopened shells.
3. Using a slotted spoon, spoon mussels evenly into 4 bowls. Pour broth evenly over mussels, and sprinkle with parsley. Serve immediately. **YIELD: 4 SERVINGS (SERVING SIZE: ABOUT 28 MUSSELS).**

PER SERVING: CAL 360 (24% from fat); FAT 9.7g (sat 1.7g); PRO 40g; CARB 22g; FIB 0.7g; CHOL 90mg; IRON 13.6mg; SOD 922mg; CALC 93mg

SEARED SCALLOPS WITH SOY-GINGER SAUCE

POINTS value: 4   *pictured on page 59*

PREP: 4 minutes ■ COOK: 6 minutes

This superfast entrée features succulent sea scallops and is perfect for an intimate gathering, since it comes together so quickly. To ensure crisp, browned scallops, pat any excess moisture from them just before seasoning and pan searing.

3 tablespoons low-sodium soy sauce
2 tablespoons chopped green onions
1 tablespoon honey
1 tablespoon chopped peeled fresh ginger
⅛ teaspoon crushed red pepper
1½ pounds large sea scallops (12 scallops)
¼ teaspoon kosher salt
¼ teaspoon freshly ground black pepper
Cooking spray
Thinly sliced green onions (optional)

1. Combine soy sauce and next 4 ingredients in a bowl.
2. Pat scallops dry with paper towels; sprinkle with salt and pepper. Heat a large skillet over medium-high heat. Coat pan with cooking spray. Add scallops to pan, and cook 3 minutes on each side until browned. Transfer scallops to a platter; drizzle with soy sauce mixture. Garnish with sliced green onions, if desired.
YIELD: 4 SERVINGS (SERVING SIZE: 3 SCALLOPS AND ABOUT 1¼ TEASPOONS SAUCE).

PER SERVING: CAL 175 (7% from fat); FAT 1.3g (sat 0.1g); PRO 29.3g; CARB 10g; FIB 0.3g; CHOL 56mg; IRON 0.8mg; SOD 792mg; CALC 46mg

GRILLED BARBECUE SHRIMP

POINTS value: 4

pictured on page 60

PREP: 23 minutes ■ **COOK:** 6 minutes
■ **OTHER:** 30 minutes

Grilling the shrimp with the shells on helps trap the zesty barbecue-flavored marinade. Serve with lemon wedges, and be sure to have plenty of napkins on hand for everyone.

  32 unpeeled jumbo shrimp (about 1½ pounds)
   2 tablespoons olive oil
   1 tablespoon brown sugar
   1 tablespoon lemon juice
   1 tablespoon ketchup
   2 teaspoons Worcestershire sauce
   1 teaspoon chili powder
   1 teaspoon black pepper
  ½ teaspoon ground cumin
  ½ teaspoon hot sauce
  ¼ teaspoon salt
  ¼ teaspoon ground allspice
  ¼ teaspoon ground cinnamon
   2 garlic cloves, minced
    Cooking spray

1. Devein shrimp by cutting a slit along the top edge of each shrimp and remove vein; leave shell intact. Place shrimp in a large bowl.
2. Combine oil and next 12 ingredients, stirring with a whisk. Pour marinade over shrimp, tossing to coat. Cover and let stand 30 minutes.
3. Prepare grill.
4. Thread shrimp onto 4 (12-inch) metal skewers. Place skewers on grill rack coated with cooking spray. Cook 3 minutes on each side or until shrimp are done. Remove from skewers, and serve immediately. **YIELD: 4 SERVINGS (SERVING SIZE: 8 SHRIMP).**

PER SERVING: CAL 188 (40% from fat); FAT 8.3g (sat 1.3g); PRO 22.8g; CARB 5.2g; FIB 0.4g; CHOL 210mg; IRON 3.8mg; SOD 482mg; CALC 58mg

DEVEINING SHRIMP

To remove the slim black vein from the back of a shrimp, take a small knife or shrimp deveiner, slit the shrimp down the back, and remove the vein. Most cooks prefer to remove the vein from larger shrimp and prawns because it can be gritty. To save time, there is the option of leaving the vein intact in smaller shrimp; it is a safe alternative.

SHRIMP TACOS

POINTS value: 6

PREP: 13 minutes ■ **COOK:** 6 minutes

Warming corn tortillas makes them pliable enough to fold around the filling without cracking. The simplest way to warm them is to place them, one at a time, between damp paper towels, and microwave at HIGH 15 to 20 seconds or until soft.

   2 pounds medium shrimp, peeled and deveined
   1 tablespoon olive oil
   2 garlic cloves, minced
   1 teaspoon ground cumin
  ¼ teaspoon salt
    Cooking spray
  12 (6-inch) corn tortillas, warmed
   2 cups shredded angel hair cabbage
  ½ cup refrigerated fresh salsa
  ½ cup light sour cream
  ¾ cup fresh guacamole (such as Wholly Guacamole)
   1 lime, cut into 6 wedges

1. Prepare grill.
2. Combine shrimp and next 3 ingredients in a medium bowl. Thread shrimp onto 8 (10-inch) metal skewers; sprinkle with salt.
3. Place skewers on grill rack coated with cooking spray. Grill 3 minutes on each side or until shrimp are done.
4. Remove shrimp from skewers, and divide evenly among tortillas. Top each with cabbage, salsa, sour cream, and guacamole. Serve immediately with lime wedges. **YIELD: 6 SERVINGS (SERVING SIZE: 2 TACOS).**

PER SERVING: CAL 283 (34% from fat); FAT 10.7g (sat 2.6g); PRO 22.2g; CARB 26.8g; FIB 4.8g; CHOL 175mg; IRON 3.1mg; SOD 522mg; CALC 79mg

With its long stalk, scallion-like base, and sweet aroma, lemongrass is an aesthetically pleasing addition to any meal. A vital element in Thai and Vietnamese cooking, lemongrass can be found in the gourmet produce section of most supermarkets. Removing the outer layers is essential in order to access the interior white part that's used in cooking.

1. Cut 1 inch from the base of the stalk using a chef's knife.

2. Pull away the tough outer layers until you reach the tender, central interior.

3. Decide how much you need; then, using the side of your knife, crush it just like you would crush a clove of garlic.

Crushed lemongrass can be added to broths, stir-fries, or rice—just remember to remove it from the dish before serving. Minced lemongrass can be used in soups or stews; removing it before serving is unnecessary.

COCONUT-LEMONGRASS SHRIMP

POINTS value: 6

PREP: 7 minutes ▪ COOK: 17 minutes

The delicate citrus flavor from lemongrass gives this Thai-inspired main dish a unique flavor. Look for lemongrass in Asian markets or near fresh herbs in your supermarket's produce section. Select stalks with firm, heavy bulbs and tightly bound green leaves.

  1 teaspoon canola oil
  ¼ cup finely chopped shallots
  1 stalk peeled fresh lemongrass
  1 cup light coconut milk
  ½ cup clam juice
  1 teaspoon grated fresh lime rind
  ½ teaspoon red curry paste
  1½ pounds medium shrimp, peeled and deveined
  1 tablespoon fresh lime juice
  1 teaspoon fish sauce
  ¼ cup chopped fresh cilantro
  2 cups hot cooked rice

1. Heat oil in a large nonstick skillet over medium heat. Add shallots; cook 2 minutes or until soft, stirring occasionally.

2. Cut lemongrass in half lengthwise; lightly crush each half with the back of a knife to release the aroma and oils. Add lemongrass and next 4 ingredients to pan; bring to a boil. Reduce heat, and simmer 7 minutes, stirring occasionally. Add shrimp; cover and simmer 6 minutes or until shrimp are done. Remove from heat; discard lemongrass. Stir in lime juice and fish sauce, and sprinkle with cilantro. Serve over rice. YIELD: 4 SERVINGS (SERVING SIZE: ABOUT ⅔ CUP SHRIMP MIXTURE AND ½ CUP RICE).

PER SERVING: CAL 262 (20% from fat); FAT 5.8g (sat 3.3g); PRO 25.7g; CARB 26.6g; FIB 0.8g; CHOL 211mg; IRON 5.5mg; SOD 432mg; CALC 61mg

SHRIMP JAMBALAYA WITH SAUSAGE

POINTS value: 5

PREP: 15 minutes ▪ COOK: 35 minutes
▪ OTHER: 5 minutes

  2 teaspoons canola oil
  1 (7-ounce) link smoked turkey sausage, cut into thin slices
  1 cup diced onion
  1 cup diced celery
  1 cup diced red bell pepper
  1 garlic clove, minced
  2 cups fat-free, less-sodium chicken broth
  1 cup uncooked long-grain rice
  1 (14.5-ounce) can diced tomatoes, undrained
  ¾ teaspoon Creole seasoning (such as Tony Chachere's)
  1 pound medium shrimp, peeled and deveined
  ⅓ cup chopped green onions
  1½ teaspoons hot sauce

1. Heat oil in a large nonstick skillet over medium-high heat. Add sausage; cook 3 minutes or until lightly browned, stirring frequently. Add onion and next 3 ingredients. Sauté 4 minutes or until vegetables are tender.

2. Add broth and next 3 ingredients to pan; bring to a boil. Cover, reduce heat, and simmer 18 minutes. Add shrimp, green onions, and hot sauce. Cover and cook 7 to 8 minutes or until shrimp are done. Remove from heat, and let stand 5 minutes. YIELD: 6 SERVINGS (SERVING SIZE: 1⅓ CUPS).

PER SERVING: CAL 259 (14% from fat); FAT 3.9g (sat 0.9.g); PRO 18.2g; CARB 36.9g; FIB 2.2g; CHOL 104mg; IRON 3.7mg; SOD 784mg; CALC 67mg

meatless main dishes

Creole Vegetables on Cheese Grits, *page 82*

CURRIED RICE WITH EXOTIC VEGETABLE MEDLEY

POINTS value: 7

PREP: 5 minutes ■ **COOK:** 22 minutes
■ **OTHER:** 5 minutes

Creamy vegetables and a subtle curry-flavored rice will satisfy your craving for something out of the ordinary. Prep the ingredients needed for Step Four while the rice cooks.

⅓ cup sliced almonds
1 cup fat-free, less-sodium chicken broth
2 large carrots, diagonally sliced
1 large red bell pepper, cut into strips
2 cups water
1⅓ cups quick-cooking brown rice
½ teaspoon curry powder
1 cup light coconut milk
¾ cup frozen petite green peas
1 tablespoon fresh lime juice
2 teaspoons cornstarch
½ cup chopped green onions
⅓ cup chopped fresh cilantro
⅓ cup chopped fresh basil
1½ tablespoons sugar
1½ tablespoons grated peeled fresh ginger
½ teaspoon salt
⅛ teaspoon crushed red pepper

1. Cook almonds in a medium nonstick skillet over medium heat 1 minute or until toasted, stirring occasionally. Set almonds aside.
2. Bring broth to a boil in a large saucepan; add carrot and bell pepper. Return to a boil. Cover, reduce heat, and simmer 6 minutes or just until tender.
3. Bring 2 cups water to a boil in a medium saucepan; stir in rice and curry powder. Cover, reduce heat, and simmer 5 minutes. Remove from heat; let stand, covered, 5 minutes. Drain.
4. Add coconut milk and peas to broth mixture. Return to a boil; cook 1 minute. Combine lime juice and cornstarch in a small bowl, stirring until smooth. Stir cornstarch mixture into broth mixture. Cook, stirring constantly, 2 minutes or until thick. Stir in reserved almonds, green onions, and next 6 ingredients. Serve over rice. **YIELD: 3 SERVINGS (SERVING SIZE: ABOUT 1 CUP VEGETABLE MIXTURE AND ¾ CUP RICE).**

PER SERVING: CAL 325 (31% from fat); FAT 11.1g (sat 4.3g); PRO 9.5g; CARB 53.6g; FIB 6.3g; CHOL 0mg; IRON 2.4mg; SOD 654mg; CALC 62mg

---

CURRY POWDER

The term "curry" means different things to different cultures. In India, where the blend of seasonings originated, "curry" refers to any number of spices, not simply the taste Americans associate with Indian food. Curry powder is not always spicy but can simply enhance flavor without adding heat.

BLACK BEAN AND SWEET TOMATO-LIME RICE

POINTS value: 6

PREP: 4 minutes ■ **COOK:** 13 minutes

2 tablespoons olive oil, divided
1 teaspoon grated fresh lime rind
2 tablespoons fresh lime juice
½ teaspoon salt
1 cup chopped onion
1 cup chopped green bell pepper
1 (10-ounce) package frozen microwave brown rice (such as Birds Eye Steamfresh)
1 (15-ounce) can black beans, rinsed and drained
1½ cups quartered grape tomatoes
1½ teaspoons chili powder
¼ cup chopped fresh cilantro

1. Combine 1 tablespoon olive oil, lime rind, lime juice, and salt in a small bowl. Set aside.
2. Heat remaining 1 tablespoon oil a large nonstick skillet over medium-high heat. Add onion and bell pepper; cook 10 minutes or until browned, stirring frequently.
3. While vegetables cook, prepare rice according to package directions.
4. Add beans to onion mixture; cook 30 seconds. Remove from heat, and stir in rice, tomatoes, and chili powder. Drizzle with reserved lime mixture, and sprinkle with cilantro. **YIELD: 3 SERVINGS (SERVING SIZE: ABOUT 1¾ CUPS).**

PER SERVING: CAL 314 (31% from fat); FAT 10.8g (sat 1.6g); PRO 9.9g; CARB 49.6g; FIB 9.7g; CHOL 0mg; IRON 2.1mg; SOD 653mg; CALC 76mg

TIJUANA BLACK BEANS AND RICE

POINTS value: 5

PREP: 8 minutes ■ **COOK:** 7 minutes

If queso quesadilla cheese is unavailable, substitute shredded Monterey Jack.

- 1 (8.8-ounce) package precooked whole-grain brown rice (such as Uncle Ben's Ready Rice)
- 1 tablespoon canola oil
- ½ cup vertically sliced red onion
- 3 garlic cloves, minced
- 1 (15-ounce) can no-salt-added black beans, drained
- 1 (14.5-ounce) can diced tomatoes with zesty green chiles
- ⅓ cup chopped fresh cilantro
- 2 tablespoons fresh lime juice
- ¼ teaspoon salt
- ½ cup (2 ounces) crumbled queso quesadilla cheese
- 1 lime, cut into wedges

1. Cook rice according to package directions.
2. Heat oil in a large nonstick skillet over medium-high heat. Add onion, and sauté 3 minutes or until browned. Stir in garlic; sauté 1 minute. Add beans and tomatoes, and cook 2 minutes or until thoroughly heated. Stir in cilantro, lime juice, and salt. Serve bean mixture over rice. Sprinkle with cheese; serve with lime wedges. **YIELD: 4 SERVINGS (SERVING SIZE: ¾ CUP BEAN MIXTURE, ½ CUP RICE, AND 2 TABLESPOONS CHEESE).**

PER SERVING: CAL 266 (32% from fat); FAT 9.4g (sat 3g); PRO 10.5g; CARB 36.5g; FIB 5.8g; CHOL 15mg; IRON 1.8mg; SOD 663mg; CALC 160mg

QUESO QUESADILLA

Queso quesadilla is a soft, mild, white cheese. It's popular throughout Mexico for both snacking and cooking, and it becomes soft and creamy when heated. Traditionally, this type of cheese is mixed into refried beans, melted between tortillas for a wonderfully creamy quesadilla, or melted into a queso dipping sauce.

TWO-BEAN QUESADILLAS WITH GREEN CHILES

POINTS value: 5

PREP: 16 minutes ■ **COOK:** 15 minutes

Drain canned beans into a colander in the sink; then rinse with cold water. This quick step reduces the sodium content of the recipe by 40 percent.

- 1 (15-ounce) can black beans, rinsed and drained
- 4 teaspoons chopped pickled jalapeño peppers
- ½ teaspoon ground cumin
- 1 (15.8-ounce) can Great Northern beans, rinsed and drained
- 1 cup chopped seeded tomato (about 1 medium)
- 1 (4-ounce) can chopped green chiles, drained
- 3 tablespoons chopped fresh cilantro
- 6 (8-inch) flour tortillas
- ¾ cup (3 ounces) reduced-fat shredded sharp Cheddar cheese
- Cooking spray
- 6 tablespoons light sour cream

1. Combine first 3 ingredients in a medium bowl; mash with a fork until most beans are mashed.
2. Combine Great Northern beans and next 3 ingredients. Spread about 2½ tablespoons black bean mixture over half of each tortilla; top each with about ½ cup white bean mixture and 2 tablespoons cheese. Fold tortillas in half.
3. Heat a large nonstick skillet over medium heat. Coat pan with cooking spray. Place 2 tortillas, folded edges together, in pan. Cook 2 to 3 minutes on each side or until lightly browned. Remove from pan, and keep warm. Repeat procedure with remaining folded tortillas. Cut each quesadilla into 4 wedges, and serve immediately with sour cream. **YIELD: 6 SERVINGS (SERVING SIZE: 4 WEDGES AND 1 TABLESPOON SOUR CREAM).**

PER SERVING: CAL 268 (17% from fat); FAT 5.2g (sat 2.9g); PRO 13.8g; CARB 42.7g; FIB 7.7g; CHOL 15.8mg; IRON 1.6mg; SOD 600mg; CALC 154mg

SPINACH QUESADILLAS WITH MANGO-AVOCADO SALSA

POINTS value: 7

PREP: 11 minutes ■ COOK: 16 minutes

Traditional quesadillas are given an update with a spinach filling and a fresh, colorful salsa. If any salsa is left over, serve it with baked tortilla chips for a quick snack.

- ½ cup chopped peeled mango
- ¼ cup diced peeled avocado
- 4 teaspoons minced jalapeño pepper, divided
- 2 teaspoons chopped fresh cilantro
- 2 teaspoons fresh lime juice
- Cooking spray
- 1 (8-ounce) package presliced mushrooms
- 1 garlic clove, minced
- 2 (6-ounce) packages fresh baby spinach
- ¼ teaspoon kosher salt
- ¼ teaspoon dried oregano
- ¾ cup (3 ounces) shredded reduced-fat Monterey Jack cheese
- 4 (8-inch) 96% fat-free whole wheat flour tortillas (such as Mission)

1. Combine mango, avocado, 2 teaspoons jalapeño pepper, cilantro, and lime juice in a small bowl. Set salsa aside.

2. Heat a large nonstick skillet over medium-high heat. Coat pan with cooking spray. Add mushrooms; sauté 6 minutes or until tender. Add garlic and remaining 2 teaspoons jalapeño pepper. Add spinach, in batches, and cook until spinach wilts and liquid almost evaporates, stirring frequently. Stir in salt and oregano. Remove from pan, and keep warm.

3. Sprinkle 3 tablespoons cheese over each of 2 tortillas. Top each with half of spinach mixture, 3 tablespoons cheese, and 1 tortilla.

4. Heat pan over medium heat. Coat pan with cooking spray. Add 1 quesadilla to pan; cook 2 minutes on each side or until lightly browned and cheese melts. Remove quesadilla from pan, and keep warm. Repeat with remaining quesadilla. Cut each quesadilla into 6 wedges. Serve with salsa. YIELD: 3 SERVINGS (SERVING SIZE: 4 WEDGES AND ABOUT 3½ TABLESPOONS SALSA).

PER SERVING: CAL 343 (31% from fat); FAT 11.8g (sat 4g); PRO 18.5g; CARB 47.5g; FIB 8.4g; CHOL 20mg; IRON 3.7mg; SOD 949mg; CALC 323mg

OPEN-FACED TORTILLA STACKERS

POINTS value: 5

PREP: 9 minutes ■ COOK: 17 minutes

Serve these hearty and filling vegetable tostadas with a guacamole salad for a quick weeknight meal. Use hot and spicy picante sauce for extra heat.

- 4 (6-inch) corn tortillas
- 2 teaspoons olive oil
- 1 medium onion, thinly sliced
- 1 medium-sized yellow squash, thinly sliced
- 1 green bell pepper, cut into strips
- 1 cup fat-free refried beans
- 6 tablespoons picante sauce, divided
- 1 tablespoon fresh lime juice
- 1 teaspoon ground cumin
- 1 cup (4 ounces) shredded part-skim mozzarella cheese
- 4 lime wedges (optional)

1. Preheat oven to 350°. Place baking sheet in oven to heat.

2. Bake tortillas on hot baking sheet at 350° for 5 minutes on each side or until toasted.

3. Heat oil in a large nonstick skillet over medium-high heat. Add onion, squash, and bell pepper; cook 10 minutes or until vegetables begin to brown on edges.

4. Combine beans, 2 tablespoons picante sauce, lime juice, and cumin. Spread bean mixture evenly on toasted tortillas, and return to baking sheet. Top evenly with vegetable mixture and cheese. Bake at 350° for 6 minutes or until cheese melts. Serve with remaining picante sauce and lime wedges, if desired. YIELD: 4 SERVINGS (SERVING SIZE: 1 TORTILLA AND 1 TABLESPOON PICANTE SAUCE).

PER SERVING: CAL 246 (32% from fat); FAT 8.8g (sat 4g); PRO 14.1g; CARB 30g; FIB 6.5g; CHOL 15mg; IRON 2.1mg; SOD 501mg; CALC 272mg

DOUBLE-STACK PORTOBELLO BURGERS

POINTS value: 6

PREP: 8 minutes ■ **COOK:** 9 minutes

Did you know that portobello mushrooms are actually large crimini mushrooms? Once crimini mushrooms grow to about 5 inches in diameter, they are marketed as portobello mushrooms.

 ¼ cup low-fat mayonnaise
 2 tablespoons commercial pesto
 8 large portobello mushroom caps
 4 (¼-inch-thick) slices sweet onion
Cooking spray
 ¼ teaspoon coarsely ground black pepper
 4 (1.8-ounce) whole wheat hamburger buns
 1 cup packed baby arugula or baby spinach
 4 (0.66-ounce) slices reduced-fat provolone cheese

1. Prepare grill.
2. Combine mayonnaise and pesto in a small bowl. Set aside.
3. Coat mushroom caps and onion slices heavily with cooking spray; sprinkle evenly with pepper. Place on grill rack coated with cooking spray. Grill 4 to 5 minutes on each side or until tender.
4. While vegetables grill, place bun halves, cut sides down, on grill, and cook 1 to 2 minutes or until toasted.
5. Spread mayonnaise mixture evenly on bottom half of each bun; top with 1 mushroom cap, ¼ cup arugula, 1 cheese slice, an additional mushroom cap, 1 onion slice, and top half of bun. YIELD: 4 SERVINGS (SERVING SIZE: 1 BURGER).

PER SERVING: CAL 295 (32% from fat); FAT 10.6g (sat 3.1g); PRO 14.3g; CARB 38.3g; FIB 5.3g; CHOL 13mg; IRON 2.4mg; SOD 611mg; CALC 264mg

EGGPLANT-POLENTA LASAGNA

POINTS value: 8

PREP: 17 minutes ■ **COOK:** 52 minutes
■ **OTHER:** 4 hours and 5 minutes

The cooked polenta prepared in Step One replaces pasta in this veggie-packed lasagna. To get a headstart on the preparation, prepare the recipe through Step Three up to two days in advance.

 1 cup vegetable broth
 1 cup water
 ¾ cup yellow cornmeal
 ¼ teaspoon salt
 ½ cup frozen whole-kernel corn
 1 (14.5-ounce) can diced tomatoes with basil, garlic, and oregano, drained
 ¼ cup coarsely chopped fresh basil
 1 tablespoon balsamic vinegar
 1 tablespoon olive oil, divided
 1 (1-pound) eggplant, finely chopped
 ½ cup chopped onion
 1 cup part-skim ricotta cheese
 ½ cup grated fresh Parmigiano-Reggiano cheese

1. Bring broth and water to a boil in a large saucepan. Add cornmeal and ¼ teaspoon salt, stirring with a whisk; cook over medium heat 6 minutes or until thick, stirring constantly. Remove from heat, and stir in corn.
2. Spoon polenta into a 9 x 5–inch nonstick loaf pan, spreading evenly. Press plastic wrap onto surface of polenta; chill 4 hours or until firm.
3. Combine tomatoes, basil, vinegar, and 1½ teaspoons oil in a blender; process until smooth. Cover and chill.
4. Preheat oven to 350°.
5. Heat remaining 1½ teaspoons oil in a large nonstick skillet over medium-high heat. Add eggplant and onion; sauté 8 to 10 minutes or until tender.
6. Invert chilled polenta onto a cutting board; cut crosswise into ¼-inch-thick slices. Spoon ⅓ cup tomato mixture into an 8-inch square baking dish. Layer half of polenta slices in pan. Add half of eggplant mixture, spreading evenly over polenta; top with ½ cup ricotta cheese and ⅓ cup tomato mixture. Repeat layers.
7. Cover with foil, and bake at 350° for 30 minutes. Uncover; sprinkle evenly with Parmigiano-Reggiano cheese. Bake an additional 6 to 8 minutes or until cheese melts and lasagna is bubbly. Let stand 5 minutes before serving. YIELD: 4 SERVINGS (SERVING SIZE: ¼ OF CASSEROLE).

PER SERVING: CAL 374 (32% from fat); FAT 13.3g (sat 5.7g); PRO 18.4g; CARB 47.1g; FIB 6.5g; CHOL 29mg; IRON 3mg; SOD 951mg; CALC 431mg

LASAGNA-STUFFED PEPPERS

POINTS value: 5

PREP: 5 minutes ∎ **COOK:** 42 minutes

For a pretty presentation, use an assortment of colored bell peppers. Red, yellow, or orange bell peppers will work as well as green for this recipe.

> 2 cups uncooked whole wheat egg noodles (such as Hodgson Mill)
> 4 large green bell peppers
> Cooking spray
> 1 (8-ounce) package presliced crimini mushrooms
> 1 medium zucchini, diced
> ½ cup chopped sun-dried tomatoes, packed without oil
> 1½ cups pasta sauce
> 1 cup (4 ounces) shredded light 4-cheese Italian blend cheese, divided
> ½ teaspoon crushed red pepper

1. Prepare noodles according to package directions. Drain.
2. While noodles cook, slice tops off peppers. Remove seeds and veins; rinse and drain peppers. Stand peppers upright in an 11 x 7–inch microwave-safe baking dish. Microwave at HIGH 7 minutes or until crisp-tender.
3. Preheat oven to 350°.
4. While peppers cook, heat a large nonstick skillet over medium-high heat. Coat pan with cooking spray. Add mushrooms, zucchini, and sun-dried tomatoes; cook 9 minutes or until tender. Stir in noodles, pasta sauce, ½ cup cheese, and crushed red pepper; cook 1 minute or until thoroughly heated.
5. Divide noodle mixture evenly among peppers; top with remaining ½ cup cheese. Bake at 350° for 25 minutes. **YIELD: 4 SERVINGS (SERVING SIZE: 1 STUFFED PEPPER).**

PER SERVING: CAL 277 (23% from fat); FAT 7.1g (sat 3.2g); PRO 16.8g; CARB 41.3g; FIB 6.9g; CHOL 15mg; IRON 2.3mg; SOD 772mg; CALC 245mg

MEDITERRANEAN STUFFED CABBAGE ROLLS

POINTS value: 6

PREP: 20 minutes ∎ **COOK:** 1 hour and 47 minutes
∎ **OTHER:** 5 minutes

> ½ cup dried lentils
> 3¼ cups water, divided
> ½ cup uncooked short-grain brown rice
> 8 large napa (Chinese) cabbage leaves
> Cooking spray
> 1 small zucchini, diced
> 2 garlic cloves, minced
> 1 teaspoon dried dill
> ½ teaspoon kosher salt
> 1 cup prepared hummus (such as Sabra), divided
> 1 (14.5-ounce) can diced tomatoes

1. Place lentils and 2¼ cups water in a medium saucepan. Bring to a boil; cover, reduce heat, and simmer 35 minutes or until tender. Drain.
2. Place rice and remaining 1 cup water in a small saucepan. Bring to a boil; cover, reduce heat, and simmer 30 minutes or until rice is tender. Remove from heat; cover and let stand 5 minutes. Drain.
3. While lentils and rice cook, cut off raised portion of the center vein of each cabbage leaf (do not cut out vein). Steam, covered, 3 minutes or until tender. Let cool.
4. Heat a medium-sized nonstick skillet over medium heat. Coat pan with cooking spray. Add zucchini; cook 5 minutes, stirring often. Add garlic, dill, and salt. Cook 5 minutes or until zucchini begins to brown.
5. Preheat oven to 350°.
6. Combine lentils, rice, zucchini mixture, and ⅓ cup hummus in a medium bowl, stirring well. Working with 1 cabbage leaf at a time, place about ⅓ cup lentil mixture in center of leaf. Fold in edges of leaf; roll up. Repeat procedure with remaining cabbage leaves and lentil mixture to form 8 cabbage rolls.
7. Place cabbage rolls in an 11 x 7–inch baking dish. Spread remaining ⅔ cup hummus over rolls. Pour tomatoes over rolls. Bake at 350° for 30 minutes or until thoroughly heated. **YIELD: 4 SERVINGS (SERVING SIZE: 2 CABBAGE ROLLS).**

PER SERVING: CAL 311 (18% from fat); FAT 6.3g (sat 0.9g); PRO 15.1g; CARB 50.4g; FIB 12.9g; CHOL 0mg; IRON 5.3mg; SOD 712mg; CALC 85mg

HOMESTYLE VEGETABLE AND TEMPEH LOAF

POINTS value: 4

PREP: 22 minutes ■ **COOK:** 1 hour and 22 minutes
■ **OTHER:** 10 minutes

This meatless version of a comfort food classic is full of protein, low in fat, and has no cholesterol thanks to tempeh, a fermented soybean cake.

> 2 red bell peppers, cut into 4 wedges
> 1 large red onion, cut into 10 wedges
> 1¼ cups cabernet marinara sauce with herbs, divided
> ¾ cup frozen whole-kernel corn
> 2 (8-ounce) packages five-grain tempeh (such as Westsoy), grated
> 1 cup dry breadcrumbs
> ⅓ cup chopped fresh parsley
> 2 large egg whites, lightly beaten
> 1½ teaspoons garlic salt
> **Cooking spray**

1. Preheat broiler.
2. Place peppers and onion on a foil-lined baking sheet. Broil 12 minutes or until browned, rearranging as necessary to prevent overbrowning.
3. Reduce oven temperature to 350°.
4. Combine browned vegetables, ½ cup marinara sauce, and corn in a blender, and pulse 4 times or until blended. Combine vegetable mixture, tempeh, and next 4 ingredients in a large bowl.
5. Place tempeh mixture in an 8½ x 4½–inch loaf pan coated with cooking spray. Spread remaining ¾ cup marinara sauce over top. Bake at 350° for 1 hour and 10 minutes. Let stand 10 minutes. Remove from pan, and cut into 8 slices. **YIELD: 8 SERVINGS (SERVING SIZE: 1 SLICE).**

PER SERVING: CAL 213 (19% from fat); FAT 4.6g (sat 0.7g); PRO 13.2g; CARB 31.5g; FIB 5.4g; CHOL 0mg; IRON 2mg; SOD 424mg; CALC 57mg

---

TEMPEH

Although tempeh and tofu both come from soybeans, they are very different in texture and nutritional characteristics. Tempeh contains soybeans that are more intact than those found in tofu; a four-ounce serving contains as much as six times more fiber than an equal portion of tofu. Also, tempeh retains its own slightly nutty flavor, while tofu reflects the tastes of the ingredients that surround it. Although tofu contains more calcium, tempeh is also a good source of calcium and can provide significant amounts of iron and protein.

HEARTY VEGETABLES AND PENNE WITH FETA

POINTS value: 5

PREP: 4 minutes ■ **COOK:** 20 minutes

Despite its sour-sounding name, balsamic vinegar is actually slightly sweet. Along with creamy feta cheese, it provides an ideal balance to the earthy flavor of the roasted vegetables.

> 8 ounces uncooked multigrain penne (such as Barilla Plus)
> 2 (8-ounce) packages mushrooms, quartered
> 3 plum tomatoes, quartered
> 2 medium zucchini, cubed
> 1 medium-sized yellow squash, cubed
> ½ medium onion, thinly sliced and separated into rings
> 1 tablespoon olive oil
> ½ teaspoon kosher salt
> ¼ cup chopped fresh basil
> 1 cup (4 ounces) crumbled feta cheese
> 1 tablespoon balsamic vinegar

1. Cook pasta according to package directions, omitting salt and fat. Drain.
2. Preheat oven to 475°.
3. While pasta cooks, combine mushrooms and next 6 ingredients in a large bowl; toss to coat. Arrange vegetables in a single layer on a jelly-roll pan. Bake at 475° for 10 minutes; stir and bake an additional 10 minutes or until lightly browned.
4. Combine pasta, vegetables, and basil in a large bowl. Sprinkle with feta, and drizzle with vinegar; toss gently. **YIELD: 5 SERVINGS (SERVING SIZE: 2 CUPS PASTA MIXTURE).**

PER SERVING: CAL 271 (32% from fat); FAT 9.7g (sat 3.9g); PRO 12.7g; CARB 41.8g; FIB 7.1g; CHOL 20mg; IRON 2.5mg; SOD 450mg; CALC 149mg

BUTTERNUT SQUASH AND LEEK RISOTTO

POINTS value: *7*   *pictured on page 64*

PREP: 12 minutes ■ **COOK:** 58 minutes

This is a great dish to prepare for a casual dinner if your friends always end up in the kitchen while you cook. Have everyone take turns with the hands-on stirring in Step Four while you attend to final dinner details.

    2 cups (1-inch) cubed peeled butternut squash
    1 tablespoon maple syrup
    2 teaspoons olive oil
    ¾ teaspoon salt, divided
    ½ teaspoon black pepper
    2 cups water
    1¾ cups vegetable broth
    1 tablespoon butter
    ¾ cup thinly sliced leek (about 1 small)
    1 cup uncooked Arborio rice
    ¼ cup dry white wine
    2 tablespoons whole milk
    ½ cup (2 ounces) preshredded fresh Parmesan cheese
    1 tablespoon snipped fresh chives

1. Preheat oven to 375°.
2. Combine squash, maple syrup, olive oil, ½ teaspoon salt, and pepper in a large bowl; toss to coat. Arrange squash in a single layer on a jelly-roll pan. Bake at 375° for 25 minutes or until squash is very tender and lightly browned, stirring after 20 minutes.
3. While squash bakes, bring water, broth, and remaining ¼ teaspoon salt to a simmer in a medium saucepan (do not boil). Keep warm over low heat.
4. Melt butter in a large saucepan over medium–high heat. Add leek; sauté 2 minutes. Add rice; sauté 1 minute. Stir in wine and ½ cup warm broth mixture; cook 3 minutes or until liquid is nearly absorbed, stirring constantly. Add remaining broth mixture, ½ cup at a time, stirring constantly until each portion is absorbed before adding the next (about 28 minutes total). Remove from heat. Add milk, cheese, and roasted butternut squash, stirring until cheese melts. Sprinkle each serving with snipped chives. YIELD: 4 SERVINGS (SERVING SIZE: ABOUT 1 CUP).

PER SERVING: CAL 333 (24% from fat); FAT 8.9g (sat 4g); PRO 9.1g; CARB 53.3g; FIB 4.2g; CHOL 17mg; IRON 1.2mg; SOD 869mg; CALC 163mg

CREOLE VEGETABLES ON CHEESE GRITS

POINTS value: *7*   *pictured on page 62*

PREP: 4 minutes ■ **COOK:** 20 minutes

Here's a secret we discovered for great grits: Always cook them in salted water. Adding salt after cooking just doesn't have the same flavor-enhancing effect.

    1 tablespoon extra-virgin olive oil
    1 cup chopped onion
    1 cup chopped green bell pepper
    4 garlic cloves, minced
    1 (15.5-ounce) can dark kidney beans, rinsed and drained
    1 (14.5-ounce) can stewed tomatoes
    1 cup frozen cut okra, thawed
    1 teaspoon dried thyme
    ¼ teaspoon salt
    ⅛ teaspoon ground red pepper
    2⅔ cups water
    ⅔ cup uncooked quick-cooking grits
    ¼ teaspoon salt
    1 cup (4 ounces) reduced-fat shredded sharp Cheddar cheese
    1 teaspoon hot sauce
    2 tablespoons chopped fresh parsley

1. Heat oil in a large nonstick skillet over medium–high heat. Add onion and bell pepper; sauté 4 minutes. Add garlic; sauté 15 seconds. Add kidney beans and next 5 ingredients. Bring to a boil; cover, reduce heat, and simmer 15 minutes or until okra is just tender.
2. While vegetable mixture simmers, bring 2⅔ cups water to a boil in a large saucepan over medium–high heat; stir in grits and salt. Cover, reduce heat, and simmer 10 minutes or until thick, stirring occasionally. Remove from heat; add cheese and hot sauce, stirring until cheese melts. Serve vegetable mixture over grits. Sprinkle with parsley. YIELD: 4 SERVINGS (SERVING SIZE: ABOUT 1 CUP VEGETABLES, ABOUT ½ CUP GRITS, AND ½ TABLESPOON PARSLEY).

PER SERVING: CAL 338 (29% from fat); FAT 10.9g (sat 5.1g); PRO 15.7g; CARB 48.2g; FIB 8.6g; CHOL 22mg; IRON 2.8mg; SOD 753mg; CALC 311mg

GARDEN OMELET
WITH GOAT CHEESE

POINTS value: 7

PREP: 9 minutes ▪ **COOK:** 11 minutes

As the egg mixture begins to cook in Step Two, gently lift the edges of the omelet with a spatula, and tilt the pan so any uncooked portion flows underneath.

- 2 teaspoons olive oil
- ½ cup packed fresh baby spinach
- ½ cup chopped seeded tomato
- 2 tablespoons finely chopped shallots
- ½ tablespoon chopped fresh basil
- ¼ teaspoon salt
- ¼ teaspoon freshly ground black pepper
- ½ cup egg substitute
- 2 tablespoons 1% low-fat milk
- 1 tablespoon goat cheese, cut into small pieces

1. Heat oil in a large nonstick skillet over medium heat. Add spinach and next 5 ingredients. Cook 4 minutes, stirring frequently. Remove from pan, and keep warm.
2. Combine egg substitute and milk, stirring with a whisk. Pour egg mixture into pan. Cook over medium heat 5 minutes or until set.
3. Spoon spinach mixture over omelet. Sprinkle with goat cheese. Loosen omelet with a spatula; fold in half. Serve immediately. **YIELD: 1 SERVING (SERVING SIZE: 1 OMELET).**

PER SERVING: CAL 277 (58% from fat); FAT 17.9g (sat 5.3g); PRO 19.7g; CARB 10.6g; FIB 1.9g; CHOL 14mg; IRON 3.8mg; SOD 894mg; CALC 182mg

HOW TO MAKE AN OMELET

Prepare your omelet's filling before you begin heating the eggs. Whisk egg substitute or eggs until slightly frothy, about 20 to 30 seconds. Be careful not to overbeat. Heat a nonstick pan over medium heat. Spray pan with cooking spray, or add a small amount of oil; pour in eggs. Gently shake pan to distribute.

1. As the omelet cooks, use a nonstick spatula to lift edges and allow uncooked egg to flow underneath. Cook until egg appears set, not runny.

2. Sprinkle filling over half of omelet; then use spatula to lift and fold the other half over filling.

3. To remove omelet from pan, carefully slide it onto a plate using the spatula to guide omelet.

GREEK FRITTATA

POINTS value: 4

pictured on page 63

PREP: 13 minutes ■ **COOK:** 28 minutes
■ **OTHER:** 5 minutes

Quick-cooking orzo, a rice-shaped pasta, is the bottom layer of this hearty frittata loaded with veggies, feta cheese, and olives. Substitute ½ teaspoon dried oregano in the frittata mixture for fresh, if you prefer.

½ cup uncooked orzo (rice-shaped pasta)
Cooking spray
2 cups grape tomatoes
1 (8-ounce) package presliced cremini mushrooms
4 large eggs
4 large egg whites
⅛ teaspoon kosher salt
⅛ teaspoon black pepper
¼ cup chopped pitted kalamata olives
2 tablespoons capers
1½ teaspoons chopped fresh oregano
1 (4-ounce) package crumbled feta cheese
Fresh oregano leaves (optional)

1. Preheat oven to 400°.
2. Cook orzo according to package directions, omitting salt and fat; drain.
3. While orzo cooks, heat a 10-inch ovenproof skillet over medium heat. Coat pan with cooking spray. Add tomatoes and mushrooms. Sauté 6 minutes or until mushrooms are tender and liquid almost evaporates. Remove tomato mixture from pan. Coat pan with cooking spray; spoon cooked orzo into pan, spreading evenly.
4. Combine eggs, egg whites, salt, and pepper in a bowl, stirring with a whisk. Stir in olives, capers, and oregano. Slowly pour egg mixture over orzo in pan; spoon tomato mixture over egg mixture, and sprinkle with feta.
5. Bake at 400° for 20 to 24 minutes or just until set. Let stand 5 minutes before cutting into wedges. Garnish with fresh oregano leaves, if desired. **YIELD: 6 SERVINGS (SERVING SIZE: 1 WEDGE).**

PER SERVING: CAL 199 (43% from fat); FAT 9.4g (sat 4.1g); PRO 12.6g; CARB 16.1g; FIB 1.5g; CHOL 158mg; IRON 1.1mg; SOD 521mg; CALC 129mg

SPINACH AND ARTICHOKE SPAGHETTI FRITTATA

POINTS value: 4

PREP: 17 minutes ■ **COOK:** 25 minutes

4 ounces uncooked multigrain thin spaghetti, broken into thirds
Cooking spray
1½ cups chopped onion
1 cup chopped green bell pepper
3 large eggs
4 large egg whites
1 (10-ounce) package frozen chopped spinach, thawed, drained, and squeezed dry
⅓ cup fat-free milk
1 (14-ounce) can quartered artichoke hearts, drained and coarsely chopped
¾ cup (3 ounces) shredded light 4-cheese Italian blend cheese, divided
¼ cup chopped fresh basil
¼ teaspoon salt
¼ teaspoon crushed red pepper
¾ cup tomato-basil pasta sauce (such as Classico), warmed
2 tablespoons grated fresh Parmesan cheese

1. Cook spaghetti according to package directions, omitting salt and fat. Drain and set aside.
2. While spaghetti cooks, heat a large nonstick skillet over medium-high heat. Coat pan with cooking spray. Add onion and bell pepper; coat onion mixture with cooking spray. Sauté 6 minutes or until vegetables are tender. Remove from heat, and cool slightly.
3. Combine eggs, egg whites, spinach, and milk in a large bowl, stirring with a whisk. Stir in artichokes, ½ cup shredded Italian blend cheese, and next 3 ingredients. Stir in onion mixture and pasta.
4. Place pan over medium-low heat. Coat pan with cooking spray. Pour egg mixture into pan. Cook 5 minutes or until edges are set. Cover and cook 10 minutes or until set.
5. Uncover and sprinkle evenly with remaining ¼ cup Italian blend cheese. Cover and cook 2 minutes or until cheese melts. Cut frittata into 6 wedges. Serve with pasta sauce and Parmesan cheese. **YIELD: 6 SERVINGS (SERVING SIZE: 1 WEDGE FRITTATA, 2 TABLESPOONS PASTA SAUCE, AND 1 TEASPOON PARMESAN CHEESE).**

PER SERVING: CAL 232 (24% from fat); FAT 6.3g (sat 2.3g); PRO 19g; CARB 25.7g; FIB 4.5g; CHOL 113mg; IRON 2.4mg; SOD 561mg; CALC 273mg

Apricot and Wasabi–Sauced Pork Tenderloin, *page 90*

PICADILLO

POINTS value: 8

pictured on page 131

PREP: 7 minutes ■ **COOK:** 23 minutes

Our version of this Latin American favorite is mildly spicy and ideal for a hungry family. The dish goes well with a wedge salad and a scoop of lime sherbet for dessert.

Cooking spray
¾ pound ground beef, extra lean
1½ cups chopped onion
1 cup chopped red bell pepper
½ teaspoon salt
½ teaspoon ground allspice
½ teaspoon ground cumin
½ teaspoon black pepper
⅛ teaspoon crushed red pepper
1 (8-ounce) can tomato sauce
½ cup water
3 tablespoons raisins
¼ cup pine nuts, toasted
1 (8.8-ounce) package precooked whole-grain brown rice (such as Uncle Ben's Ready Rice)
Chopped fresh parsley (optional)

1. Heat a large nonstick skillet over medium-high heat. Coat pan with cooking spray. Add beef, onion, and bell pepper; cook 7 minutes or until browned, stirring to crumble.
2. Stir in salt and next 4 ingredients. Cook 1 minute. Add tomato sauce, water, and raisins, stirring well. Bring to a boil; cover, reduce heat, and simmer 10 minutes or until mixture thickens. Stir in pine nuts.
3. Cook rice according to package directions. Spoon beef mixture into shallow bowls. Top with rice and, if desired, garnish with parsley. **YIELD: 4 SERVINGS (SERVING SIZE: ABOUT 1 CUP BEEF MIXTURE AND ½ CUP RICE).**

PER SERVING: CAL 371 (38% from fat); FAT 15.7g (sat 3.8g); PRO 22.9g; CARB 36.9g; FIB 4.4g; CHOL 31mg; IRON 3.7mg; SOD 657mg; CALC 40mg

BEEF AND BACON PIE WITH CORNBREAD CRUST

POINTS value: 6

PREP: 5 minutes ■ **COOK:** 38 minutes

4 bacon slices, chopped
1½ pounds ground beef, extra lean
1 cup chopped onion
1¼ cups fat-free, less-sodium beef broth, divided
½ cup white wine
1 teaspoon garlic salt
1 teaspoon dried thyme
2 tablespoons all-purpose flour
Cooking spray
½ cup fat-free milk
2 large egg whites
1½ teaspoons butter, melted
1 cup self-rising yellow cornmeal mix

1. Preheat oven to 400°.
2. Heat a large nonstick skillet over medium-high heat. Add bacon; cook 5 minutes. Add beef; cook 2 minutes, stirring to crumble. Add onion; cook 7 minutes or until beef is browned, stirring occasionally. Stir in 1 cup broth and next 3 ingredients.
3. Combine remaining ¼ cup broth and flour, stirring with a whisk until smooth. Add to beef mixture, and bring to a boil. Reduce heat, and simmer 3 minutes or until mixture thickens, stirring constantly. Spoon beef mixture into an 11 x 7–inch baking dish coated with cooking spray.
4. Combine milk, egg whites, and butter in a medium bowl; add cornmeal mix, stirring until blended. Drizzle cornmeal mixture on top of meat mixture. Bake at 400° for 20 minutes or until golden brown. **YIELD: 8 SERVINGS (SERVING SIZE: ⅛ OF CASSEROLE).**

PER SERVING: CAL 252 (35% from fat); FAT 9.7g (sat 3.9g); PRO 22g; CARB 15.6g; FIB 1.6g; CHOL 37mg; IRON 2.9mg; SOD 514mg; CALC 95mg

SELF-RISING CORNMEAL MIX

Self-rising cornmeal mix has cornmeal, all-purpose flour, salt, baking powder, and baking soda already added in, allowing you to save measuring and mixing time and still achieve consistent results. As a substitute for 1 cup self-rising cornmeal, use a mixture of ¾ cup plain cornmeal, ¼ cup all-purpose flour, ½ teaspoon salt, ½ teaspoon baking powder, and ¼ teaspoon baking soda.

STEAK FAJITAS WITH FRESH PICO DE GALLO

POINTS value: 5

PREP: 27 minutes ■ **COOK:** 6 minutes
■ **OTHER:** 30 minutes

Serve any extra Pico de Gallo with baked tortilla chips for a quick snack or appetizer.

       2 tablespoons fresh lime juice
       1 tablespoon olive oil
       1 teaspoon ground cumin
       1 teaspoon chili powder
       ½ teaspoon crushed red pepper
       ¼ teaspoon salt
       1 pound flank steak, trimmed
       2 teaspoons olive oil
       1 cup thinly sliced red onion
       1 cup thinly sliced green bell pepper
       6 (7-inch) flour tortillas
    Fresh Pico de Gallo

1. Combine first 6 ingredients in a large heavy-duty zip-top plastic bag.
2. Cut steak diagonally across grain into thin slices. Add steak to marinade in bag; seal and marinate in refrigerator at least 30 minutes, turning occasionally.
3. Heat 2 teaspoons oil in a large nonstick skillet over medium–high heat. Add steak with marinade, onion, and bell pepper. Sauté 5 to 7 minutes or until steak is done and vegetables are tender.
4. Divide steak mixture evenly among tortillas. Top each tortilla with Pico de Gallo. YIELD: 6 SERVINGS (SERV-ING SIZE: 1 FAJITA AND ¼ CUP PICO DE GALLO).

PER SERVING: CAL 248 (38% from fat); FAT 10.6g (sat 2.5g); PRO 19.2g; CARB 19.6g; FIB 2.4g; CHOL 25mg; IRON 2.4mg; SOD 414mg; CALC 34mg

Fresh Pico de Gallo

POINTS value: 0

PREP: 5 minutes

       4 plum tomatoes, seeded and diced
       1 cup chopped red onion
       2 garlic cloves, minced
       1 jalapeño pepper, seeded and minced
       2 tablespoons chopped fresh cilantro
       2 tablespoons fresh lime juice
       2 teaspoons olive oil
       ½ teaspoon salt

1. Combine all ingredients in a medium bowl; cover and chill. YIELD: 12 SERVINGS (SERVING SIZE: ¼ CUP).

PER SERVING: CAL 18 (45% from fat); FAT 0.9g (sat 0.1g); PRO 0.4g; CARB 2.7g; FIB 0.5g; CHOL 0mg; IRON 0.1mg; SOD 100mg; CALC 6mg

MARSALA BEEF TENDERLOIN STEAKS WITH MUSHROOMS

POINTS value: 5

PREP: 4 minutes ■ **COOK:** 16 minutes
■ **OTHER:** 30 minutes

Seared on the outside, juicy on the inside—that's the perfect steak. To get that result, let the steaks stand at room temperature for about 30 minutes so they are an even temperature throughout before cooking.

       4 (4-ounce) beef tenderloin steaks (about 1 inch thick), trimmed
       ¼ teaspoon salt
       ¼ teaspoon pepper
    Butter-flavored cooking spray
       1 (8-ounce) package presliced mushrooms
       3 medium shallots, thinly sliced
       ½ cup Marsala wine
       2 teaspoons butter
       2 tablespoons chopped fresh parsley

1. Let steaks stand at room temperature for 30 minutes.
2. Sprinkle steaks with salt and pepper. Heat a large nonstick skillet over medium–high heat. Coat pan with cooking spray. Add steaks, and cook 2 to 3 minutes on each side or until desired degree of doneness. Remove steaks from pan; keep warm.
3. Add mushrooms and shallots to pan; coat vegetables with cooking spray. Sauté 5 to 6 minutes or until mushrooms are browned and tender. Add Marsala; cook 1 minute or until liquid almost evaporates. Add butter, and cook 1 minute, stirring constantly. Spoon mushroom sauce over steaks. Sprinkle with parsley.
YIELD: 4 SERVINGS (SERVING SIZE: 1 STEAK AND ABOUT ¼ CUP MUSHROOM SAUCE).

PER SERVING: CAL 238 (32% from fat); FAT 8.5g (sat 3.6g); PRO 23.5g; CARB 7.8g; FIB 0.5g; CHOL 64mg; IRON 1.9mg; SOD 212mg; CALC 33mg

GRILLED SIRLOIN WITH ADOBO AÏOLI

POINTS value: 4

PREP: 8 minutes ■ **COOK:** 8 minutes
■ **OTHER:** 5 minutes

If the weather outside is chilly, cook the steak on the stovetop using a grill pan or skillet over medium-high heat for the same amount of time.

⅓ cup fat-free sour cream
2 tablespoons light mayonnaise
1 garlic clove, minced
2 teaspoons adobo sauce
½ teaspoon salt, divided
2 teaspoons chili powder
1 teaspoon ground cumin
1 pound boneless lean sirloin steak (about ¾ inch thick)
4 lemon wedges

1. Prepare grill.
2. Combine sour cream, mayonnaise, garlic, adobo sauce, and ¼ teaspoon salt in a small bowl. Set aside.
3. Combine chili powder, cumin, and remaining ¼ teaspoon salt in a small bowl. Rub mixture on both sides of steak.
4. Place steak on grill rack, and grill 4 to 5 minutes on each side or until desired degree of doneness. Let steak stand 5 minutes. Cut steak diagonally across grain into thin slices. Serve with reserved adobo aïoli and lemon wedges. **YIELD: 4 SERVINGS (SERVING SIZE: 3 OUNCES STEAK AND 2 TABLESPOONS AÏOLI).**

PER SERVING: CAL 171 (31% from fat); FAT 5.9g (sat 1.9g); PRO 23.5g; CARB 5.5g; FIB 0.5g; CHOL 44mg; IRON 1.6mg; SOD 486mg; CALC 51mg

DRY RUBS

If you're looking for a fat-free addition to grilled meats that packs a whopping punch of flavor, look no farther than dry rubs. While they were originally used for preservation purposes, today, rubs add an appealing taste and create a delightful crust for your meats. Dry rubs are a healthy alternative to marinades that are oil-based and high in fat. Dry rubs work best when the rub is massaged fully into the surface of meats prior to cooking.

SKILLET SIRLOIN, ONIONS, AND MUSHROOMS

POINTS value: 4

PREP: 14 minutes ■ **COOK:** 23 minutes

Adding a small amount of instant coffee granules to the steak along with freshly ground black pepper boosts the flavor of the pan juices. If you serve the juicy steak over a single serving of ½ cup mashed potatoes, the **POINTS** value will be 6.

12 ounces boneless sirloin steak, cut diagonally across grain into thin strips
2 teaspoons instant coffee granules
½ teaspoon freshly ground black pepper
Cooking spray
1¼ cups thinly sliced onion
1 (8-ounce) package presliced mushrooms
2 garlic cloves, minced
¼ teaspoon salt
¼ cup bourbon
2 tablespoons low-sodium soy sauce
1 tablespoon sugar
¼ cup chopped green onions

1. Combine steak, coffee granules, and pepper in a medium bowl; toss gently to coat.
2. Heat a large nonstick skillet over medium-high heat. Coat pan with cooking spray. Add steak to pan; sauté 4 minutes or until browned on all sides. Remove steak from pan; set aside, and keep warm.
3. Recoat pan with cooking spray. Add onion; coat onion with cooking spray. Sauté 4 minutes or until tender, stirring frequently. Add mushrooms, garlic, and salt; coat mushrooms with cooking spray. Sauté 4 minutes or until tender. Add vegetables to reserved beef; keep warm.
4. Add bourbon, soy sauce, and sugar to pan. Cook over medium-high heat 1 minute or until reduced to ¼ cup. Pour over beef mixture, and sprinkle evenly with green onions. **YIELD: 4 SERVINGS (SERVING SIZE: 1 CUP).**

PER SERVING: CAL 187 (17% from fat); FAT 3.5g (sat 1.3g); PRO 19g; CARB 11g; FIB 1.3g; CHOL 31mg; IRON 1.7mg; SOD 453mg; CALC 40mg

TACO-SEASONED SIRLOIN WITH FRESH TOMATOES

POINTS value: 4

PREP: 5 minutes ■ **COOK:** 12 minutes
■ **OTHER:** 3 minutes

Zippy taco seasoning and fresh lime juice enhance the flavor of this quick sirloin steak main dish.

>   1 **pound boneless sirloin steak**
>   2 **tablespoons low-sodium taco seasoning**
> **Cooking spray**
>   1 **cup grape tomatoes, halved**
>   6 **tablespoons water**
>   2 **teaspoons olive oil**
>   1 **large lime**

1. Coat both sides of steak evenly with taco seasoning.
2. Heat a large nonstick skillet over medium–high heat. Coat pan with cooking spray. Cook steak 4 minutes on each side or until desired degree of doneness. Let stand 3 minutes. Cut steak diagonally across grain into thin slices. Set aside, and keep warm.
3. Recoat pan with cooking spray. Add tomatoes and water; cook 3 minutes or until tomatoes are soft, scraping pan to loosen browned bits. Remove from heat; stir in oil.
4. Cut lime in half lengthwise. Cut 1 half into 4 wedges. Squeeze remaining lime half evenly over steak slices. Serve steak slices with tomato mixture and lime wedges. **YIELD: 4 SERVINGS (SERVING SIZE: 3 OUNCES STEAK AND 2 TABLESPOONS TOMATO MIXTURE).**

PER SERVING: CAL 179 (35% from fat); FAT 6.9g (sat 2g); PRO 22.7g; CARB 5.4g; FIB 0.5g; CHOL 42mg; IRON 1.6mg; SOD 347mg; CALC 18mg

BUYING, COOKING, AND STORING PARSNIPS

Parsnips are root vegetables with a sweet, nutty flavor. They are available year-round, but their peak seasons are fall and winter. Shaped like carrots with beige-white skin, they are suitable for baking, boiling, roasting, and steaming, and they are often boiled and mashed like potatoes. Parsnips can be refrigerated in a plastic bag up to a month.

BOILED CORNED BEEF DINNER WITH HORSERADISH SAUCE

POINTS value: 6

PREP: 23 minutes ■ **COOK:** 3 hours and 5 minutes
■ **OTHER:** 15 minutes

Use a very large Dutch oven with a 12-quart capacity for this recipe to ensure there's enough room to add the vegetables in Step Four.

>   1 **(3-pound) corned beef brisket, trimmed**
>   1 **tablespoon black peppercorns**
>   3 **bay leaves**
>   ¼ **cup prepared horseradish**
>   ¼ **cup cider vinegar**
>   2 **tablespoons sugar**
>   5 **large carrots, cut into 1-inch pieces**
>   3 **large parsnips, cut into 1-inch pieces**
>   8 **pearl onions**
>   1 **medium head green cabbage, cut into 8 wedges**

1. Place corned beef in a very large Dutch oven; add peppercorns and bay leaves. Cover with water to 2 inches above beef; bring to a boil. Partially cover, reduce heat, and simmer 2½ hours or until beef is tender. Remove beef from pan. Cool slightly.
2. While beef cooks, combine horseradish, vinegar, and sugar. Set aside.
3. Place a large heavy-duty zip-top plastic bag inside a large bowl. Strain cooking liquid through a sieve into bag; discard peppercorns and bay leaves. Place bowl in refrigerator for 15 minutes (fat will rise to the top). Seal bag; carefully snip off 1 bottom corner of bag. Drain liquid into pan, stopping before fat layer reaches opening; discard fat.
4. Add beef, carrot, parsnip, and onions to pan; bring to a boil. Cover, reduce heat, and simmer 15 minutes. Add cabbage; cover and simmer 15 minutes or until cabbage is tender.
5. Remove beef from pan, and cut diagonally across grain into slices. Remove vegetables from cooking liquid with a slotted spoon. Serve beef and vegetables with reserved horseradish sauce. **YIELD: 8 SERVINGS (SERVING SIZE: 3 OUNCES CORNED BEEF, ⅛ OF VEGETABLES, AND ABOUT 1½ TABLESPOONS HORSERADISH SAUCE).**

PER SERVING: CAL 336 (18% from fat); FAT 6.9g (sat 2.5g); PRO 39.5g; CARB 26.9g; FIB 7.2g; CHOL 70mg; IRON 4.4mg; SOD 221mg; CALC 131mg

FRESH LEMON AND BASIL PORK CHOPS

POINTS value: 4

PREP: 5 minutes ■ **COOK:** 10 minutes

    4 (4-ounce) boneless loin pork chops (about 1 inch thick)
    ½ garlic clove, halved
    1 tablespoon salt-free steak seasoning blend
    ¼ teaspoon salt
Cooking spray
    4 teaspoons fresh lemon juice
    2 teaspoons olive oil
    2 tablespoons chopped fresh basil

1. Prepare grill.
2. Pat pork chops dry with a paper towel. Rub both sides with garlic clove quarters; sprinkle evenly with seasoning blend and salt.
3. Place pork chops on grill rack coated with cooking spray; grill 5 minutes on each side or until done.
4. Drizzle pork chops with lemon juice and olive oil; sprinkle with basil. YIELD: 4 SERVINGS (SERVING SIZE: 1 CHOP).

PER SERVING: CAL 182 (43% from fat); FAT 8.7g (sat 2.7g); PRO 24g; CARB 0.6g; FIB 0.1g; CHOL 65mg; IRON 0.7mg; SOD 193mg; CALC 28mg

PORK CHOPS WITH POMEGRANATE-ORANGE REDUCTION

POINTS value: 4

PREP: 4 minutes ■ **COOK:** 9 minutes

You can find pomegranate juice blends in the refrigerated section of the grocery store alongside the orange juice. If you select a blueberry-pomegranate blend, you can use any remaining juice to prepare the highly-rated Blueberry-Pomegranate Sorbet on page 48.

    ½ teaspoon chili powder
    ¼ teaspoon ground allspice
    ¼ teaspoon ground red pepper
    ¼ teaspoon salt
    4 (4-ounce) boneless center-cut loin pork chops
        (½ inch thick)
Cooking spray
    ½ cup blueberry-pomegranate juice
    2 tablespoons balsamic vinegar
    1 tablespoon sugar
    1 teaspoon grated fresh orange rind

1. Combine first 4 ingredients in a small bowl, and sprinkle over both sides of pork.
2. Heat a large nonstick skillet over medium-high heat. Coat pan with cooking spray. Add pork chops, and cook 3 to 4 minutes on each side or until done. Remove chops from pan; keep warm.
3. Add blueberry-pomegranate juice, vinegar, and sugar to pan; bring to a boil over medium heat. Cook 3 minutes or until slightly syrupy. Remove pan from heat, and stir in orange rind. Drizzle sauce evenly over pork chops. YIELD: 4 SERVINGS (SERVING SIZE: 1 CHOP AND ABOUT 2 TEASPOONS SAUCE).

PER SERVING: CAL 198 (29% from fat); FAT 6.4g (sat 2.3g); PRO 24g; CARB 9g; FIB 0.2g; CHOL 65mg; IRON 0.8mg; SOD 207mg; CALC 31mg

REDUCTIONS

A reduction is created when juice, wine, vinegar, or other liquids are added to pan drippings from meats or juices from vegetables, then simmered until the volume of liquid is "reduced" to about half. This concentrates the flavors so that very little sauce is needed to give your dish a smooth, flavorful finish.

APRICOT AND WASABI–SAUCED PORK TENDERLOIN

POINTS value: 4

pictured on page 129

PREP: 15 minutes ■ **COOK:** 28 minutes
■ **OTHER:** 20 minutes

    1 (1-pound) pork tenderloin
    2 tablespoons low-sodium soy sauce
    2 teaspoons salt-free steak seasoning
    ¾ teaspoon ground cinnamon
    ¼ teaspoon salt
Cooking spray
    1 teaspoon dark sesame oil
    1 tablespoon cider vinegar
    1 teaspoon wasabi powder (dried Japanese horseradish)
    ¼ cup low-sugar apricot preserves
    ½ teaspoon grated fresh orange rind

1. Preheat oven to 425°.
2. Place tenderloin and soy sauce in a large zip-top plastic bag; seal bag. Let stand 15 minutes, turning bag occasionally.

3. Combine steak seasoning, cinnamon, and salt in a small bowl. Remove pork from plastic bag, discarding soy sauce. Place pork on a platter. Sprinkle with seasoning mixture.

4. Heat a large nonstick skillet over medium-high heat. Coat pan with cooking spray. Add sesame oil. Cook pork 2 minutes on each side or until lightly browned.

5. Place pork in an 11 x 7–inch baking dish coated with cooking spray. Bake at 425° for 22 minutes or until a thermometer registers 160°. Remove pork to a cutting board; let stand 5 minutes before slicing.

6. Combine vinegar and wasabi powder in a small bowl, stirring with a whisk. Stir in preserves and orange rind. Add apricot mixture to baking dish, scraping bottom to remove browned bits. Serve with pork. YIELD: 4 SERVINGS (SERVING SIZE: 3 OUNCES PORK AND ABOUT 1 TABLESPOON SAUCE).

PER SERVING: CAL 170 (26% from fat); FAT 5g (sat 1.5g); PRO 22.7g; CARB 6.7g; FIB 0.3g; CHOL 63mg; IRON 1.4mg; SOD 289mg; CALC 11mg

TACOS AL PASTOR WITH GRILLED PINEAPPLE SALSA

POINTS value: 3

PREP: 20 minutes ■ **COOK:** 20 minutes ■ **OTHER:** 8 hours and 10 minutes

Tacos al Pastor is a Mexican street food featuring marinated and spit-roasted meat. Our version uses grilled pork tenderloins.

  1 cup fresh orange juice
  ½ cup white vinegar
  ½ medium-sized red onion, finely chopped
  2 chipotle chiles, canned in adobo sauce, chopped
  1 tablespoon adobo sauce
  2 teaspoons dried oregano
  2 teaspoons ground cumin
  1 teaspoon garlic salt
  2 (1-pound) pork tenderloins
  4 (½-inch-thick) fresh pineapple slices
Cooking spray
 10 (6-inch) corn tortillas
  ¾ cup chopped fresh cilantro
Reduced-fat sour cream (optional)

1. Combine first 8 ingredients in a medium bowl. Divide juice mixture among 2 large zip-top plastic bags; add pork to 1 bag. Seal both bags, and refrigerate at least 8 hours.

2. Prepare grill.

3. Remove pork from bag, discarding marinade. Place pork and pineapple slices on grill rack coated with cooking spray. Grill pineapple 4 minutes on each side. Grill pork 20 minutes or until a thermometer registers 160°, turning once. Let stand 10 minutes.

4. Grill tortillas 30 seconds on each side. Chop grilled pineapple slices, and add chopped pineapple and cilantro to remaining zip-top plastic bag filled with juice mixture.

5. Cut pork crosswise into ¼-inch-thick slices. Divide pork evenly among tortillas, and top with pineapple salsa. Serve with sour cream, if desired. YIELD: 10 SERVINGS (SERVING SIZE: 1 TORTILLA, 3 OUNCES PORK, AND ABOUT 2½ TABLESPOONS SALSA).

PER SERVING: CAL 176 (20% from fat); FAT 3.9g (sat 1.1g); PRO 19.5g; CARB 16g; FIB 1.9g; CHOL 51mg; IRON 1.4mg; SOD 172mg; CALC 31mg

GRILLED LAMB CHOPS WITH GREMOLATA

POINTS value: 4   *pictured on page 130*

PREP: 16 minutes ■ **COOK:** 8 minutes

Gremolata is a finely minced combination of garlic, lemon rind, and parsley. It adds a fresh, zesty flavor to these lamb chops and has a **POINTS** value of 0. Round out your meal by serving the chops over pasta.

  8 (3-ounce) lamb loin chops, trimmed
  2 teaspoons olive oil
  ½ teaspoon salt
  ½ teaspoon freshly ground black pepper
  5 garlic cloves
  ½ cup fresh parsley leaves
  2 teaspoons grated fresh lemon rind

1. Prepare grill.

2. Rub lamb chops with olive oil; sprinkle with salt and pepper.

3. Drop garlic through food chute of a food processor with processor on. Process until minced. Add parsley and lemon rind; process until parsley is minced. Set gremolata aside.

4. Place lamb chops on grill rack. Grill 4 minutes on each side or to desired degree of doneness. Serve with gremolata. YIELD: 4 SERVINGS (SERVING SIZE: 2 LAMB CHOPS AND ABOUT 1½ TABLESPOONS GREMOLATA).

PER SERVING: CAL 184 (46% from fat); FAT 9.4g (sat 2.8g); PRO 21.9g; CARB 2.1g; FIB 0.5g; CHOL 68mg; IRON 1.9mg; SOD 356mg; CALC 33mg

BRAISED LAMB SHANKS WITH ROASTED BUTTERNUT SQUASH

POINTS value: 7

PREP: 13 minutes ■ **COOK:** 2 hours and 45 minutes

Before preparing this recipe, adjust the racks in your oven so there will be enough room for both a large ovenproof Dutch oven and a baking sheet.

    3   (15-ounce) lamb shanks
    1   teaspoon freshly ground black pepper, divided
    ¾   teaspoon garlic salt, divided
    1½ teaspoons olive oil
    1¾ cups chopped onion
    1   cup chopped carrot
    ½   cup chopped celery
    3   tablespoons tomato paste
    1½ cups dry red wine
    4   cups fat-free, less-sodium chicken broth
    1   (2½-pound) butternut squash
  Cooking spray

1. Sprinkle lamb with ½ teaspoon pepper and ¼ teaspoon garlic salt. Heat oil in a large ovenproof Dutch oven over medium-high heat. Add lamb, and cook 4 minutes on each side or until browned. Remove lamb from pan, reserving drippings.
2. Preheat oven to 350°.
3. Add onion, carrot, and celery to pan, and cook over medium-high heat, stirring constantly, 6 minutes or until lightly browned. Stir in tomato paste; cook 1 minute. Stir in red wine; bring to a boil over high heat. Boil 5 minutes or until liquid is slightly thick, stirring often.
4. Add chicken broth. Return lamb to pan; bring to a boil. Cover and bake at 350° for 2 hours.
5. While lamb cooks, peel and cut squash into 1-inch cubes, discarding seeds and pulp. Place squash on a baking sheet coated with cooking spray. Coat squash generously with cooking spray, tossing well. During the last 45 minutes, add squash to oven along with lamb mixture, stirring squash cubes after 20 minutes.
6. Remove lamb from pan; set aside, and keep warm. Add remaining ½ teaspoon garlic salt and ½ teaspoon pepper to pan, and bring to a boil over high heat. Reduce heat, and simmer, uncovered, 15 minutes or until slightly thick, stirring often.
7. Add lamb and squash to pan. Cook 2 minutes or just until thoroughly heated. YIELD: 6 SERVINGS (SERVING SIZE: ½ LAMB SHANK AND 1½ CUPS VEGETABLE MIXTURE).

PER SERVING: CAL 352 (24% from fat); FAT 9.2g (sat 3.3g); PRO 35.6g; CARB 24.6g; FIB 5.9g; CHOL 98mg; IRON 4.1mg; SOD 720mg; CALC 99mg

SAUSAGE, OKRA, AND TOMATO SAUTÉ

POINTS value: 6

PREP: 8 minutes ■ **COOK:** 38 minutes

Smoked turkey sausage keeps these Creole-style dishes low in fat but still big on flavor.

    4   center-cut bacon slices, chopped
    2   (14-ounce) packages smoked turkey sausage, cut into 2-inch pieces
    2   cups frozen cut okra
    2   medium tomatoes, cut into 1-inch pieces
    1   medium Vidalia or other sweet onion, cut into 8 wedges
    1   tablespoon Cajun seasoning
    3   cups water
    ¾   cup uncooked quick-cooking grits
    ¾   cup (3 ounces) reduced-fat shredded sharp Cheddar cheese
    2   teaspoons butter
    ¼   teaspoon garlic powder
  Dash of salt

1. Cook bacon in a large nonstick skillet over medium heat until crisp. Remove bacon from pan; crumble and set aside. Add sausage to drippings in pan; sauté 4 minutes or until browned. Stir in okra and next 3 ingredients. Bring to a boil; cover, reduce heat, and simmer 18 minutes, stirring occasionally. Uncover and simmer 5 minutes or until sauce thickens.
2. While turkey sausage mixture cooks, combine 3 cups water and grits in a 3-quart saucepan. Bring to a boil; cover, reduce heat, and simmer 5 minutes or until thick, stirring occasionally. Remove pan from heat. Add cheese and next 3 ingredients, stirring until cheese melts. Serve sausage mixture over grits. Sprinkle with bacon.
YIELD: 8 SERVINGS (SERVING SIZE: ABOUT ⅓ CUP GRITS, ABOUT ⅓ CUP TOMATO MIXTURE, 2 PIECES SAUSAGE, AND ABOUT 2 TEASPOONS CRUMBLED BACON).

PER SERVING: CAL 274 (29% from fat); FAT 8.8g (sat 4.3g); PRO 18.7g; CARB 28.8g; FIB 1.8g; CHOL 57mg; IRON 2.2mg; SOD 1,298mg; CALC 149mg

PROCESSED MEATS

Be careful when using processed meats such as sausage, bacon, and ham. While they add wonderful flavor to recipes, using them in excessive amounts can prove detrimental to a healthy diet because they are typically high in fat and sodium. They're a perfectly acceptable addition to any diet when eaten in moderation.

poultry

Wild Rice–Stuffed Chicken Breasts, *page 95*

JAPANESE ONE-POT CHICKEN

POINTS value: 6

pictured on page 133

PREP: 15 minutes ■ **COOK:** 15 minutes

Sriracha adds a kick to this family meal. The Thai-style hot sauce is typically made from sun-dried chili peppers, vinegar, garlic, sugar, and salt. Use it on noodles, pizza, eggs, soup, or anything that needs a spicy kick.

  1¾ cups water
    1 (14-ounce) can fat-free, less-sodium chicken broth
  ¼ cup mirin (sweet rice wine)
    2 tablespoons low-sodium soy sauce
    1 tablespoon minced peeled fresh ginger
    1 teaspoon Sriracha (hot chile sauce)
  1½ cups matchstick-cut carrots
    6 ounces snow peas, trimmed and cut in half on the diagonal
    3 cups chopped cooked chicken
  ¼ cup chopped fresh cilantro
    1 cup cooked udon noodles (thick, round, fresh Japanese wheat noodles)
  ¼ cup thinly sliced green onions

1. Combine first 6 ingredients in a large saucepan. Bring to a boil over medium-high heat. Stir in carrots and snow peas; reduce heat, and simmer 8 minutes or until vegetables are tender. Add chicken; simmer 2 minutes or until thoroughly heated. Remove from heat; stir in cilantro.
2. Divide noodles evenly among 4 bowls. Pour chicken mixture evenly over noodles, and top with green onions. **YIELD: 4 SERVINGS (SERVING SIZE: ¼ CUP NOODLES, ABOUT 1½ CUPS SOUP, AND 1 TABLESPOON GREEN ONIONS).**

PER SERVING: CAL 292 (12% from fat); FAT 4g (sat 1.1g); PRO 37g; CARB 20.6g; FIB 1.9g; CHOL 89mg; IRON 2.1mg; SOD 739mg; CALC 61mg

FRESH GINGER

Ginger adds a tangy snap to any dish. In the produce section of your supermarket, look for fresh ginger with skin that feels hard and is free of cracks and wrinkles. To prepare the ginger, use a vegetable peeler or the tip of a teaspoon to peel away the tough outer skin. Then mince, grate, or slice the gingerroot—or crush it for the most intense flavor.

DIJON CHICKEN TENDERS

POINTS value: 5

PREP: 7 minutes ■ **COOK:** 20 minutes
■ **OTHER:** 10 minutes

If you serve the crisp chicken tenders with 2 tablespoons honey mustard per serving, the **POINTS** value will be 6.

    2 large egg whites
    1 tablespoon Dijon mustard
    2 teaspoons cornstarch
  ¾ teaspoon garlic salt
  ¼ teaspoon freshly ground black pepper
    1 cup panko (Japanese breadcrumbs)
  ¼ cup chopped fresh parsley
  1½ pounds chicken breast tenders
Cooking spray
Honey mustard (optional)

1. Preheat oven to 400°.
2. Combine first 5 ingredients in a large bowl, stirring with a whisk. Combine panko and parsley in a shallow dish.
3. Dip each tender in egg white mixture. Dredge chicken in panko mixture, pressing firmly to coat. Place chicken on a wire rack; let stand 10 minutes. While chicken stands, place a baking sheet in oven to heat.
4. Coat chicken tenders well with cooking spray. Place chicken on hot pan in a single layer. Bake at 400° for 20 minutes or until chicken is done. Serve with honey mustard, if desired. **YIELD: 4 SERVINGS (SERVING SIZE: ABOUT 2 TENDERS).**

PER SERVING: CAL 261 (9% from fat); FAT 2.7g (sat 0.6g); PRO 43.2g; CARB 12.4g; FIB 0.7g; CHOL 99mg; IRON 1.5mg; SOD 455mg; CALC 26mg

TERIYAKI CHICKEN AND ORANGE KEBABS

POINTS value: 5

PREP: 13 minutes ■ **COOK:** 8 minutes
■ **OTHER:** 30 minutes

    6 tablespoons low-sodium soy sauce
    2 tablespoons rice vinegar
    2 tablespoons fresh orange juice
    2 tablespoons honey
    1 teaspoon minced peeled fresh ginger
    1 garlic clove, minced
  1½ pounds chicken breast tenders, cut into 1-inch pieces
    3 navel oranges, cut into 1-inch wedges
Cooking spray

1. Combine first 6 ingredients in a medium bowl. Add chicken, and let stand at least 30 minutes.

2. Prepare grill.

3. Remove chicken from marinade, reserving marinade. Transfer marinade to a small saucepan. Bring to a boil; boil 1 minute or until slightly thick.

4. Thread chicken and orange wedges alternately onto each of 8 (10-inch) metal skewers. Place kebabs on grill rack coated with cooking spray. Grill 3 to 4 minutes or until chicken is done, turning and basting frequently with reserved marinade. YIELD: 4 SERVINGS (SERVING SIZE: 2 KEBABS).

PER SERVING: CAL 290 (7% from fat); FAT 2.2g (sat 0.6g); PRO 41.4g; CARB 27.7g; FIB 5.5g; CHOL 99mg; IRON 2.1mg; SOD 912mg; CALC 71mg

WILD RICE–STUFFED CHICKEN BREASTS

POINTS value: 6   pictured on page 132

PREP: 34 minutes ■ COOK: 1 hour and 14 minutes

It takes almost an hour to cook wild rice, so we suggest cooking the entire package and freezing the leftovers. You'll save time later in other recipes that use wild rice for soups and side dishes.

  1 (4-ounce) package wild rice
1½ tablespoons olive oil, divided
  1 (8-ounce) package presliced mushrooms
2½ tablespoons chopped fresh thyme, divided
  2 tablespoons sweetened dried cranberries
  1 tablespoon chopped walnuts
  ½ teaspoon salt, divided
  4 (6-ounce) skinless, boneless chicken breast halves
  ¼ teaspoon black pepper

1. Cook wild rice according to package directions, omitting salt and fat; drain. Measure ⅓ cup rice, and place in a small bowl; cool slightly. Reserve remaining rice for other uses.

2. Heat 1½ teaspoons oil in a large nonstick skillet over medium-high heat. Add mushrooms; cook without stirring 5 minutes. Stir mushrooms, and cook 3 minutes or until browned. Remove pan from heat, and cool. Finely chop enough mushrooms to measure 2 tablespoons. Set aside all mushrooms.

3. Combine ⅓ cup cooked wild rice, finely chopped mushrooms, 2 tablespoons thyme, cranberries, walnuts, and ¼ teaspoon salt in a bowl, stirring well.

4. Cut a horizontal slit through thickest portion of each breast half to form a pocket. Stuff one-fourth of rice mixture into each pocket. Secure with wooden picks.

Sprinkle chicken with remaining 1½ teaspoons thyme, ¼ teaspoon salt, and pepper.

5. Add remaining 1 tablespoon oil to pan; heat over medium-high heat. Add chicken; cook 5 minutes or until browned on one side. Turn chicken, cover, and cook 5 minutes or until done. Add remaining mushrooms; cook 1 minute or until thoroughly heated. Transfer chicken to plates; top with mushrooms. YIELD: 4 SERVINGS (SERVING SIZE: 1 STUFFED CHICKEN BREAST HALF AND ⅓ CUP MUSHROOMS).

PER SERVING: CAL 285 (28% from fat); FAT 8.9g (sat 1.5g); PRO 42g; CARB 8.6g; FIB 1.2g; CHOL 99mg; IRON 1.7mg; SOD 405mg; CALC 41mg

CHICKEN WITH PROSCIUTTO, ROSEMARY, AND TOMATOES

POINTS value: 6

PREP: 8 minutes ■ COOK: 46 minutes

  1 ounce very thinly sliced prosciutto
  4 (6-ounce) skinless, boneless chicken breast halves
  ½ teaspoon freshly ground black pepper
  ¼ teaspoon salt
  2 teaspoons olive oil
  3 garlic cloves, minced
  ¾ cup dry white wine
  1 cup fat-free, less-sodium chicken broth
  1 (14.5-ounce) can no-salt-added fire-roasted diced tomatoes, undrained (such as Muir Glen)
  1 tablespoon chopped fresh rosemary

1. Cook prosciutto in a large nonstick skillet over medium heat 9 minutes or until crisp. Remove prosciutto from pan; crumble.

2. Sprinkle chicken with pepper and salt. Add oil to pan, and place over medium-high heat. Add chicken; cook 6 minutes on each side or until chicken is done. Remove from pan; keep warm.

3. Add garlic to pan; sauté 1 minute or until lightly browned. Add wine; cook until liquid almost evaporates, scraping pan to loosen browned bits. Stir in broth, tomatoes, and rosemary. Bring to a boil. Reduce heat, and simmer 15 minutes or until thick, stirring frequently. Spoon sauce into bowls; top with chicken and prosciutto. YIELD: 4 SERVINGS (SERVING SIZE: ½ CUP SAUCE, 1 CHICKEN BREAST HALF, AND ABOUT ½ TABLESPOON PROSCIUTTO).

PER SERVING: CAL 292 (16% from fat); FAT 5.3g (sat 1.2g); PRO 43.1g; CARB 7.3g; FIB 1g; CHOL 102mg; IRON 1.4mg; SOD 538mg; CALC 26mg

CHICKEN-VEGETABLE STIR-FRY

POINTS value: 8

PREP: 10 minutes ■ COOK: 13 minutes

    1 tablespoon olive oil
    2 tablespoons minced peeled fresh ginger
    2 garlic cloves, minced
    4 (6-ounce) skinless, boneless chicken breast halves,
        cut into ¼-inch strips
    1 cup snow peas, trimmed
    1 cup matchstick-cut carrots
    1 cup red bell pepper strips
    3 tablespoons low-sodium soy sauce
    1 tablespoon brown sugar
    1 tablespoon fresh lime juice
    2 teaspoons cornstarch
    2 cups cooked brown rice

1. Heat oil in a large nonstick skillet over medium-high heat. Add ginger and garlic; sauté 1 minute. Add chicken; cook 5 minutes, stirring frequently. Add snow peas, carrots, and bell pepper; cook 3 minutes, stirring frequently.
2. Combine soy sauce and next 3 ingredients; add to chicken mixture. Cook 3 minutes or until sauce thickens, stirring constantly. Serve immediately over rice. YIELD: 4 SERVINGS (SERVING SIZE: 1¼ CUPS CHICKEN MIXTURE AND ½ CUP RICE).

PER SERVING: CAL 372 (19% from fat); FAT 7.8g (sat 1.3g); PRO 43.4g; CARB 30.8g; FIB 2.9g; CHOL 99mg; IRON 2.3mg; SOD 517mg; CALC 40mg

CARAMELIZED ONION–RASPBERRY GRILLED CHICKEN

POINTS value: 6

PREP: 6 minutes ■ COOK: 1 hour

    1 tablespoon olive oil
Cooking spray
    1½ pounds sweet onions, thinly sliced
    ⅓ cup raspberry preserves
    1 tablespoon brown sugar
    1 tablespoon raspberry vinegar
    ½ teaspoon chili powder
    ¼ teaspoon dry mustard
    4 (8-ounce) skinless, bone-in chicken breast halves
    ¼ teaspoon salt
    ¼ teaspoon freshly ground black pepper

1. Prepare grill.
2. Heat oil in a large nonstick skillet coated with cooking spray over medium-low heat. Add onion; cook 25 minutes or until browned, stirring occasionally. Add raspberry preserves and next 4 ingredients; cook 2 minutes or until brown sugar melts and mixture is thoroughly heated. Set aside; keep warm.
3. Sprinkle chicken evenly with salt and pepper. Place chicken, bone side up, on grill rack coated with cooking spray. Grill 15 minutes on each side or until done. Serve chicken with sauce. YIELD: 4 SERVINGS (SERVING SIZE: 1 CHICKEN BREAST HALF AND ABOUT 3 TABLESPOONS SAUCE).

PER SERVING: CAL 278 (29% from fat); FAT 8.9g (sat 1.9g); PRO 18.5g; CARB 31.6g; FIB 1.3g; CHOL 72mg; IRON 1.4mg; SOD 240mg; CALC 46mg

CHICKEN VÉRONIQUE

POINTS value: 7

PREP: 11 minutes ■ COOK: 17 minutes

    4 (6-ounce) skinless, boneless chicken breast halves
    ¼ teaspoon salt
    ¼ teaspoon freshly ground black pepper
    3 tablespoons all-purpose flour
    1 tablespoon olive oil
    1 cup sliced mushrooms
    2 shallots, minced
    3 garlic cloves, minced
    ¾ cup dry white wine
    1 cup fat-free, less-sodium chicken broth
    2 teaspoons cornstarch
    1½ cups seedless red grapes, halved

1. Sprinkle chicken with salt and pepper, and dredge in flour.

2. Heat oil in a large nonstick skillet over medium-high heat. Add chicken; cook 4 to 5 minutes on each side or until browned. Remove from pan, and keep warm.

3. Add mushrooms, shallots, and garlic to drippings in pan. Sauté 2 to 3 minutes or until tender. Add wine; cook 3 minutes or until liquid is reduced by half.

4. Combine chicken broth and cornstarch; add mixture to pan. Bring to a boil; add chicken and grapes. Cover, reduce heat, and simmer 3 minutes or until chicken is done. Serve immediately. **YIELD: 4 SERVINGS (SERVING SIZE: 1 CHICKEN BREAST HALF AND ABOUT ½ CUP SAUCE).**

PER SERVING: CAL 321 (16% from fat); FAT 5.8g (sat 1.1g); PRO 41.9g; CARB 19.9g; FIB 1g; CHOL 99mg; IRON 1.9mg; SOD 402mg; CALC 36mg

TURN, DON'T STAB

Use tongs or a spatula to turn chicken and other meats as they are cooking. Avoid using a carving fork because once the meat has been pierced, the flavorful juices seep out too early.

LEMON-BRAISED CHICKEN AND ARTICHOKES

POINTS value: 7   *pictured on page 134*

PREP: 7 minutes ■ **COOK:** 56 minutes

  ¼ cup all-purpose flour
2½ pounds chicken pieces, skinned
  1 tablespoon olive oil
Cooking spray
  5 garlic cloves, minced
  2 cups fat-free, less-sodium chicken broth
  2 tablespoons fresh lemon juice
  1 (14-ounce) can quartered artichoke hearts, drained
  3 tablespoons chopped fresh thyme
  ½ teaspoon grated fresh lemon rind
  2 tablespoons coarsely chopped pitted kalamata olives
  2 tablespoons chopped fresh parsley

1. Place flour in a shallow dish, and dredge chicken in flour.

2. Heat oil in a large Dutch oven over medium-high heat. Add chicken; cook 5 minutes. Turn chicken; cook 3 minutes or until browned.

3. Remove chicken from pan; set aside, and keep warm. Coat pan with cooking spray. Add garlic, and sauté 1 minute.

4. Add broth and lemon juice, scraping pan to loosen browned bits. Return chicken to pan. Add artichokes, thyme, and lemon rind. Bring to a boil. Cover, reduce heat, and simmer 45 minutes or until chicken is done.

5. Ladle into bowls; sprinkle with olives and parsley. **YIELD: 4 SERVINGS (SERVING SIZE: 1 CHICKEN BREAST HALF OR 2 THIGHS OR 2 LEGS AND ¾ CUP ARTICHOKE MIXTURE).**

PER SERVING: CAL 340 (29% from fat); FAT 10.8g (sat 2.3g); PRO 42.8g; CARB 16.4g; FIB 3g; CHOL 116mg; IRON 2.4mg; SOD 878mg; CALC 39mg

TURKEY CUTLETS WITH LEMON-CAPER SAUCE

POINTS value: 6

PREP: 6 minutes ■ **COOK:** 14 minutes

Complete the meal with couscous, brown rice, or orzo and steamed carrots.

  ¼ cup all-purpose flour
1¼ pounds turkey breast cutlets (about 12)
  ¼ teaspoon salt
  ¼ teaspoon black pepper
  1 tablespoon olive oil, divided
  ½ cup dry white wine
  3 tablespoons fresh lemon juice
1½ tablespoons cold butter, cut into small pieces
  ⅛ teaspoon salt
1½ tablespoons drained capers

1. Place flour in a shallow dish. Sprinkle turkey with ¼ teaspoon salt and pepper; dredge in flour.

2. Heat 1½ teaspoons oil in a large nonstick skillet over medium-high heat; add half of turkey cutlets. Reduce heat to medium; cook 5 minutes, turning after 3 minutes. Remove turkey from pan; keep warm. Repeat procedure with remaining turkey and oil.

3. Add white wine and lemon juice to pan, scraping pan to loosen browned bits. Cook 2 minutes or until sauce is reduced by half. Remove from heat; stir in butter, ⅛ teaspoon salt, and capers. Serve sauce with turkey cutlets. **YIELD: 4 SERVINGS (SERVING SIZE: ABOUT 3 TURKEY BREAST CUTLETS AND ABOUT 1 TABLESPOON SAUCE).**

PER SERVING: CAL 254 (30% from fat); FAT 8.5g (sat 3.2g); PRO 35.6g; CARB 4.7g; FIB 0.3g; CHOL 68mg; IRON 2.1mg; SOD 469mg; CALC 5mg

TURKEY MARSALA

POINTS value: 7

PREP: 7 minutes ■ COOK: 22 minutes

Turkey cutlets vary in thickness and number of cutlets per pound depending on brand and store. We tested with cutlets that were very thin. If your cutlets are thicker than ¼ inch, place them between plastic wrap and pound to ⅛- to ¼-inch thickness with a meat mallet or rolling pin.

> 2 tablespoons butter, divided
> Cooking spray
> 1 (8-ounce) package presliced mushrooms
> 2 tablespoons minced shallots
> ¾ teaspoon garlic salt, divided
> ½ teaspoon black pepper, divided
> ⅓ cup all-purpose flour
> 1½ pounds turkey breast cutlets
> 1 cup fat-free, less-sodium chicken broth
> ½ cup dry Marsala wine

1. Melt 1 tablespoon butter in a large skillet coated with cooking spray over medium heat. Add mushrooms, shallots, ¼ teaspoon garlic salt, and ¼ teaspoon pepper; sauté 4 minutes or until mushrooms are tender. Remove from pan, and keep warm.
2. Combine flour, remaining ½ teaspoon garlic salt, and remaining ¼ teaspoon pepper in a shallow dish; dredge turkey in flour mixture.
3. Melt 1½ teaspoons butter in pan coated with cooking spray over medium–high heat. Add half of turkey cutlets; cook 2 minutes on each side or until lightly browned. Remove turkey from pan, and keep warm. Repeat procedure with remaining 1½ teaspoons butter and turkey cutlets.
4. Add broth and Marsala to pan, scraping pan to loosen browned bits. Return mushroom mixture and turkey to pan; cook 4 minutes or until sauce thickens slightly. Serve mushroom sauce over turkey. YIELD: 4 SERVINGS (SERVING SIZE: ABOUT 3 TURKEY BREAST CUTLETS AND ABOUT ⅓ CUP SAUCE).

PER SERVING: CAL 336 (18% from fat); FAT 6.7g (sat 3.6g); PRO 45.9g; CARB 15.1g; FIB 1g; CHOL 83mg; IRON 3.1mg; SOD 521mg; CALC 10mg

TURKEY-SAUSAGE MEAT LOAF

POINTS value: 4   *pictured on page 133*

PREP: 11 minutes ■ COOK: 1 hour and 10 minutes
■ OTHER: 5 minutes

To make cleanup even simpler, line the bottom of the broiler pan with foil and coat with cooking spray before baking.

> 1 pound ground turkey breast
> 1 pound hot Italian turkey sausage, casings removed and crumbled (such as Jennie-O)
> 1 cup tomato-basil pasta sauce, divided
> ⅔ cup finely chopped onion
> ½ cup seasoned breadcrumbs
> ⅓ cup chopped fresh parsley
> 1¼ teaspoons dried Italian seasoning
> ¼ teaspoon salt
> ¼ teaspoon black pepper
> 1 large egg
> Cooking spray

1. Preheat oven to 350°.
2. Combine ground turkey breast, turkey sausage, ½ cup pasta sauce, and next 7 ingredients in a large bowl. Shape into a 9 x 5–inch loaf, and place on a broiler pan coated with cooking spray. Bake at 350° for 45 minutes. Spread remaining pasta sauce over top of meat loaf. Bake an additional 25 minutes. Let stand 5 minutes. Cut into 10 slices. YIELD: 10 SERVINGS (SERVING SIZE: 1 SLICE).

PER SERVING: CAL 167 (41% from fat); FAT 7.7g (sat 2g); PRO 17.4g; CARB 7g; FIB 0.9g; CHOL 73mg; IRON 1.8mg; SOD 520mg; CALC 40mg

MAKE EXERCISE FUN

Remember how effortless movement was as a child? You didn't even have to think about it—somehow exercise was as natural as breathing. Experts recommend finding activities that bring back that sense of fun and freedom to help you look forward to incorporating fitness into your daily routine. Why not think of exercise as "recess" and revisit some activities you enjoyed as a child, such as bike riding, skating, or dancing?

salads

Sweet Lime Summer Fruits, *page 102*

WEDGE SALAD WITH AVOCADO-CILANTRO DRESSING

POINTS value: 2

PREP: 16 minutes

This salad makes more dressing than needed for 6 servings. Refrigerate the leftover dressing for up to 1 week, and use as a spread for sandwiches or as a dip for fresh vegetables. Keep plastic wrap pressed to the surface of the dressing to prevent the avocado from turning brown.

    1 ripe peeled avocado, coarsely mashed
    1 cup fat-free sour cream
    ½ cup packed cilantro leaves
    ¼ cup light mayonnaise
    ¼ cup fat-free milk
    3 tablespoons fresh lemon juice
    1 tablespoon hot sauce
    1 garlic clove, halved
    1 (0.4-ounce) package dry ranch dressing mix
    1 medium head iceberg lettuce, cut into 6 wedges
    1½ cups finely chopped red bell pepper
       Freshly ground black pepper

1. Combine first 9 ingredients in a blender; process until smooth. Cover and chill until ready to serve.
2. Place 1 lettuce wedge on each of 6 plates; top each with 2 tablespoons avocado dressing. Sprinkle with red bell pepper and freshly ground black pepper. YIELD: 6 SERVINGS (SERVING SIZE: 1 LETTUCE WEDGE, ¼ CUP BELL PEPPER, AND 2 TABLESPOONS DRESSING).

PER SERVING: CAL 98 (41% from fat); FAT 4.2g (sat 0.6g); PRO 3.7g; CARB 14.6g; FIB 3g; CHOL 5mg; IRON 0.8mg; SOD 383mg; CALC 84mg

THE POPULARITY OF WEDGE SALADS

There is a growing trend to update the original wedge salad first served in steak house restaurants. During the 1950s and 1960s, it was typically served smothered in creamy, high-calorie dressings. The salad lost its popularity in the mid-1970s when Americans discovered substitutes for iceberg lettuce such as arugula, leaf, and Romaine lettuce. Today, restaurants and home cooks have revived the quick-to-fix favorite by adorning crisp wedges with creamy, low-calorie dressings and more filling veggies.

SPRING GREENS WITH SWEET LIME VINAIGRETTE AND BERRIES

POINTS value: 2

PREP: 15 minutes ■ COOK: 2 minutes

The classic flavors of strawberries and mint are updated with fresh lime for a refreshing salad that earned our Test Kitchens' highest rating.

    4 cups spring greens
    2 cups sliced strawberries
    ½ cup thinly sliced red onion
    ¼ cup chopped fresh mint
    1 teaspoon grated fresh lime rind
    ¼ cup fresh lime juice
    3 tablespoons sugar
    1 tablespoon canola oil
    ⅛ teaspoon crushed red pepper
    2 tablespoons sliced almonds, toasted

1. Place greens on a large serving platter; top with strawberries, onion, and mint.
2. Combine lime rind and next 4 ingredients in a small bowl, stirring with a whisk. Drizzle vinaigrette over salad; sprinkle with almonds. YIELD: 6 SERVINGS (SERVING SIZE: 1 CUP SALAD, ABOUT 1 TABLESPOON DRESSING, AND 1 TEASPOON ALMONDS).

PER SERVING: CAL 111 (43% from fat); FAT 5.3g (sat 1.1g); PRO 2.7g; CARB 15.3g; FIB 2.6g; CHOL 4mg; IRON 0.7mg; SOD 34mg; CALC 66mg

CAJUN GREEN SALAD WITH CAPERS

POINTS value: 2

PREP: 18 minutes

A generous amount of hot sauce adds volume and a punch of flavor to this big, low-calorie side salad.

    2 tablespoons olive oil
    1½ tablespoons hot sauce
    1 tablespoon water
    1 teaspoon cider vinegar
    1 medium garlic clove, minced
    4 cups torn romaine lettuce
    2 medium plum tomatoes, diced
    ½ cup chopped green bell pepper
    ½ cup chopped red onion
    ¼ cup chopped fresh parsley
    3 tablespoons drained capers

1. Combine first 5 ingredients in a large bowl, stirring with a whisk. Add lettuce and remaining ingredients. Toss well. Serve immediately. YIELD: 4 SERVINGS (SERVING SIZE: ABOUT 1½ CUPS).

PER SERVING: CAL 93 (72% from fat); FAT 7.4g (sat 1.1g); PRO 1.7g; CARB 6.9g; FIB 2.5g; CHOL 0mg; IRON 1.2mg; SOD 342mg; CALC 36mg

CITRUS KALE

POINTS value: 2

PREP: 6 minutes ■ COOK: 12 minutes

Serve this calcium-rich wilted salad with grilled or roasted chicken.

    Cooking spray
    6 cups chopped kale
    ¼ cup water
    1 orange
    1 teaspoon honey Dijon mustard
    1 teaspoon honey
    ⅛ teaspoon kosher salt
    ⅛ teaspoon crushed red pepper
    ¼ cup sliced almonds, toasted

1. Heat a large nonstick skillet over medium-high heat. Coat pan with cooking spray. Add kale and ¼ cup water. Cover and cook 10 minutes or until tender, stirring occasionally. Drain.
2. While kale cooks, peel and section orange over a large bowl; squeeze membranes to extract juice. Set sections aside; reserve 2 tablespoons juice. Discard membranes.
3. Combine orange juice, mustard, and next 3 ingredients in a small bowl, stirring with a whisk.
4. Combine kale and orange sections in a large bowl; drizzle with orange juice mixture, tossing to coat. Sprinkle with almonds. YIELD: 4 SERVINGS (SERVING SIZE: ½ CUP).

PER SERVING: CAL 110 (34% from fat); FAT 4.2g (sat 0.4g); PRO 4.9g; CARB 16.8g; FIB 3.5g; CHOL 0mg; IRON 2mg; SOD 111mg; CALC 164mg

KALE

Don't relegate the curly leaves of kale to the side of the plate as a garnish. Its earthy flavor is delicious in soups, stews, and even salads. Since kale is a relatively tough green, it's a good idea to steam or cook the leaves in a small amount of water to tenderize them while preserving their abundance of vitamins A and K.

PANZANELLA

POINTS value: 5

PREP: 21 minutes ■ COOK: 2 minutes

Serve this Italian salad as soon as it's tossed so the bread soaks up the dressing without becoming soggy. Turn it into a main dish by adding grilled steak or chicken.

    3 tablespoons olive oil
    3 tablespoons white wine vinegar
    2 garlic cloves, crushed
    1 tablespoon capers
    ½ teaspoon freshly ground black pepper
    ¼ teaspoon salt
    4 cups (1-inch) cubed Italian bread, toasted
    2 cups chopped seeded tomato
    1½ cups chopped red onion
    1 cup chopped seeded peeled cucumber
    ½ cup chopped pepperoncini peppers
    2 tablespoons chopped fresh basil

1. Combine first 6 ingredients in a large bowl, stirring with a whisk. Add Italian bread and remaining ingredients, tossing to coat. Serve immediately. YIELD: 4 SERVINGS (SERVING SIZE: ABOUT 1¾ CUPS).

PER SERVING: CAL 220 (49% from fat); FAT 11.9g (sat 1.8g); PRO 4.5g; CARB 26.1g; FIB 3.5g; CHOL 0mg; IRON 1.5mg; SOD 384mg; CALC 57mg

COLESLAW WITH FETA

POINTS value: 3

PREP: 5 minutes ■ OTHER: 4 hours

    3 tablespoons olive oil
    2 tablespoons white vinegar
    2 tablespoons water
    1 garlic clove, crushed
    ½ teaspoon Greek seasoning
    ¼ teaspoon black pepper
    1 (10-ounce) package angel hair coleslaw
    ½ cup (2 ounces) crumbled feta cheese

1. Combine first 6 ingredients in a large bowl, stirring with a whisk. Add coleslaw and feta cheese; toss well. Cover and chill 4 to 6 hours before serving. YIELD: 5 SERVINGS (SERVING SIZE: 1 CUP).

PER SERVING: CAL 117 (84% from fat); FAT 10.9g (sat 2.9g); PRO 2.4g; CARB 4g; FIB 1.5g; CHOL 10mg; IRON 0.4mg; SOD 145mg; CALC 80mg

SWEET AND SPICY SLAW

POINTS value: 0

PREP: 10 minutes

2 tablespoons "measures-like-sugar" calorie-free sweetener (such as Splenda)
2 tablespoons cider vinegar
2 teaspoons canola oil
½ teaspoon celery seed
¼ teaspoon salt
¼ teaspoon crushed red pepper
½ (16-ounce) package coleslaw
½ cup preshredded carrot
½ medium-sized red bell pepper, thinly sliced and cut into 2-inch strips
½ medium poblano chile, thinly sliced and cut into 2-inch strips

1. Combine first 6 ingredients in a large bowl, stirring with a whisk. Add coleslaw and remaining ingredients; toss well. Serve immediately or chill up to 1 hour. YIELD: 6 SERVINGS (SERVING SIZE: ABOUT ¾ CUP).

PER SERVING: CAL 32 (0.7% from fat); FAT 1.7g (sat 0.1g); PRO 0.7g; CARB 4g; FIB 1.5g; CHOL 0mg; IRON 0.3mg; SOD 130mg; CALC 22mg

SWEET LIME SUMMER FRUITS

POINTS value: 1

pictured on page 136

PREP: 4 minutes

4 cups cubed seeded watermelon
1 cup blueberries
¼ cup white grape juice
1 tablespoon sugar
1 tablespoon grated fresh lime zest
2 tablespoons fresh lime juice

1. Combine watermelon cubes and blueberries in a medium bowl.
2. Combine grape juice and next 3 ingredients in a small bowl. Pour over fruit mixture; toss gently to coat. Cover and chill. YIELD: 5 SERVINGS (SERVING SIZE: ABOUT 1 CUP).

PER SERVING: CAL 77 (1% from fat); FAT 0.1g (sat 0g); PRO 1.1g; CARB 22.5g; FIB 1.9g; CHOL 0mg; IRON 0.7mg; SOD 12mg; CALC 28mg

NECTARINES AND SALAD GREENS WITH MOLASSES-BALSAMIC VINAIGRETTE

POINTS value: 6

PREP: 9 minutes ■ **COOK:** 2 minutes

Molasses may seem like an odd ingredient in a salad dressing, but in this vinaigrette, it provides some body and highlights the tangy-hot flavor. If nectarines are unavailable, peaches make an ideal substitute.

8 cups mixed salad greens
4 small nectarines, thinly sliced
½ cup thinly sliced red onion
¼ cup balsamic vinegar
1 tablespoon sugar
2 tablespoons molasses
2 tablespoons water
¼ teaspoon salt
¼ teaspoon crushed red pepper
½ cup (2 ounces) crumbled goat cheese
¼ cup chopped pecans, toasted

1. Combine greens, nectarine, and onion in a large bowl. Combine vinegar and next 5 ingredients in a small bowl, stirring with a whisk. Pour over salad; toss gently to coat.
2. Divide salad mixture evenly among 4 plates; sprinkle with cheese and pecans. YIELD: 4 SERVINGS (SERVING SIZE: 2 CUPS SALAD, 1 TABLESPOON CHEESE, AND 1 TABLESPOON PECANS).

PER SERVING: CAL 291 (46% from fat); FAT 14.8g (sat 6g); PRO 9.6g; CARB 33.6g; FIB 4.8g; CHOL 24mg; IRON 2.1mg; SOD 325mg; CALC 205mg

FRUITY SALAD WITH WATERMELON DRESSING

POINTS value: 1

PREP: 20 minutes ■ **COOK:** 2 minutes

2½ cups diced seeded watermelon, divided
2 cups seedless red grapes
1 cup blueberries
¼ cup fat-free Greek yogurt
1 tablespoon balsamic vinegar
1 teaspoon chopped fresh rosemary
12 cups torn romaine lettuce
1 (4-ounce) package goat cheese, crumbled
¼ cup chopped walnuts, toasted

1. Combine 2 cups watermelon, grapes, and blueberries in a medium bowl.

2. Mash remaining ½ cup watermelon in a small bowl with a potato masher, reserving ¼ cup juice. Discard solids. Combine ¼ cup reserved watermelon juice, yogurt, vinegar, and rosemary, stirring with a whisk until well blended.

3. Arrange lettuce on plates. Top with fruit, cheese, walnuts, and dressing. YIELD: 4 SERVINGS (SERVING SIZE: 3 CUPS LETTUCE, 1¼ CUPS FRUIT, 2 TABLESPOONS CHEESE, 1 TABLESPOON WALNUTS, AND ABOUT 2 TABLESPOONS DRESSING).

PER SERVING: CAL 59 (38% from fat); FAT 2.5g (sat 0.1g); PRO 2.6g; CARB 8.4g; FIB 1.9g; CHOL 8mg; IRON 1.6mg; SOD 359mg; CALC 36mg

GREEK YOGURT

Greek yogurt is triple-strained to remove the watery whey. What results is a slightly sweet yogurt with the thick, velvety consistency of sour cream. Enjoy it with cereal instead of milk, or stir in a small amount of honey or maple syrup to eat as a pudding. It's also a great substitute for mayonnaise.

LEAN AND GREEN PASTA SALAD

POINTS value: 5

PREP: 13 minutes ■ COOK: 16 minutes

A lean pesto made with basil and spinach smothers whole-grain pasta and blanched veggies for a salad that tastes as healthy as it looks.

    3 cups uncooked multigrain fusilli
    2 cups (1-inch) cut green beans (about ½ pound)
    1 cup frozen shelled edamame (green soybeans)
    ⅔ cup frozen petite green peas
    2 cups fresh basil leaves
    1 cup baby spinach
    3 tablespoons preshredded fresh Parmesan cheese
    3 tablespoons fresh lemon juice
    2 tablespoons chopped walnuts
    2 garlic cloves, halved
    1 tablespoon olive oil
    ½ teaspoon kosher salt
    ½ teaspoon black pepper

1. Cook pasta according to package directions, omitting salt and fat, for 10 minutes. Add green beans, edamame, and peas; return to a boil. Boil 3 minutes or until vegetables are crisp-tender and pasta is done. Drain and rinse with cold water. Pour into a large bowl.

2. While pasta and vegetables cook, combine basil and next 8 ingredients in a food processor; process until blended. Add basil mixture to pasta mixture, tossing gently to coat. Serve immediately. YIELD: 6 SERVINGS (SERVING SIZE: 1⅓ CUPS).

PER SERVING: CAL 259 (27% from fat); FAT 7.7g (sat 1.2g); PRO 11.8g; CARB 38.1g; FIB 7.8g; CHOL 3mg; IRON 1.6mg; SOD 246mg; CALC 82mg

ASPARAGUS SPEAR SALAD WITH CAESAR-STYLE DRESSING

POINTS value: 1   pictured on page 134

PREP: 8 minutes ■ COOK: 5 minutes

Just a small amount of anchovy paste adds the essential briny flavor to this Caesar-style dressing. We added a small amount of light mayonnaise in place of the raw egg found in traditional Caesar dressing.

    1 pound asparagus spears, trimmed
    ¼ cup light mayonnaise
    2 tablespoons fat-free sour cream
    2 tablespoons fresh lemon juice
    2 teaspoons water
    1½ teaspoons anchovy paste
    1 teaspoon Dijon mustard
    1 garlic clove, crushed
    ¼ teaspoon freshly ground black pepper
    ⅛ teaspoon salt
    ½ cup finely chopped red bell pepper

1. Place asparagus in a Dutch oven filled with boiling water; cook 2 to 3 minutes or until crisp-tender. Remove asparagus with a slotted spoon. Plunge into ice water; drain. Pat asparagus dry with paper towels.

2. Combine mayonnaise and next 8 ingredients in a bowl, stirring with a whisk.

3. Arrange asparagus on a platter; top with dressing, and sprinkle with bell pepper. YIELD: 4 SERVINGS (SERVING SIZE: ABOUT 10 ASPARAGUS SPEARS, ABOUT 2 TABLESPOONS DRESSING, AND 2 TABLESPOONS CHOPPED BELL PEPPER).

PER SERVING: CAL 59 (38% from fat); FAT 2.5g (sat 0.1g); PRO 2.6g; CARB 8.4g; FIB 1.9g; CHOL 8mg; IRON 1.6mg; SOD 359mg; CALC 36mg

BEET SALAD WITH CITRUS AND GOAT CHEESE

POINTS value: 2

PREP: 15 minutes ■ **COOK:** 30 minutes
■ **OTHER:** 20 minutes

Serve this vibrant salad at room temperature, and dress it just before serving to keep the colors distinct.

 3 small red beets, peeled and cut into wedges
 3 small golden beets, peeled and cut into wedges
 Cooking spray
 1 tablespoon olive oil
 1 tablespoon orange juice
 1 tablespoon water
 1 tablespoon sherry vinegar
 1 teaspoon Dijon mustard
 ½ teaspoon freshly ground black pepper
 ¼ teaspoon salt
 2 navel oranges, peeled and sliced crosswise into ⅛-inch-thick slices
 1 (6-ounce) package baby spinach
 ½ cup (2 ounces) crumbled goat cheese

1. Preheat oven to 450°.
2. Place beets on a roasting pan coated with cooking spray; coat beets with cooking spray. Bake at 450° for 30 minutes or until beets are tender and lightly browned, stirring once. Cool to room temperature (about 20 minutes).
3. While beets cool, combine oil and next 6 ingredients in a small bowl; stir well with a whisk.
4. Combine roasted beets, oranges, and spinach in a large bowl. Add vinaigrette, tossing gently to coat. Divide salad among plates; sprinkle with cheese. **YIELD: 6 SERVINGS (SERVING SIZE: 1⅔ CUPS SALAD AND 1 TABLESPOON GOAT CHEESE).**

PER SERVING: CAL 128 (37% from fat); FAT 5.3g (sat 2.3g); PRO 4.4g; CARB 18.6g; FIB 6g; CHOL 7mg; IRON 1.9mg; SOD 275mg; CALC 82mg

BLACK BEAN SALSA SALAD

POINTS value: 1

PREP: 8 minutes

Queso fresco is a Mexican cheese that is mild, crumbly, and a bit salty. If it's unavailable, shredded Monterey Jack is a good substitute.

 2 cups grape tomatoes, halved
 1 cup canned no-salt-added black beans
 ½ cup (2 ounces) crumbled queso fresco
 ¼ cup chopped red onion
 ¼ cup chopped fresh cilantro
 2 tablespoons chopped jalapeño peppers
 1 tablespoon cider vinegar
 2 teaspoons olive oil
 ⅛ teaspoon salt

1. Combine all ingredients in a large bowl. Cover and chill. **YIELD: 7 SERVINGS (SERVING SIZE: ½ CUP).**

PER SERVING: CAL 66 (31% from fat); FAT 2.3g (sat 0.7g); PRO 3.6g; CARB 8.3g; FIB 2.3g; CHOL 3mg; IRON 0.8mg; SOD 62mg; CALC 48mg

MARINATED GREEN BEAN AND RED ONION SALAD

POINTS value: 1

PREP: 8 minutes ■ **COOK:** 5 minutes
■ **OTHER:** 2 hours

 1 (12-ounce) package trimmed fresh green beans
 ½ cup thinly sliced red onion
 ¼ cup raspberry vinegar
 3 tablespoons sugar
 3½ tablespoons crumbled blue cheese
 ¼ teaspoon salt
 ⅛ teaspoon crushed red pepper
 3 tablespoons chopped pecans, toasted

1. Microwave green beans according to package directions. Place beans in a colander; rinse with cold water. Drain.
2. Place green beans and onion in a large bowl. Add vinegar and next 4 ingredients; toss well. Cover and chill 2 hours before serving. Stir in pecans just before serving. Serve with a slotted spoon. **YIELD: 8 SERVINGS (SERVING SIZE: ½ CUP).**

PER SERVING: CAL 80 (38% from fat); FAT 3.4g (sat 1g); PRO 2.1g; CARB 11.7g; FIB 2g; CHOL 4.4mg; IRON 0.5mg; SOD 138mg; CALC 42mg

SWEET-HOT CUCUMBER SALAD

POINTS value: 1

PREP: 10 minutes ▪ **OTHER:** 1 hour

Anaheim peppers are moderately hot, although their heat depends on where they are grown and how mature they are. Select deep green Anaheim chiles, and avoid those that look wrinkled or soft.

- ¼ cup water
- 2 tablespoons sugar
- 2 tablespoons cider vinegar
- 2 teaspoons canola oil
- ¼ teaspoon salt
- ¼ teaspoon freshly ground black pepper
- 2¼ cups thinly sliced peeled cucumber
- ½ cup chopped red bell pepper
- ½ cup thinly sliced seeded Anaheim chile
- ⅓ cup chopped green onions

1. Combine first 6 ingredients in a medium bowl. Add cucumber and remaining ingredients; stir well. Cover and chill 1 hour. Stir well before serving. YIELD: 8 SERVINGS (SERVING SIZE: ½ CUP).

PER SERVING: CAL 34 (34% from fat); FAT 1.3g (sat 0.1g); PRO 0.5g; CARB 5.4g; FIB 0.7g; CHOL 0mg; IRON 0.3mg; SOD 75mg; CALC 10mg

LEMON–CRACKED WHEAT SALAD

POINTS value: 2

PREP: 11 minutes ▪ **COOK:** 16 minutes

Bulgur comes from wheat berries that have been steamed, dried, and then cracked. It's essentially precooked, so preparation is quick.

- 2 cups water
- 1 cup uncooked bulgur (cracked wheat)
- 1 medium tomato, seeded and chopped
- ½ cup chopped fresh mint
- ⅓ cup finely chopped red onion
- ¼ cup pine nuts, toasted
- ¼ cup (1 ounce) crumbled reduced-fat feta cheese
- 2 tablespoons olive oil
- 1 tablespoon grated fresh lemon rind
- 2 tablespoons fresh lemon juice
- ½ teaspoon salt
- ¼ teaspoon crushed red pepper

1. Bring 2 cups water to a boil in a medium saucepan. Add bulgur; cover, reduce heat, and simmer 12 minutes or until water is almost evaporated. Drain and rinse with cold water; drain well.

2. While bulgur cooks, combine tomato and next 9 ingredients in a large bowl. Add bulgur, and toss well. YIELD: 8 SERVINGS (SERVING SIZE: ABOUT ½ CUP).

PER SERVING: CAL 134 (48% from fat); FAT 7.2g (sat 1.1g); PRO 3.8g; CARB 15.9g; FIB 4g; CHOL 1mg; IRON 0.8mg; SOD 199mg; CALC 24mg

EDAMAME SALAD

POINTS value: 3

PREP: 6 minutes ▪ **COOK:** 10 minutes

Edamame is just another word for heart-healthy soybeans. Look for them in the frozen vegetable case.

- 4 cups frozen shelled edamame (green soybeans)
- 2 tablespoons minced fresh parsley
- 2 tablespoons fresh lemon juice
- 1 tablespoon olive oil
- ½ teaspoon freshly ground black pepper
- ⅛ teaspoon salt
- ½ cup (2 ounces) shredded fresh pecorino Romano cheese

1. Cook edamame in boiling water to cover 3 minutes. Drain and plunge into ice water; drain.

2. Combine parsley and next 4 ingredients in a medium bowl, stirring with a whisk. Add edamame, and toss well. Sprinkle with cheese. YIELD: 8 SERVINGS (SERVING SIZE: ½ CUP EDAMAME SALAD AND 1 TABLESPOON CHEESE).

PER SERVING: CAL 174 (47% from fat); FAT 9.1g (sat 2g); PRO 13.8g; CARB 11.5g; FIB 5.8g; CHOL 5mg; IRON 0.1mg; SOD 159mg; CALC 65mg

EDAMAME

Edamame (eh-dah-MAH-meh) are soybeans that are not fully mature. The bean pod looks like a large, fuzzy sugar snap pea. Whether fresh or frozen, this healthful legume adds fiber, vitamin K, and protein to any nutritious diet. Find edamame in your supermarket's frozen vegetable aisle, and use it for an extra boost in salads, pastas, and casseroles. It also makes a healthy, nutty-tasting snack.

CARROT SALAD WITH CURRANTS AND WALNUTS

POINTS value: 3

PREP: 19 minutes ■ **COOK:** 2 minutes

This carrot salad is unlike the ordinary, sweet version. With a subtle lemon-honey undertone, it's best served immediately. If you prefer to make it in advance and refrigerate, let it return to room temperature, and then stir in the walnuts just before serving.

  ¼ cup lemon juice
  1 tablespoon honey
  1 teaspoon olive oil
  ⅛ teaspoon ground cumin
  2 cups shredded carrot
  ⅓ cup dried currants
  ¼ cup chopped walnuts, toasted
  2 tablespoons chopped green onions
  2 tablespoons chopped fresh parsley

1. Combine first 4 ingredients in a large bowl, stirring with a whisk.
2. Add carrot and remaining ingredients; toss gently.
YIELD: 4 SERVINGS (SERVING SIZE: ABOUT ½ CUP).

PER SERVING: CAL 136 (40% from fat); FAT 6.1g (sat 0.6g); PRO 2.2g; CARB 21.3g; FIB 2.9g; CHOL 0mg; IRON 1mg; SOD 40mg; CALC 45mg

RED POTATO–CAULIFLOWER SALAD

POINTS value: 1

pictured on page 135

PREP: 15 minutes ■ **COOK:** 8 minutes
■ **OTHER:** 15 minutes

  2¼ cups diced red potato (about 12 ounces)
  1 (10-ounce) bag cauliflower florets (about 3 cups)
  ½ cup chopped celery
  ½ cup chopped green bell pepper
  ¼ cup light mayonnaise
  ¼ cup fat-free sour cream
  ¼ cup chopped dill pickles
  1 tablespoon cider vinegar
  1 tablespoon prepared mustard
  ½ teaspoon salt
  ¼ teaspoon black pepper

1. Place potato and cauliflower in a microwave-safe bowl. Cover with wax paper; microwave at HIGH 8 minutes or until tender. Drain and rinse with cold water; drain.
2. While vegetable mixture cooks, combine celery and next 8 ingredients in a large bowl. Add potato and cauliflower; stir to combine. Let stand 15 minutes before serving. YIELD: 6 SERVINGS (SERVING SIZE: ABOUT 1 CUP).

PER SERVING: CAL 80 (19% from fat); FAT 1.7g (sat 0.1g); PRO 2.7g; CARB 15.7g; FIB 2.5g; CHOL 1mg; IRON 0.8mg; SOD 420mg; CALC 37mg

CONVENIENT VEGETABLES

Thanks to modern technology, food companies are now packaging frozen vegetables that steam directly in a specially designed microwavable bag. The process leaves nothing to clean up and produces colorful, crisp-tender vegetables every time. They are a superquick way to round out a well-balanced meal.

FRESH FENNEL SALAD WITH ORANGE ESSENCE

POINTS value: 2

PREP: 8 minutes ■ **OTHER:** 15 minutes

The feathery foliage from fennel stems makes a graceful garnish for this salad.

  3 cups thinly sliced fennel bulb
  2 cups thinly sliced green bell pepper
  1 cup thinly sliced red onion
  1 cup matchstick-cut carrots
  ¼ cup sugar
  ¼ cup white balsamic raspberry vinegar
  2 tablespoons canola oil
  2 teaspoons grated fresh orange rind
  ¼ teaspoon salt
  ¼ teaspoon freshly ground black pepper

1. Combine first 4 ingredients in a large bowl. Combine sugar and next 5 ingredients in a small bowl, stirring with a whisk. Pour dressing over vegetables. Let stand 15 minutes before serving. YIELD: 7 SERVINGS (SERVING SIZE: 1 CUP).

PER SERVING: CAL 103 (36% from fat); FAT 4.1g (sat 0.3g); PRO 1g; CARB 16.6g; FIB 2.2g; CHOL 0mg; IRON 0.5mg; SOD 105mg; CALC 30mg

WHEAT BERRY, SPINACH, AND SWEET POTATO SALAD

POINTS value: 6

PREP: 5 minutes ▪ **COOK:** 1 hour and 15 minutes

Chewy wheat berries add texture, and sweet potatoes lend an earthy flavor to this fabulous autumn salad. The wheat berries are simple to prepare and require little attention while cooking.

½ cup uncooked wheat berries
1½ cups water
2 medium-sized sweet potatoes, peeled and cut into 1-inch pieces
⅓ cup water
½ cup raisins
¼ cup balsamic vinegar
2 tablespoons maple syrup
2 tablespoons honey Dijon mustard
¼ teaspoon kosher salt
Cooking spray
3 tablespoons pine nuts, toasted
1 (5-ounce) bag baby spinach

1. Combine wheat berries and 1½ cups water in a medium saucepan; bring to a boil. Cover, reduce heat, and simmer 55 minutes or until berries are plump and tender.
2. Place potato and ⅓ cup water in a microwave-safe bowl; cover and microwave at HIGH 10 minutes or until tender. Drain.
3. While potato cooks, place raisins in a small bowl, and add just enough hot water to cover raisins. Let stand 10 minutes. Drain.
4. Combine vinegar and next 3 ingredients in a small bowl. Heat a large nonstick skillet over medium-high heat. Coat pan with cooking spray. Add potato; sauté 4 minutes or until lightly browned. Add wheat berries, raisins, pine nuts, spinach, and vinegar mixture. Cook 2 to 3 minutes or until spinach wilts. Serve warm. **YIELD: 4 SERVINGS (SERVING SIZE: ABOUT 1⅓ CUPS).**

PER SERVING: CAL 300 (17% from fat); FAT 5.5g (sat 0.5g); PRO 6.7g; CARB 62g; FIB 7.7g; CHOL 0.2mg; IRON 2.6mg; SOD 283mg; CALC 70mg

SOUTHWESTERN SALAD

POINTS value: 7

PREP: 22 minutes ▪ **COOK:** 10 minutes

This generous salad is perfect for a casual meal with friends. Toss it just before serving in a big festive serving bowl.

1 pound lean ground beef
3 garlic cloves, minced and divided
1 (15-ounce) can no-salt-added black beans
½ cup refrigerated fresh salsa
2½ teaspoons ground cumin, divided
2 teaspoons chili powder
¾ teaspoon kosher salt
½ teaspoon ground red pepper
1 cup light sour cream
2 tablespoons chopped fresh cilantro
1 tablespoon lime juice
3 cups shredded romaine lettuce
1½ cups chopped tomato
1 small peeled avocado, diced
21 baked tortilla chips, crushed (such as Guiltless Gourmet)

1. Cook beef and half of garlic in a large nonstick skillet over medium-high heat 10 minutes or until browned, stirring to crumble. Stir in black beans, salsa, 2 teaspoons cumin, chili powder, salt, and red pepper. Remove from heat.
2. While beef mixture cooks, combine sour cream, cilantro, lime juice, remaining garlic, and remaining ½ teaspoon cumin in a small bowl; stir until blended.
3. Place lettuce and tomato in a large bowl; add beef mixture, and toss well. Add sour cream mixture and avocado; toss gently. Sprinkle with tortilla chips, and serve immediately. **YIELD: 6 SERVINGS (SERVING SIZE: ABOUT 1½ CUPS).**

PER SERVING: CAL 312 (44% from fat); FAT 15.4g (sat 5.6g); PRO 21.7g; CARB 22.8g; FIB 5.9g; CHOL 41mg; IRON 3.4mg; SOD 447mg; CALC 66mg

TOMATILLO-AVOCADO SALSA SALAD

POINTS value: 4

PREP: 16 minutes

3 medium tomatillos
¾ cup chopped seeded peeled cucumber
¾ cup diced peeled avocado
½ cup chopped green onions
¼ cup chopped fresh cilantro
1 teaspoon grated fresh lime rind
2 tablespoons fresh lime juice
1 tablespoon olive oil
1 garlic clove, minced
½ teaspoon salt

1. Discard husks and stems from tomatillos.
2. Finely chop tomatillos, and place in a large bowl. Add cucumber and remaining ingredients; toss gently.
YIELD: 3 SERVINGS (SERVING SIZE: ABOUT ⅔ CUP).

PER SERVING: CAL 183 (77% from fat); FAT 15.6g (sat 2.4g); PRO 2.6g; CARB 12.6g; FIB 5.5g; CHOL 0mg; IRON 1.5mg; SOD 399mg; CALC 36mg

SHRIMP SALAD

POINTS value: 4

PREP: 18 minutes

2½ cups chopped cooked shrimp (about 1¼ pounds unpeeled medium shrimp)
½ cup reduced-fat mayonnaise
¼ cup diced celery
1 tablespoon chopped fresh dill
1 tablespoon fresh lemon juice
¼ teaspoon salt
¼ teaspoon freshly ground black pepper
8 (¼-inch-thick) slices tomato
1 cucumber, peeled and quartered lengthwise

1. Combine first 7 ingredients in a medium bowl, and stir well.
2. Divide tomato slices among 4 plates; top with about ½ cup shrimp mixture. Arrange 1 cucumber spear on each plate. YIELD: 4 SERVINGS (SERVING SIZE: ½ CUP SHRIMP MIXTURE, 2 TOMATO SLICES, AND 1 CUCUMBER SPEAR).

PER SERVING: CAL 168 (29% from fat); FAT 5.4g (sat 0.4g); PRO 245g; CARB 7.3g; FIB 1g; CHOL 221mg; IRON 3.8mg; SOD 668mg; CALC 59mg

FRUITED CHICKEN SALAD

POINTS value: 4

PREP: 20 minutes ■ COOK: 16 minutes
■ OTHER: 1 hour and 15 minutes

3 (6-ounce) skinless, boneless chicken breast halves
3 tablespoons light creamy Caesar dressing (such as Wish-Bone)
1 cup red grapes, halved
½ cup finely chopped celery
⅓ cup light mayonnaise
¼ cup sliced green onions
¼ cup (1 ounce) preshredded fresh Parmesan cheese
1 tablespoon spicy brown mustard
¼ teaspoon garlic powder
¼ teaspoon black pepper
Cooking spray
3 tablespoons sliced almonds, toasted
3 cups shredded romaine lettuce

1. Prepare grill.
2. Brush chicken breast halves with Caesar dressing, and let stand 15 minutes.
3. While chicken stands, combine grapes and next 7 ingredients in a large bowl; toss gently to coat.
4. Place chicken on grill rack coated with cooking spray. Grill 7 minutes on each side or until chicken is done. Cool slightly. Coarsely chop chicken. Add chicken to grape mixture; stir well. Cover and chill 1 hour.
5. Sprinkle with almonds just before serving. Serve chicken mixture over lettuce. YIELD: 6 SERVINGS (SERVING SIZE: ABOUT ⅔ CUP CHICKEN SALAD, ½ CUP LETTUCE, AND 1½ TEA-SPOONS ALMONDS).

PER SERVING: CAL 189 (30% from fat); FAT 6.3g (sat 1.3g); PRO 22.6g; CARB 10.9g; FIB 1.5g; CHOL 56mg; IRON 1.2mg; SOD 352mg; CALC 86mg

GREEK STEAK SALAD

POINTS value: 4   *pictured on page 137*

PREP: 10 minutes ▪ COOK: 16 minutes
▪ OTHER: 2 hours and 5 minutes

Each of the optional ingredients adds 1 to the total **POINTS** value.

  ¾ cup red wine vinegar
  3 tablespoons chopped fresh parsley, divided
  2 tablespoons Dijon mustard
  1 tablespoon olive oil
  1½ teaspoons Greek seasoning (such as Cavender's)
  1 pound flank steak, trimmed
  Cooking spray
  8 cups torn romaine lettuce
  1 cup chopped cucumber
  1 cup grape tomatoes, halved
  2 tablespoons chopped fresh mint
  ¼ cup pitted kalamata olives, chopped (optional)
  ¼ cup (1 ounce) crumbled feta cheese (optional)

1. Combine red wine vinegar, 2 tablespoons parsley, and next 3 ingredients in a small bowl, stirring with a whisk. Place flank steak in a large zip-top plastic bag. Pour 7 tablespoons vinegar mixture over steak, and seal bag. Marinate in refrigerator 2 to 8 hours, turning bag occasionally.
2. Prepare grill.
3. Remove steak from bag, discarding marinade. Place on grill rack coated with cooking spray; grill 8 minutes on each side or until desired degree of doneness. Let steak stand 5 minutes. Cut steak diagonally across grain into thin slices.
4. Combine lettuce, cucumber, tomatoes, mint, and remaining 1 tablespoon parsley in a large bowl; add steak slices and, if desired, olives or feta. Pour remaining 7 tablespoons dressing over salad; toss well. YIELD: 4 SERVINGS (SERVING SIZE: 2¾ CUPS).

PER SERVING: CAL 213 (35% from fat); FAT 8.4g (sat 2.7g); PRO 26.4g; CARB 6.9g; FIB 3g; CHOL 37mg; IRON 3.3mg; SOD 182mg; CALC 77mg

SHRIMP, OLIVE, AND BARLEY SALAD

POINTS value: 5

PREP: 18 minutes ▪ COOK: 17 minutes
▪ OTHER: 5 minutes

  1 cup uncooked quick-cooking barley
  Cooking spray
  1½ pounds large shrimp, peeled and deveined
  1 English cucumber, chopped
  1 red bell pepper, chopped
  ¾ cup (3 ounces) crumbled feta cheese with basil and sun-dried tomatoes
  ¼ cup pitted kalamata olives, chopped
  2 tablespoons capers
  1 tablespoon canola oil
  2 teaspoons grated fresh lemon rind
  ¼ cup fresh lemon juice
  1½ teaspoons dried oregano
  ¼ teaspoon salt
  ¼ teaspoon black pepper

1. Cook barley according to package directions, omitting salt and fat. Drain.
2. Heat a large nonstick skillet over medium–high heat. Coat pan with cooking spray. Add shrimp; cook 4 to 5 minutes or until lightly browned, stirring frequently.
3. Combine barley, shrimp, cucumber, and remaining ingredients in a large bowl; toss well. Cover and chill. YIELD: 6 SERVINGS (SERVING SIZE: 1½ CUPS).

PER SERVING: CAL 245 (31% from fat); FAT 8.4g (sat 2.5g); PRO 21g; CARB 23.6g; FIB 3.9g; CHOL 150mg; IRON 3.2mg; SOD 598mg; CALC 94mg

SPRING ROLL SALAD

POINTS value: 4

PREP: 31 minutes ■ **COOK:** 6 minutes
■ **OTHER:** 10 minutes

Serve this fresh-tasting salad with soy sauce at the table, and remember that a small amount goes a long way in flavor. We found that ½ to 1 teaspoon per serving was plenty.

  ½ cup chopped seeded peeled cucumber
  ½ cup preshredded carrot
  ½ cup chopped red bell pepper
  ¼ cup rice vinegar
  ¼ cup water
 12 ounces peeled and deveined large shrimp
  6 teaspoons sweet red chili sauce, divided
Cooking spray
  3 ounces dried rice noodles, broken into 3-inch pieces
  ¼ cup packed fresh mint leaves
  ¼ cup fresh lime juice
  2 tablespoons minced peeled fresh ginger
  2 teaspoons dark sesame oil
  4 cups shredded iceberg lettuce
  2 tablespoons chopped unsalted, dry-roasted peanuts

1. Combine first 5 ingredients in a small bowl, tossing well. Let stand 10 minutes, stirring often.
2. Combine shrimp and 2 teaspoons chili sauce in a medium bowl, stirring to coat.
3. Heat a large nonstick skillet over medium-high heat. Coat pan with cooking spray. Add shrimp; cook 6 minutes or until shrimp turn pink, stirring frequently.
4. Soften noodles in boiling water in a large saucepan according to package directions. Drain noodles in a sieve, and rinse with cold water; drain. Pour cucumber mixture over noodles in sieve, discarding liquid. Set noodle mixture aside.
5. Combine remaining 4 teaspoons chili sauce, mint, and next 3 ingredients in a blender; process until mint is minced.
6. Combine noodle mixture and mint mixture in a large bowl; toss well. Divide lettuce among 4 bowls; spoon noodle mixture over lettuce, top with shrimp, and sprinkle with peanuts. YIELD: 4 SERVINGS (SERVING SIZE: 1½ CUPS NOODLE MIXTURE, 1 CUP LETTUCE, ABOUT 6 SHRIMP, AND 1½ TEASPOONS PEANUTS).

PER SERVING: CAL 217 (23% from fat); FAT 5.6g (sat 0.9g); PRO 16.9g; CARB 25.3g; FIB 2.2g; CHOL 126mg; IRON 3mg; SOD 166mg; CALC 55mg

GRILLED SHRIMP AND VEGETABLE SPINACH SALAD WITH LEMON DRESSING

POINTS value: 5

PREP: 16 minutes ■ **COOK:** 14 minutes

This salad is almost too pretty to eat, but you won't want to miss the fresh lemon dressing, smoky grilled vegetables, and tangy-sweet shrimp.

  6 tablespoons fresh lemon juice
  2 tablespoons olive oil
  1 teaspoon kosher salt
  ½ teaspoon freshly ground black pepper
 1½ pounds medium shrimp, peeled and deveined
  2 carrots, cut lengthwise into ¼-inch-thick strips
  2 ears shucked corn
  1 large red bell pepper, quartered
Cooking spray
  1 (6-ounce) package fresh baby spinach
  ¼ cup chopped fresh cilantro

1. Prepare grill.
2. Combine first 4 ingredients in a small bowl, stirring with a whisk. Place shrimp in a large zip-top plastic bag; pour ¼ cup lemon dressing over shrimp, seal bag, and shake to coat. Thread shrimp evenly onto 4 (12-inch) metal skewers.
3. Place carrot, corn, and bell pepper on grill rack coated with cooking spray; grill 8 minutes, turning vegetables occasionally. Add shrimp skewers to grill rack; grill 3 minutes on each side or until shrimp are done and vegetables are lightly charred.
4. Cut carrot and bell pepper into bite-sized pieces. Cut kernels from ears of corn. Discard cobs.
5. Divide spinach evenly among 4 plates; drizzle each with remaining ¼ cup lemon dressing. Top spinach evenly with shrimp skewers and vegetables. Sprinkle with cilantro. YIELD: 4 SERVINGS (SERVING SIZE: 1¼ CUPS SPIN-ACH, ½ CUP GRILLED VEGETABLES, ¼ OF SHRIMP, 1 TABLESPOON LEMON DRESSING, AND 1 TABLESPOON CILANTRO).

PER SERVING: CAL 264 (33% from fat); FAT 9.7g (sat 1.4g); PRO 26.5g; CARB 22.2g; FIB 5.2g; CHOL 210mg; IRON 5.2mg; SOD 811mg; CALC 92mg

sandwiches

Italian Steak Sandwiches, *page 114*

TOMATO-PESTO PANINI

POINTS value: 5

PREP: 11 minutes ■ **COOK:** 4 minutes
■ **OTHER:** 5 minutes

It isn't necessary to have a panini press for this recipe. A countertop electric grill, such as the George Foreman®, works just as well. Or use a large nonstick skillet over medium heat. To do so, place sandwiches in the hot skillet with a piece of foil over the top. Place a heavy skillet on top of the sandwiches to weigh them down, and cook 2 to 3 minutes on each side or until golden.

½ cup boiling water
¼ cup sun-dried tomato halves, packed without oil
2 tablespoons light mayonnaise
2 tablespoons commercial pesto
8 (1-ounce) slices ciabatta, cut diagonally
2 (¾-ounce) slices reduced-fat provolone cheese, cut in half
8 slices plum tomato
8 fresh basil leaves
Cooking spray

1. Combine water and sun-dried tomatoes in a small bowl; cover and let stand 5 minutes. Drain and chop tomatoes; discard liquid.
2. Combine tomatoes, mayonnaise, and pesto in a small bowl; stir well.
3. Preheat panini press.
4. Spread pesto mixture evenly on each slice of bread. Top each of 4 bread slices with ½ slice cheese, 2 slices plum tomato, and 2 basil leaves. Top with remaining bread slices, pesto-mixture sides down.
5. Coat sandwiches with cooking spray, place on panini press, and cook 4 to 6 minutes or until golden brown.
YIELD: 4 SERVINGS (SERVING SIZE: 1 SANDWICH).

PER SERVING: CAL 249 (33% from fat); FAT 9.1g (sat 2.1g); PRO 9.4g; CARB 35.7g; FIB 2.1g; CHOL 8mg; IRON 2.4mg; SOD 671mg; CALC 111mg

COOKING WITH COOKING SPRAY

Whether it's keeping cookies from sticking to a baking sheet or helping honey slide off a measuring spoon, cooking spray is one of the handiest ingredients in the kitchen. It prevents foods like chicken breasts, pork chops, fish, and vegetables from sticking to the pan while providing crispness, browning, and flavor with a very small amount of calories.

OVEN-FRIED GREEN TOMATO BLTS

POINTS value: 6

PREP: 15 minutes ■ **COOK:** 25 minutes
■ **OTHER:** 10 minutes

Enjoy the same crunch as a deep-fried green tomato, without all the fat, in this stacked "BLGreen-T" sandwich.

¼ cup light mayonnaise
2 tablespoons fat-free sour cream
2 teaspoons hot sauce
1 garlic clove, crushed
¼ teaspoon black pepper
2 large egg whites
¼ cup nonfat buttermilk
¼ teaspoon salt
¼ teaspoon ground red pepper
½ cup yellow cornmeal
½ cup panko (Japanese breadcrumbs)
2 medium-sized green tomatoes, cut into 8 (½-inch-thick) slices
Cooking spray
8 (1-ounce) slices whole wheat double-fiber bread (such as Nature's Own), toasted
4 red leaf lettuce leaves
8 center-cut bacon slices, cooked

1. Preheat oven to 450°.
2. Combine first 5 ingredients in a small bowl; set aside.
3. Combine egg whites and next 3 ingredients in a shallow dish. Combine cornmeal and panko in another shallow dish.
4. Dip tomatoes in egg white mixture. Dredge tomatoes in cornmeal mixture, pressing firmly to coat. Place tomatoes on a wire rack, and let stand 10 minutes.
5. While tomatoes stand, place a jelly-roll pan in oven to heat.
6. Coat both sides of tomatoes heavily with cooking spray. Remove hot pan from oven; coat pan with cooking spray. Place tomatoes on pan in a single layer. Bake at 450° for 25 minutes or until tomatoes are crisp and golden, turning after 12 minutes.
7. Spread about ¾ tablespoon mayonnaise mixture onto bread slices. Top 4 bread slices with 1 lettuce leaf, 2 bacon slices, and 2 oven-fried green tomato slices. Top with remaining bread slices, mayonnaise-mixture sides down. YIELD: 4 SERVINGS (SERVING SIZE: 1 SANDWICH).

PER SERVING: CAL 301 (19% from fat); FAT 6.5g (sat 1.1g); PRO 16.3g; CARB 54.9g; FIB 12g; CHOL 11mg; IRON 3.5mg; SOD 865mg; CALC 47mg

ROASTED PEAR AND RICOTTA SANDWICHES

POINTS value: 6

PREP: 19 minutes ■ COOK: 40 minutes
■ OTHER: 45 minutes

For added texture and flavor, stir 2 tablespoons chopped, toasted walnuts into the ricotta cheese mixture. The **POINTS** value will increase to 7.

- 1 teaspoon butter
- 2 teaspoons sugar
- 3 peeled pears, cored and cut in half
- 1 teaspoon balsamic vinegar
- ¼ teaspoon dried thyme
- 1 cup fat-free ricotta cheese
- 1 tablespoon honey
- ¼ teaspoon salt
- ¼ teaspoon dried rubbed sage
- ¼ teaspoon freshly ground black pepper
- ¼ cup (1 ounce) crumbled blue cheese
- 8 (1-ounce) slices whole wheat bread, toasted (such as Arnold 100% Whole Wheat)
- 2 cups loosely packed arugula

1. Preheat oven to 350°.
2. Coat bottom of an 11 x 7–inch baking dish with butter. Sprinkle evenly with sugar. Place pears, cut sides down, in dish; drizzle with vinegar, and sprinkle with thyme. Cover pan with foil; bake at 350° for 40 minutes or until tender. Cool in pan 45 minutes. Cut each pear half lengthwise into 4 slices.
3. Combine ricotta cheese, honey, and next 3 ingredients in a small bowl, stirring until smooth. Fold in blue cheese.
4. Top each of 4 bread slices with about ¼ cup ricotta mixture, 6 pear slices, ½ cup arugula, and a remaining bread slice. YIELD: 4 SERVINGS (SERVING SIZE: 1 SANDWICH).

PER SERVING: CAL 331 (19% from fat); FAT 7.1g (sat 2.3g); PRO 16.6g; CARB 53.5g; FIB 14.1g; CHOL 19mg; IRON 1.8mg; SOD 612mg; CALC 262mg

SALMON BURGERS

POINTS value: 7 *pictured on page 138*

PREP: 18 minutes ■ COOK: 8 minutes

Each pulse on the food processor in Step Two should last as long as it takes you to say "one-thousand-one." This will help ensure that all of the ingredients are chopped coarsely and evenly.

- ½ cup light mayonnaise
- 1 tablespoon fresh lemon juice
- 1 tablespoon capers
- 1 tablespoon sweet pickle relish
- 1 cup panko (Japanese breadcrumbs)
- ¼ cup chopped onion
- 1 large egg white
- 1 teaspoon hot sauce
- ½ teaspoon kosher salt
- ½ teaspoon freshly ground black pepper
- 1 pound salmon fillets, skinned and cut into 1-inch pieces
- Cooking spray
- Lettuce leaves, tomato slices, red onion slices (optional)
- 5 (1½-ounce) light whole wheat hamburger buns

1. Combine first 4 ingredients in a small bowl; cover and chill.
2. Place breadcrumbs and next 5 ingredients in a food processor; process until minced. Add salmon; pulse 5 times or until salmon is coarsely chopped.
3. Divide salmon mixture into 5 equal portions; shape each portion into a 1-inch-thick patty.
4. Heat a large nonstick skillet over medium–high heat. Coat pan with cooking spray. Add patties to pan; cook 4 minutes on each side or until done.
5. Arrange lettuce, tomato, and onion on bottom half of each bun, if desired. Top each with 1 salmon patty, about 2 tablespoons mayonnaise mixture, and top half of bun. YIELD: 5 SERVINGS (SERVING SIZE: 1 BURGER).

PER SERVING: CAL 339 (27% from fat); FAT 10.2g (sat 1.3g); PRO 26.9g; CARB 36.5g; FIB 1.7g; CHOL 53mg; IRON 1.7mg; SOD 812mg; CALC 108mg

HERBED LOBSTER ROLLS

POINTS value: 4

PREP: 15 minutes ■ **COOK:** 2 minutes

- ½ pound cooked lobster meat, cut into bite-sized pieces
- ⅓ cup minced green onions
- ¼ cup light mayonnaise
- 1 tablespoon lemon juice
- 2 teaspoons minced fresh tarragon
- 2 teaspoons minced fresh chives
- 2 teaspoons minced fresh parsley
- ⅛ teaspoon salt
- ⅛ teaspoon black pepper
- 1 cup shredded iceberg lettuce
- 4 slices tomato, cut in half
- 4 whole wheat hot dog buns, toasted

1. Combine first 9 ingredients in a medium bowl. Arrange lettuce and tomato in each bun; top evenly with lobster mixture. Serve immediately. YIELD: 4 SERVINGS (SERVING SIZE: 1 SANDWICH).

PER SERVING: CAL 199 (20% from fat); FAT 4.5g (sat 0.4g); PRO 15.8g; CARB 27g; FIB 3.9g; CHOL 41mg; IRON 1.6mg; SOD 628mg; CALC 100mg

DIJON-PEPPERCORN STEAK WRAPS

POINTS value: 5

PREP: 23 minutes ■ **COOK:** 10 minutes
■ **OTHER:** 2 hours and 10 minutes

- ¼ cup Dijon mustard, divided
- 1 tablespoon cracked black pepper, divided
- 1 pound flank steak
- 6 (½-inch-thick) red onion slices
- Cooking spray
- ¼ cup light mayonnaise
- 1 teaspoon grated fresh lemon rind
- 1 tablespoon fresh lemon juice
- 6 (7-inch) fat-free whole wheat tortillas
- 1½ cups chopped plum tomatoes
- 24 (⅛-inch-thick) slices cucumber

1. Stir together 2 tablespoons mustard and 2 teaspoons cracked pepper; rub evenly over steak. Cover and chill 2 hours.
2. Prepare grill.
3. Place steak and onion slices on grill rack coated with cooking spray; grill 5 minutes on each side or until desired degree of doneness. Let stand 10 minutes; cut steak diagonally across grain into thin slices, and separate onion into rings.
4. Combine mayonnaise, lemon rind, lemon juice, remaining 2 tablespoons mustard, and remaining 1 teaspoon cracked pepper, stirring well.
5. Arrange steak slices evenly down center of each tortilla. Top steak evenly with grilled onion, tomato, and cucumber slices. Spread about 1 tablespoon mayonnaise mixture on top. Roll up tortillas; secure with wooden picks. YIELD: 6 SERVINGS (SERVING SIZE: 1 WRAP).

PER SERVING: CAL 280 (24% from fat); FAT 7.6g (sat 1.6g); PRO 21.1g; CARB 32.9g; FIB 4.1g; CHOL 25mg; IRON 1.5mg; SOD 712mg; CALC 31mg

ITALIAN STEAK SANDWICHES

POINTS value: 7   *pictured on page 140*

PREP: 6 minutes ■ **COOK:** 8 minutes
■ **OTHER:** 1 hour and 35 minutes

Always marinate food in the refrigerator, not on the countertop.

- 2 (8-ounce) rib-eye steaks, trimmed
- ¼ cup Worcestershire sauce
- ¼ cup balsamic vinegar
- ¼ cup light mayonnaise
- 2 tablespoons chopped sun-dried tomatoes
- 4 teaspoons crumbled blue cheese
- 8 (0.8-ounce) slices Italian bread
- 1 cup baby arugula or chopped iceberg lettuce
- 2 tomatoes, thinly sliced

1. Combine steaks, Worcestershire sauce, and vinegar in a large zip-top plastic bag; seal and marinate in refrigerator at least 1½ hours. Remove steaks from bag; discard marinade.
2. Combine mayonnaise, sun-dried tomatoes, and blue cheese in a small bowl. Set aside.
3. Prepare grill.
4. Grill steaks 4 minutes on each side or until desired degree of doneness. Let stand 5 minutes before cutting across the grain into thin strips.
5. While steak stands, grill bread slices 1 to 2 minutes on each side or until toasted.

6. Spread mayonnaise mixture evenly onto bread slices. Top 4 bread slices with steak, arugula, and tomatoes. Top with remaining bread slices, mayonnaise-mixture sides down. YIELD: 4 SERVINGS (SERVING SIZE: 1 SANDWICH).

PER SERVING: CAL 318 (32% from fat); FAT 11.2g (sat 3.4g); PRO 24.7g; CARB 29.9g; FIB 2.2g; CHOL 64mg; IRON 3.3mg; SOD 559mg; CALC 85mg

PORK FRENCH DIP AU JUS

POINTS value: 8

PREP: 10 minutes ■ COOK: 35 minutes
■ OTHER: 5 minutes

This flavorful jus tastes like it simmered for hours instead of just minutes. Serve it alongside the sandwich for dipping.

     2 garlic cloves, minced and divided
     1 tablespoon olive oil
     1 teaspoon grated fresh lemon rind
     ¼ teaspoon salt
     ¼ teaspoon freshly ground black pepper
     1 pound pork tenderloin, trimmed
  Cooking spray
     ½ cup diced onion
     ½ cup diced celery
     ½ cup diced carrot
     2 tablespoons tomato paste
     2 cups fat-free, less-sodium beef broth
     1 cup fat-free, less-sodium chicken broth
     2 bay leaves
     ¼ teaspoon black peppercorns
     5 (3-ounce) whole wheat hoagie rolls, toasted

1. Preheat oven to 500°.
2. Combine 1 garlic clove, olive oil, and next 3 ingredients. Pat tenderloin dry with paper towels; rub with olive oil mixture. Place tenderloin on broiler pan coated with cooking spray. Bake at 500° for 25 minutes or until thermometer registers 160°. Let stand 5 minutes; shred pork with 2 forks.
3. While pork cooks, heat a large saucepan over medium-high heat. Coat pan with cooking spray. Add onion, celery, and carrot; cook 8 minutes, stirring frequently. Add tomato paste; cook 2 minutes, stirring constantly. Add remaining garlic, beef broth, and next 3 ingredients. Bring to a boil; reduce heat and simmer, uncovered, 15 minutes or until reduced by half. Strain through a colander into a bowl; discard solids.

4. Divide shredded pork evenly among rolls, and serve with jus. YIELD: 5 SERVINGS (SERVING SIZE: 1 SANDWICH AND ¼ CUP JUS).

PER SERVING: CAL 404 (26% from fat); FAT 11.5g (sat 4.6g); PRO 28.8g; CARB 44.5g; FIB 3.7g; CHOL 51mg; IRON 2.6mg; SOD 932mg; CALC 120mg

---

AU JUS

Au jus literally means "with the juice," referring to the sauce created from juices remaining in the pan after meat is cooked. The savory sauce is often served as a dip alongside a sandwich made of crusty bread to contribute rich flavor without adding a lot of calories.

PROSCIUTTO AND SHARP PROVOLONE FRENCH WHEAT SANDWICHES

POINTS value: 4

PREP: 10 minutes

We used sandwich-sized flatbreads for this trendy sandwich. If they are unavailable, substitute whole wheat English muffins.

     ¼ cup light balsamic vinaigrette
     1 garlic clove, finely minced
     4 (1½-ounce) presliced whole wheat sandwich thin flatbreads (such as Arnold Select 100% Whole Wheat Sandwich Thins)
     4 (¼-inch-thick) slices tomato
    16 large basil leaves
     2 ounces thinly sliced prosciutto
     4 (½-ounce) slices sharp provolone cheese
     2 cups packed baby arugula
     1 cup thinly sliced green bell pepper

1. Combine vinaigrette and garlic in a small bowl. Brush evenly on 1 side of each flatbread half. Top 4 bottom halves with 1 slice tomato, 4 basil leaves, ½ ounce prosciutto, 1 slice cheese, ½ cup arugula, and ¼ cup bell pepper. Top with remaining flatbread halves. YIELD: 4 SERVINGS (SERVING SIZE: 1 SANDWICH).

PER SERVING: CAL 211 (35% from fat); FAT 8.3g (sat 3.2g); PRO 12.7g; CARB 25.1g; FIB 6.9g; CHOL 18mg; IRON 1.8mg; SOD 808mg; CALC 179mg

MEDITERRANEAN-STYLE PITAS

POINTS value: 3

PREP: 22 minutes ■ COOK: 32 minutes
■ OTHER: 15 minutes

If you don't want to make all six servings at once, keep the chicken salad in the refrigerator and assemble the sandwiches when you're ready.

     3 cups water
     1 cup fat-free, less-sodium chicken broth
     2 (6-ounce) skinless, boneless chicken breast halves
     ⅓ cup finely chopped red onion
     ⅓ cup finely chopped celery
     ¼ cup finely chopped carrot
     ¼ cup sliced ripe olives
     2 tablespoons balsamic vinegar
     1½ tablespoons lemon juice
     1½ tablespoons Dijon mustard
     1 tablespoon light mayonnaise
     1 tablespoon finely chopped fresh parsley
     ¼ teaspoon chopped fresh thyme
     3 (6-inch) whole wheat pitas, cut in half
     1½ cups arugula leaves

1. Combine 3 cups water and chicken broth in a Dutch oven; add chicken and bring to a boil. Cover, reduce heat, and simmer 25 minutes or until chicken is done. Let stand 15 minutes. Remove chicken from pan, discarding broth mixture. Shred chicken with 2 forks.
2. Combine shredded chicken, onion, and next 9 ingredients in a large bowl, tossing to coat.
3. Fill each pita half with ¼ cup arugula leaves and ½ cup chicken salad. YIELD: 6 SERVINGS (SERVING SIZE: 1 PITA HALF).

PER SERVING: CAL 162 (9% from fat); FAT 1.7g (sat 0.3g); PRO 17g; CARB 20.2g; FIB 2.3g; CHOL 33mg; IRON 1.7mg; SOD 371mg; CALC 49mg

TURKEY, CHEDDAR, ROMAINE, AND APPLE WRAPS

POINTS value: 6

PREP: 6 minutes

     2 tablespoons creamy mustard blend (such as Dijonnaise)
     6 (7½-inch) fat-free whole wheat tortillas
     12 ounces thinly sliced deli turkey breast
     2 cups chopped romaine lettuce
     1 cup (4 ounces) reduced-fat shredded sharp Cheddar cheese
     2 Granny Smith apples, cored and sliced

1. Spread mustard blend evenly over each tortilla. Arrange turkey and next 3 ingredients evenly down center of each tortilla. Roll up; secure with wooden picks. Chill until ready to serve. YIELD: 6 SERVINGS (SERVING SIZE: 1 WRAP).

PER SERVING: CAL 317 (21% from fat); FAT 7.4g (sat 2.9g); PRO 22.8g; CARB 38.5g; FIB 5.1g; CHOL 35mg; IRON 0.7mg; SOD 767mg; CALC 156mg

THANKSGIVING WRAPS

POINTS value: 4   *pictured on page 139*

PREP: 15 minutes ■ COOK: 5 minutes

To roll these wraps up easily, place each tortilla on a square of parchment or wax paper as you assemble it. After rolling up the wraps, twist the ends of the paper to hold them together. Cut through the paper, and peel it back to serve.

     1 (8-ounce) sweet potato
     4 (8-inch) whole wheat tortillas
     ½ cup cranberry-orange crushed fruit (such as Ocean Spray Cran-Fruit)
     ¼ cup sweetened dried cranberries
     2 tablespoons chopped walnuts
     8 ounces thinly sliced deli turkey breast
     1 cup bagged baby spinach

1. Scrub sweet potato; pat dry. Wrap potato in heavy-duty plastic wrap (do not prick potato). Microwave at HIGH 5 minutes or until tender. Unwrap potato; peel and mash with a fork until smooth.
2. Spread mashed sweet potato evenly over each tortilla. Top each with crushed fruit; sprinkle with cranberries and walnuts. Arrange turkey and spinach over filling. Fold in edges of tortillas; roll up and cut diagonally in half. YIELD: 4 SERVINGS (SERVING SIZE: 1 WRAP).

PER SERVING: CAL 231 (29% from fat); FAT 7.3g (sat 0.2g); PRO 18.8g; CARB 21.1g; FIB 4.8g; CHOL 20mg; IRON 1.7mg; SOD 634mg; CALC 159mg

side dishes

Artichokes with Garlic Aïoli, *page 118*

ASPARAGUS WITH TARRAGON VINAIGRETTE

POINTS value: 1

PREP: 9 minutes ■ **COOK:** 10 minutes

This classic side dish is topped off with chopped hard-cooked egg. To make it quick to prepare, purchase precooked eggs found in the dairy case at your supermarket.

- 8 cups water
- 5 cups (2-inch) diagonally cut asparagus (about 2 pounds)
- 3 tablespoons tarragon vinegar
- 1 tablespoon olive oil
- ½ teaspoon ground mustard
- ½ teaspoon ground black pepper
- ¼ teaspoon salt
- 1 tablespoon finely shredded Parmesan cheese
- 1 hard-cooked large egg, chopped

1. Bring 8 cups water to a boil in a Dutch oven; add asparagus. Cook 3 minutes or until crisp-tender.
2. Drain and plunge asparagus into ice water; drain.
3. Combine vinegar and next 4 ingredients in a large bowl, stirring with a whisk. Add asparagus, tossing gently to coat. Sprinkle with Parmesan cheese, and top with hard-cooked egg. YIELD: 8 SERVINGS (SERVING SIZE: ABOUT ⅔ CUP).

PER SERVING: CAL 46 (53% from fat); FAT 2.7g (sat 0.6g); PRO 2.7g; CARB 3.1g; FIB 1.6g; CHOL 27mg; IRON 1.7mg; SOD 96mg; CALC 28mg

ARTICHOKES WITH GARLIC AÏOLI

POINTS value: 1   *pictured on page 141*

PREP: 6 minutes ■ **COOK:** 45 minutes

The ritual of eating artichokes—tear off a leaf, eat the tender flesh, and repeat—is as much a part of the experience as the flavor. The creamy texture and flavor of aïoli enhance the process.

- 2 large artichokes (about 1½ pounds)
- 8 garlic cloves, peeled
- ⅓ cup light mayonnaise
- 2 tablespoons chopped fresh tarragon
- 1 tablespoon fresh lemon juice
- 4 lemon wedges

1. Cut off stems of artichokes, and remove bottom leaves. Trim about ½ inch from tops of artichokes. Place artichokes, stem ends down, in a large Dutch

oven. Fill with water to cover artichokes; bring to a boil. Cover, reduce heat, and simmer 25 minutes. Turn artichokes over, and add garlic. Cover and simmer 15 minutes or until tender. Drain.
2. Cut artichokes in half. Mash garlic cloves. Combine mashed garlic, mayonnaise, tarragon, and lemon juice in a medium bowl. Serve artichokes with aïoli and lemon wedges. YIELD: 4 SERVINGS (SERVING SIZE: ½ ARTICHOKE AND 2 TABLESPOONS AÏOLI).

PER SERVING: CAL 71 (19% from fat); FAT 1.5g (sat 0g); PRO 3.2g; CARB 14.2g; FIB 4.5g; CHOL 0mg; IRON 1.1mg; SOD 251mg; CALC 52mg

AÏOLI

Pronounced "ay-OH-lee," this garlic mayonnaise has its roots in the Provence region of France, an area known for intense, distinctive flavors. Traditionally, aïoli was prepared using a mortar and pestle to crush fresh garlic cloves before adding in raw egg and olive oil, but cooks have abandoned that practice because of concerns about the safety of eating raw eggs. Most aïolis are now prepared with a base of mayonnaise in which the eggs have already been pasteurized. Aïoli is usually served as an accompaniment to vegetables, fish, or chicken dishes.

RED LENTIL DAL

POINTS value: 4

PREP: 3 minutes ■ **COOK:** 30 minutes

Throughout India, a meal is not complete without some variation of this spice-tempered legume dish. Cumin and turmeric provide slightly bitter notes, and crushed red pepper heats it up.

- 2 teaspoons canola oil
- 1 cup chopped onion
- 2 teaspoons minced peeled fresh ginger
- ½ teaspoon ground cumin
- ½ teaspoon ground turmeric
- ¼ teaspoon crushed red pepper
- 2 cups less-sodium organic vegetable broth (such as Swanson Organic)
- 1 cup red lentils, rinsed and drained
- ¼ cup chopped fresh cilantro

1. Heat oil in a medium saucepan over medium heat. Add onion; sauté 5 minutes. Add ginger and next 3 ingredients; sauté 1 minute. Add vegetable broth; bring to a boil. Stir in lentils; return mixture to a boil. Cover, reduce heat, and simmer 20 minutes or until

lentils are tender and broth is almost absorbed. Stir in cilantro. **YIELD: 4 SERVINGS (SERVING SIZE: ABOUT ⅔ CUP).**

PER SERVING: CAL 208 (11% from fat); FAT 2.5g (sat 0.2g); PRO 12.6g; CARB 32.8g; FIB 3.4g; CHOL 0mg; IRON 1.7mg; SOD 292mg; CALC 33mg

ROASTED YELLOW BEETS WITH HAZELNUT GREMOLATA

POINTS value: 1

PREP: 13 minutes ■ **COOK:** 1 hour

Gremolata is an herb garnish of chopped parsley, lemon rind, and garlic. We've added hazelnuts to our version for added texture and flavor. Substitute red beets for the yellow beets, if you like.

- 2 pounds small yellow beets
- 1 lemon
- 2 tablespoons finely chopped toasted hazelnuts
- 1 tablespoon chopped fresh parsley
- 2 teaspoons olive oil
- ½ teaspoon garlic salt
- ¼ teaspoon freshly ground black pepper

1. Preheat oven to 450°.
2. Leave roots and 1-inch stems on beets; scrub with a brush. Wrap beets in foil. Roast at 450° for 1 hour or until tender. Trim off beet roots; rub off skins. Cut beets into ½-inch wedges.
3. While beets roast, grate ½ teaspoon lemon rind; squeeze 4 teaspoons juice from lemon. Reserve remaining lemon for another use. Combine lemon rind, lemon juice, hazelnuts, and next 4 ingredients in a medium bowl. Add warm beets; toss gently to coat. **YIELD: 6 SERVINGS (SERVING SIZE: ½ CUP).**

PER SERVING: CAL 58 (48% from fat); FAT 3.1g (sat 0.4g); PRO 1.5g; CARB 7.2g; FIB 2.2g; CHOL 0mg; IRON 0.7mg; SOD 126mg; CALC 15mg

BEETS

Beets ripen during mid-summer and early autumn instead of being a predominantly cold-weather crop like most other root vegetables. You can find fresh beets in the supermarket year-round; choose ones that are small to medium in size and have smooth skins. They are a particularly nutrient-dense food, low in calories and high in beta-carotene, vitamin C, iron, and calcium. Don't throw away the leafy green tops; beet greens can be used in salads or cooked as a side dish.

BROCCOLI FLORETS WITH CREAMY CURRY MUSTARD SAUCE

POINTS value: 1

PREP: 5 minutes ■ **COOK:** 8 minutes

- 7 cups broccoli florets (about 1 pound)
- ¼ cup light mayonnaise
- 2 tablespoons fat-free milk
- 1 tablespoon honey
- 1½ teaspoons prepared mustard
- ¼ teaspoon curry powder
- ¼ teaspoon salt

1. Place broccoli in a vegetable steamer. Steam, covered, 8 minutes or until tender. Drain.
2. While broccoli cooks, combine mayonnaise and next 5 ingredients in a small saucepan, stirring with a whisk. Cook over medium heat 2 minutes or until thoroughly heated and smooth, stirring frequently (do not boil). Spoon sauce over broccoli. **YIELD: 6 SERVINGS (SERVING SIZE: 1 CUP BROCCOLI AND ABOUT 1½ TABLESPOONS SAUCE).**

PER SERVING: CAL 44 (18% from fat); FAT 0.9g (sat 0g); PRO 2.5g; CARB 8.5g; FIB 2.2g; CHOL 0mg; IRON 0.7mg; SOD 222mg; CALC 43mg

BRUSSELS SPROUTS WITH LEMON

POINTS value: 3

PREP: 5 minutes ■ **COOK:** 28 minutes

To trim Brussels sprouts, discard the tough outer leaves and trim about ¼ inch from the stems. Don't trim too much, or the sprouts will fall apart when halved.

- 2 tablespoons olive oil
- 2 cups chopped sweet onion
- 1 garlic clove, minced
- 1 pound trimmed Brussels sprouts
- ¼ cup (1 ounce) grated fresh Parmigiano-Reggiano cheese
- 1¼ teaspoons grated fresh lemon rind

1. Heat oil in a large nonstick skillet over medium heat. Add onion; cook 5 minutes, stirring occasionally. Add garlic; cook 30 seconds.
2. While onion mixture cooks, cut Brussels sprouts in half.
3. Add Brussels sprouts to pan; cover and cook 20 minutes or until tender, stirring often.
4. Remove from heat. Add cheese and rind; toss gently. Serve immediately. **YIELD: 4 SERVINGS (SERVING SIZE: ¾ CUP).**

PER SERVING: CAL 167 (51% from fat); FAT 9.4g (sat 2.1g); PRO 7.6g; CARB 16.7g; FIB 5.1g; CHOL 5mg; IRON 1.8mg; SOD 162mg; CALC 168mg

ROASTED CAULIFLOWER

POINTS value: 2

PREP: 5 minutes ■ **COOK:** 30 minutes

Roasted cauliflower has a savory caramelized crust and is tender and creamy inside. Don't let the simplicity of this dish fool you; it got one of our highest ratings.

- 4½ cups cauliflower florets
- 2 tablespoons olive oil
- 1 teaspoon grated fresh lemon rind
- 1 tablespoon lemon juice
- ½ teaspoon freshly ground black pepper
- ¼ teaspoon salt
- 3 tablespoons grated fresh Parmesan cheese

1. Preheat oven to 425°.
2. Combine first 6 ingredients in a 13 x 9–inch baking dish, and toss to coat. Bake at 425° for 30 minutes or until cauliflower is golden brown and tender. Sprinkle with cheese. Serve immediately. YIELD: 4 SERVINGS (SERVING SIZE: ABOUT ¾ CUP).

PER SERVING: CAL 120 (65% from fat); FAT 8.7g (sat 1.8g); PRO 5.2g; CARB 8.2g; FIB 3.7g; CHOL 4mg; IRON 0.7mg; SOD 282mg; CALC 109mg

STEAMED CAULIFLOWER WITH CHEDDAR SAUCE

POINTS value: 1

PREP: 5 minutes ■ **COOK:** 10 minutes

Adding butter at the very end makes this Cheddar sauce rich and silky smooth.

- 5 cups cauliflower florets (about 1¾ pounds)
- 4 teaspoons all-purpose flour
- ¼ teaspoon salt
- ⅛ teaspoon ground red pepper
- ⅔ cup fat-free milk
- ½ cup (2 ounces) reduced-fat shredded sharp Cheddar cheese
- 2 teaspoons butter

1. Steam cauliflower florets, covered, 5 minutes or until tender. Keep warm.
2. Place flour, salt, and red pepper in a small saucepan; gradually add milk, stirring with a whisk until blended.

Bring to a boil over medium–high heat, stirring constantly. Reduce heat; cook 4 minutes or until thick, stirring constantly. Remove from heat; add cheese, stirring until smooth. Add butter, stirring until butter melts. YIELD: 6 SERVINGS (SERVING SIZE: ½ CUP CAULIFLOWER AND 2 TABLESPOONS SAUCE).

PER SERVING: CAL 86 (42% from fat); FAT 4g (sat 2.4g); PRO 6.1g; CARB 8.4g; FIB 2.9g; CHOL 11mg; IRON 0.5mg; SOD 140mg; CALC 127mg

ORANGE-GLAZED CARROTS

POINTS value: 1

PREP: 2 minutes ■ **COOK:** 19 minutes

Using convenient, precut carrots helps this recipe come together quickly. If you prefer, substitute a 1-pound bag of whole carrots, cut into ¼-inch slices, for the crinkle-cut carrots.

- 1 (16-ounce) package crinkle-cut carrots
- ¼ cup sugar-free orange marmalade
- 2 teaspoons butter
- 1 teaspoon Dijon mustard

1. Place carrots in a medium saucepan; cover with water. Bring to a boil. Cover, reduce heat, and cook 16 minutes or until tender; drain.
2. Return carrots to pan; add marmalade, butter, and mustard. Cook over medium heat 1 to 2 minutes or until carrots are glazed, stirring frequently. YIELD: 6 SERVINGS (SERVING SIZE: ½ CUP).

PER SERVING: CAL 45 (28% from fat); FAT 1.4g (sat 0.8g); PRO 0.5g; CARB 9.7g; FIB 2.3g; CHOL 2.3mg; IRON 0.7mg; SOD 88mg; CALC 25mg

CARROTS AND KIDS

You can find prewashed, precut carrots in nearly any supermarket; this saves the trouble of doing those chores yourself. Carrots are a member of the parsley family and are high in nutrients like beta-carotene and vitamin A. They also have the advantage of being a kid-friendly veggie, so they are a great side dish for parents trying to watch their weight as well as those trying to instill healthy eating habits in their children. To store uncut carrots, cut off and discard the tops, and refrigerate in plastic bags for up to 2 weeks.

SOUTHWESTERN-STYLE SUCCOTASH

POINTS value: 2

PREP: 7 minutes ■ COOK: 12 minutes

Succotash gets a spicy update with jalapeño, garlic, cumin, and cilantro. Don't discard the jalapeño seeds if you'd like this fiery hot.

> 2 teaspoons canola oil
> ½ cup chopped onion
> ½ cup chopped red bell pepper
> 2 garlic cloves, minced
> 1 jalapeño pepper, seeded and minced
> 1 cup frozen whole-kernel corn
> 1 cup frozen baby lima beans
> ½ teaspoon salt
> ½ teaspoon ground cumin
> ½ cup water, divided
> 2 tablespoons chopped fresh cilantro

1. Heat oil in a large nonstick skillet over medium heat. Add onion and next 3 ingredients; sauté 2 minutes.
2. Add corn, lima beans, salt, and cumin; sauté 3 minutes. Add 1 tablespoon water to pan; cook over medium heat about 1 minute or until pan becomes almost dry. Repeat procedure with remaining water until vegetables are tender. Stir in cilantro. **YIELD: 4 SERVINGS (SERVING SIZE: ABOUT ½ CUP).**

PER SERVING: CAL 121 (22% from fat); FAT 2.9g (sat 0.3g); PRO 4.7g; CARB 21.4g; FIB 4.6g; CHOL 0mg; IRON 1.4mg; SOD 307mg; CALC 25mg

FRESH CORN SAUTÉ

POINTS value: 2

PREP: 10 minutes ■ COOK: 19 minutes

Everyone loves fresh sweet corn, and it's fun to take it beyond basic. This dish adds smoky bacon to complement the corn's sweetness. It's perfect served alongside anything from the grill.

> 1 applewood-smoked bacon slice
> ½ cup chopped sweet onion
> ¼ cup finely chopped red bell pepper
> 2 cups fresh corn kernels
> ½ teaspoon dried thyme
> ¼ teaspoon salt
> ¼ teaspoon freshly ground black pepper

1. Cook bacon in a large nonstick skillet over medium heat until crisp. Remove bacon from pan; crumble.
2. Add onion and bell pepper to drippings in pan; sauté 5 minutes. Add corn and next 3 ingredients; sauté 4 minutes or until tender. Stir in crumbled bacon. **YIELD: 4 SERVINGS (SERVING SIZE: ½ CUP).**

PER SERVING: CAL 104 (30% from fat); FAT 3.5g (sat 1.2g); PRO 3.4g; CARB 17.5g; FIB 2.8g; CHOL 3.3mg; IRON 0.6mg; SOD 184mg; CALC 16mg

SWEET-SPICED ROASTED VEGETABLES

POINTS value: 1

PREP: 12 minutes ■ COOK: 30 minutes

> 2 carrots, peeled
> 2 medium eggplants, cubed
> 1 cauliflower, cored and chopped
> ½ cup raisins
> 4 garlic cloves, minced
> 1 tablespoon olive oil
> 2 teaspoons honey
> ½ teaspoon ground cinnamon
> ¼ teaspoon kosher salt
> Cooking spray

1. Preheat oven to 450°.
2. Using a vegetable peeler, slice carrots lengthwise into thin strips to form ribbons. Combine carrot, eggplant, and next 7 ingredients in a large bowl; toss well. Spread vegetables in a single layer on a large rimmed baking sheet coated with cooking spray. Bake at 450° for 30 minutes or until tender and browned. **YIELD: 8 SERVINGS (SERVING SIZE: 1 CUP).**

PER SERVING: CAL 100 (21% from fat); FAT 2.3g (sat 0.3g); PRO 2.7g; CARB 20.3g; FIB 5.8g; CHOL 0mg; IRON 0.8mg; SOD 81mg; CALC 33mg

HONEY

The flavor of honey can differ widely depending on the kind of flowers that provided the nectar—such as clover, orange blossoms, or sage flowers—and the climate and location where the flowers were grown. When choosing a honey, pay attention to the color: Lighter honey has a more delicate flavor than the darker varieties. To minimize waste and promote accuracy in measuring, coat utensils with cooking spray before pouring in the honey; this allows the honey to slide out easily. Avoid storing honey in the refrigerator, as it will crystallize; a dry location at room temperature is best.

An ancient Greek myth maintains that a fennel stalk held the fiery coal that carried knowledge to man from Olympus. Whether or not you believe in Greek mythology, this vegetable is a wonderful flavor source for many dishes—its taste has often been likened to licorice. The large bulbous base can be braised, sliced into salads, or chopped into a soup, while the feathery tops are good for seasoning. Fresh fennel should be stored in the refrigerator in plastic, and kept for no longer than 5 days.

ROASTED FENNEL, CARROTS, AND SHALLOTS

POINTS value: 1

PREP: 13 minutes ■ **COOK:** 45 minutes

After some trial and error, we found that by not turning the veggies as they roast, they become caramelized on both sides more quickly.

> 2 **fennel bulbs, trimmed and cut into ½-inch-thick wedges**
> 4 **carrots, cut into 4 x ½–inch sticks**
> 4 **ounces shallots, peeled and halved**
> **Butter-flavored cooking spray**
> ¼ **teaspoon salt**
> ¼ **teaspoon black pepper**

1. Preheat oven to 450°.
2. Arrange fennel, carrots, and shallots in a single layer on a large rimmed baking sheet coated with cooking spray. Bake at 450° for 45 minutes (do not turn vegetables).
3. Transfer vegetables to a medium bowl; sprinkle with salt and pepper. YIELD: 4 SERVINGS (SERVING SIZE: 1 CUP).

PER SERVING: CAL 77 (8% from fat); FAT 0.7g (sat 0g); PRO 2.6g; CARB 17.2g; FIB 5.7g; CHOL 0mg; IRON 1.3mg; SOD 251mg; CALC 85mg

KALE WITH CRANBERRIES, APRICOTS, AND ALMONDS

POINTS value: 2

PREP: 5 minutes ■ **COOK:** 14 minutes

Chewy kale, tangy cranberries, and sweet apricots combine to make a healthy and nutritious side dish.

> ½ **cup water**
> 1 **tablespoon balsamic vinegar**
> 1 **pound kale, trimmed and cut into 2-inch pieces (about 12 cups)**
> ¼ **cup slivered almonds**
> ¼ **cup dried cranberries**
> ¼ **cup finely chopped dried apricots**

1. Combine water and vinegar in a large Dutch oven; bring to a boil over medium-high heat. Add kale; cover, reduce heat, and simmer 12 minutes or until tender and liquid almost evaporates, stirring occasionally.
2. While kale cooks, heat a medium nonstick skillet over medium-high heat. Add almonds; cook 4 minutes or until toasted, stirring constantly.
3. Add toasted almonds, cranberries, and apricots to kale; toss gently to combine. Serve immediately. YIELD: 6 SERVINGS (SERVING SIZE: ¾ CUP).

PER SERVING: CAL 86 (28% from fat); FAT 2.7g (sat 0.3g); PRO 3.1g; CARB 13.9g; FIB 1.8g; CHOL 0mg; IRON 1.3mg; SOD 23mg; CALC 128mg

COLLARD GREENS WITH FIGS AND BACON CRUMBLES

POINTS value: 2

PREP: 5 minutes ■ **COOK:** 30 minutes

This updated Southern side has a perfect blend of sweet and salty flavors and is quick to assemble. Serve it with roasted or grilled pork.

> 2 **bacon slices**
> 1 **(16-ounce) package chopped collard greens**
> ½ **cup dried figs, chopped**
> ⅓ **cup water**
> 2 **teaspoons maple syrup**

1. Cook bacon in a large nonstick skillet over medium heat until crisp. Crumble bacon, and return to pan. Add greens and remaining ingredients; cover and cook over

medium heat 20 minutes or until greens are tender, stirring occasionally. **YIELD: 4 SERVINGS (SERVING SIZE: 1 CUP).**

PER SERVING: CAL 134 (24% from fat); FAT 3.5g (sat 1.2g); PRO 4.6g; CARB 24.6g; FIB 6.1g; CHOL 5mg; IRON 2.1mg; SOD 70mg; CALC 227mg

SPINACH WITH RAISINS AND PINE NUTS

POINTS value: 2

PREP: 4 minutes ■ **COOK:** 7 minutes

This side dish coupled with a rotisserie chicken and whole-grain couscous makes a quick weeknight meal with a Mediterranean flair.

- 1 tablespoon olive oil
- ½ cup thinly sliced red onion
- 2 (6-ounce) packages fresh baby spinach
- ¼ cup golden raisins
- ⅜ teaspoon salt, divided
- 2 tablespoons pine nuts, toasted
- ¼ teaspoon freshly ground black pepper

1. Heat oil in a Dutch oven over medium-high heat. Add onion; sauté 3 minutes or until browned. Stir in spinach, raisins, and ⅛ teaspoon salt; cook 2 to 4 minutes or until spinach wilts, stirring occasionally.
2. Add pine nuts, pepper, and remaining ¼ teaspoon salt to spinach mixture; toss gently to combine. Serve immediately. **YIELD: 6 SERVINGS (SERVING SIZE: ½ CUP).**

PER SERVING: CAL 77 (53% from fat); FAT 4.5g (sat 0.5g); PRO 2.4g; CARB 9g; FIB 1.8g; CHOL 0mg; IRON 1.9mg; SOD 191mg; CALC 63mg

OKRA AND SUN-DRIED TOMATO SAUTÉ

POINTS value: 2

PREP: 6 minutes ■ **COOK:** 14 minutes

- ⅔ cup water
- 1 (16-ounce) package frozen cut okra
- 1½ cups frozen whole-kernel corn
- 1 tablespoon sun-dried tomato oil
- ½ cup chopped red onion
- 6 oil-packed sun-dried tomato halves, coarsely chopped
- 2 tablespoons chopped fresh thyme
- ¼ teaspoon salt
- ¼ teaspoon freshly ground black pepper

1. Combine water, okra, and corn in a large saucepan; bring to a boil. Cover, reduce heat, and simmer 10 minutes. Drain and rinse.
2. While vegetables cook, heat 1 tablespoon sun-dried tomato oil in a large nonstick skillet over medium-high heat. Add onion; sauté 5 minutes or until browned.
3. Stir in okra mixture, chopped sun-dried tomatoes, thyme, salt, and pepper; cook 2 to 3 minutes or until thoroughly heated. **YIELD: 8 SERVINGS (SERVING SIZE: ½ CUP).**

PER SERVING: CAL 91 (44% from fat); FAT 4.4g (sat 0.6g); PRO 2g; CARB 12.6g; FIB 3.4g; CHOL 0mg; IRON 0.5mg; SOD 110mg; CALC 8mg

SUN-DRIED TOMATOES

Sun-dried tomatoes are either oil- or dry-packed. If you use sun-dried tomatoes packed in oil, here's a tip to eliminate unnecessary calories: After draining, pat them dry with a paper towel to soak up the extra oil. You can keep already-opened jars of the oil-packed variety in the refrigerator for up to 2 weeks. The dry-packed kind will keep up to 12 months in a moisture-proof container stored in a cool, dry area. The sweet, intense flavor of sun-dried tomatoes adds interest to dishes like appetizers and salads, and richness to sauces for pizza and pasta.

LEMON-HERB POTATOES

POINTS value: 2

PREP: 7 minutes ■ **COOK:** 10 minutes

- 12 ounces Yukon gold potatoes, cut into ½-inch cubes
- 1½ cups chopped onion
- ¼ cup chopped parsley
- 1½ tablespoons butter, softened
- 1 tablespoon grated fresh lemon rind
- ½ teaspoon chopped fresh rosemary
- ¼ teaspoon dried oregano, crushed
- ¼ teaspoon salt

1. Steam potato and onion, covered, 10 minutes or until tender. Drain and return to pan.
2. While potatoes steam, combine parsley and next 5 ingredients in a medium bowl. Add potato mixture; toss gently until butter melts and mixture is blended. **YIELD: 6 SERVINGS (SERVING SIZE: ½ CUP).**

PER SERVING: CAL 90 (29% from fat); FAT 2.9g (sat 1.8g); PRO 1.9g; CARB 14.1g; FIB 1.6g; CHOL 8mg; IRON 0.8mg; SOD 124mg; CALC 16mg

ROASTED PURPLE POTATOES AND PARSNIPS WITH ROSEMARY

POINTS value: 2

PREP: 6 minutes ■ **COOK:** 30 minutes

Purple-fleshed potatoes, also known as Peruvian blue potatoes, are now available in most supermarkets. If you are unable to find them, substitute baby red potatoes.

- ½ pound purple potatoes, cut into 1-inch wedges
- 2 parsnips, cut into 1-inch pieces
- 2 red bell peppers, cut into 1-inch pieces
- 1 tablespoon olive oil
- 2 teaspoons chopped fresh rosemary
- ½ teaspoon kosher salt
- ¼ teaspoon freshly ground black pepper
- Cooking spray

1. Preheat oven to 400°.
2. Combine first 3 ingredients in a large bowl; drizzle with oil. Sprinkle with rosemary, salt, and black pepper, tossing gently to coat.
3. Arrange vegetables in a single layer on a large rimmed baking sheet coated with cooking spray. Bake at 400° for 30 minutes or until vegetables are browned. **YIELD: 4 SERVINGS (SERVING SIZE: 1 CUP).**

PER SERVING: CAL 140 (26% from fat); FAT 4g (sat 0.6g); PRO 2.5g; CARB 25.6g; FIB 5.7g; CHOL 0mg; IRON 1.2mg; SOD 248mg; CALC 40mg

---

EASY-TO-GROW BASIL

Fresh basil is an ideal ingredient for making fresh meals with a distinct flavor. The really good news is that it's simple to grow fresh basil yourself—all you need is plenty of sunlight, small starter basil plants, a few sturdy pots, good soil, and water. Be careful not to overwater basil; once a week is usually sufficient for smaller plants. Besides its culinary attributes, the aroma of a fresh basil plant adds an invigorating scent to a kitchen garden, sunroom, patio, or wherever you decide it should live.

SAUTÉED SUMMER SQUASH WITH BASIL AND TOMATOES

POINTS value: 1

pictured on page 141

PREP: 5 minutes ■ **COOK:** 13 minutes

This recipe is a wonderful way to use up the bounty of fresh garden produce.

- 2 teaspoons olive oil
- 2 small zucchini, cut into ¼-inch slices
- 1 large yellow squash, cut into ¼-inch chunks
- ½ cup chopped sweet onion
- 2 garlic cloves, minced
- 1 cup grape tomatoes
- ¼ teaspoon salt
- ¼ teaspoon freshly ground black pepper
- ¼ cup (1 ounce) shredded Asiago cheese
- 2 tablespoons chopped fresh basil

1. Heat oil in a large nonstick skillet over medium-high heat. Add zucchini, yellow squash, and onion; sauté 6 minutes. Add garlic; sauté 4 minutes or until vegetables are tender.
2. Add tomatoes, salt, and pepper to pan; sauté 2 minutes or until thoroughly heated. Stir in cheese and basil. **YIELD: 6 SERVINGS (SERVING SIZE: ⅔ CUP).**

PER SERVING: CAL 52 (52% from fat); FAT 3g (sat 1.1g); PRO 2.5g; CARB 4.8g; FIB 1.3g; CHOL 4mg; IRON 0.4mg; SOD 115mg; CALC 61mg

SUMMER SQUASH AND EDAMAME SUCCOTASH

POINTS value: 1

PREP: 7 minutes ■ COOK: 15 minutes

1¼ pounds yellow squash (about 5)
1 cup frozen shelled edamame (green soybeans)
⅓ cup finely chopped red bell pepper
⅓ cup finely chopped onion
2 tablespoons chopped fresh basil
2 teaspoons butter
2 teaspoons fresh lemon juice
1 teaspoon extra-virgin olive oil
¼ teaspoon salt
¼ teaspoon black pepper

1. Cut squash lengthwise into quarters. Cut quarters crosswise into ½-inch slices, creating chunks.
2. Add water to a large saucepan, filling two-thirds full; bring to a boil. Add squash, edamame, bell pepper, and onion. Return to a boil; cover, reduce heat, and simmer 9 minutes or until vegetables are tender. Drain vegetables and return to pan.
3. Add basil and remaining ingredients; toss gently until butter melts. YIELD: 6 SERVINGS (SERVING SIZE: ABOUT ⅔ CUP).

PER SERVING: CAL 61 (47% from fat); FAT 3.2g (sat 1g); PRO 3.4g; CARB 6.4g; FIB 2.4g; CHOL 3mg; IRON 0.8mg; SOD 110mg; CALC 31mg

VEGETABLE RIBBONS WITH MUSTARD BUTTER

POINTS value: 1

PREP: 10 minutes ■ COOK: 4 minutes

Graceful ribbons of yellow squash and zucchini make a pretty side dish that's surprisingly easy to make. Just use a vegetable peeler to cut long paper-thin strips of each vegetable.

3 small yellow squash
2 small zucchini
2 teaspoons butter
2 teaspoons Dijon mustard
¼ teaspoon salt
⅛ teaspoon freshly ground black pepper

1. Cut yellow squash and zucchini into very thin slices using a vegetable peeler.
2. Place sliced vegetables and butter in a microwave-safe bowl. Cover dish with a double layer of moistened paper towels. Microwave at HIGH 3 minutes. Add

mustard, salt, and pepper, tossing to coat. Cover with moistened paper towels and cook at HIGH 1 minute or until crisp-tender. YIELD: 4 SERVINGS (SERVING SIZE: ABOUT ½ CUP).

PER SERVING: CAL 38 (50% from fat); FAT 2.1g (sat 1.2g); PRO 1.4g; CARB 4.3g; FIB 1.3g; CHOL 5mg; IRON 0.4mg; SOD 226mg; CALC 18mg

THYME-ROASTED ROOT VEGETABLES

POINTS value: 2

PREP: 9 minutes ■ COOK: 30 minutes

Roasting root vegetables at a high temperature browns them while concentrating and sweetening their flavor in a way that just might entice picky youngsters to give them a try.

4 parsnips, peeled and cut into 1-inch pieces
1 large turnip, peeled and cut into 1-inch pieces
1 small red onion, cut into thin wedges
1 cup baby carrots
1 tablespoon olive oil
1 teaspoon dried thyme
¼ teaspoon salt
¼ teaspoon freshly ground black pepper
Cooking spray

1. Preheat oven to 425°.
2. Combine first 8 ingredients in a large bowl, and toss to coat.
3. Arrange vegetables in a single layer on a large rimmed baking sheet coated with cooking spray. Bake at 425° for 30 minutes or until tender and browned. YIELD: 4 SERVINGS (SERVING SIZE: ¾ CUP).

PER SERVING: CAL 107 (33% from fat); FAT 3.9g (sat 0.6g); PRO 1.7g; CARB 17.9g; FIB 5.2g; CHOL 0mg; IRON 1mg; SOD 219mg; CALC 69mg

VEGETABLE COUSCOUS

POINTS value: 2

PREP: 6 minutes ■ **COOK:** 15 minutes
■ **OTHER:** 5 minutes

Purchase a fennel bulb with plenty of bright green fronds attached. The fronds are sprinkled over the finished dish just before serving, giving it a beautiful and aromatic finish.

    2 teaspoons canola oil
    1 cup chopped fennel bulb
    ¾ cup thinly sliced carrot (about 2 medium)
    ½ cup thinly sliced shallots
    1¼ cups low-sodium vegetable juice (such as V-8)
    ½ cup water
    ½ teaspoon salt
    1 cup frozen petite green peas, thawed
    1 cup uncooked whole wheat couscous
    2 tablespoons chopped fennel fronds

1. Heat oil in a large saucepan over medium heat. Add chopped fennel bulb, carrot, and shallots; sauté 5 minutes or until tender. Add vegetable juice, water, and salt; bring mixture to a boil. Cover, reduce heat, and simmer 8 to 10 minutes or until vegetables are tender.
2. Stir in peas and couscous. Remove from heat. Cover and let stand 5 minutes or until liquid is absorbed. Fluff with a fork. Sprinkle with fennel fronds. YIELD: 6 SERVINGS (SERVING SIZE: 1 CUP).

PER SERVING: CAL 133 (14% from fat); FAT 2.1g (sat 0.1g); PRO 4.8g; CARB 25.4g; FIB 4.8g; CHOL 0mg; IRON 1.5mg; SOD 270mg; CALC 39mg

COOKING COUSCOUS

The tiny semolina grains of couscous cook quickly, a trait that makes this traditional North African food an increasingly attractive option for busy cooks looking for fast, healthy meals. Besides the always reliable package instructions for the stovetop, our Test Kitchens staff also recommends this oven-cooked technique for even fluffier results: Measure equal parts of salted water and couscous (3 cups of each, for instance) into a wide oven-safe dish, using a fork to stir and break up any lumps. Let stand at room temperature about 15 minutes. While couscous stands, preheat oven to 400°. After the standing time, add 3 tablespoons of vegetable oil to couscous mixture, rubbing the couscous between your hands to break up any remaining lumps. Place the uncovered dish in oven and bake for 15 to 20 minutes, fluffing once with a fork after 10 minutes.

ASIAN NOODLES AND VEGETABLES

POINTS value: 2

PREP: 12 minutes ■ **COOK:** 9 minutes

Chilled leftovers of this pasta salad make a great addition to a brown-bag lunch.

    8 ounces multigrain thin spaghetti, uncooked (such as Barilla)
  Cooking spray
    1 red bell pepper, cut into thin strips
    2 cups snow peas, cut lengthwise into thirds
    2 garlic cloves, minced
    1 teaspoon minced peeled fresh ginger
    ¼ teaspoon crushed red pepper
    ¼ cup chopped fresh cilantro
    ¼ cup fat-free, less-sodium chicken broth
    2 tablespoons low-sodium soy sauce
    1 tablespoon dark sesame oil

1. Cook spaghetti according to package directions, omitting salt and fat. Drain and return to pan.
2. While spaghetti cooks, heat a large nonstick skillet over medium-high heat. Coat pan with cooking spray. Add bell pepper and snow peas; stir-fry 2 minutes. Stir in garlic, ginger, and red pepper; stir-fry 2 minutes or until crisp-tender.
3. Add vegetables, cilantro, and next 3 ingredients to spaghetti. Toss well. YIELD: 8 SERVINGS (SERVING SIZE: ¾ CUP).

PER SERVING: CAL 136 (19% from fat); FAT 2.9g (sat 0.3g); PRO 6g; CARB 22g; FIB 2.8g; CHOL 0mg; IRON 0.5mg; SOD 165mg; CALC 10mg

BROWN RICE PILAF

POINTS value: 2

PREP: 5 minutes ■ **COOK:** 58 minutes

Resist the temptation to lift the lid and stir after adding the rice. Lifting the lid allows steam to escape, and stirring the rice causes the grains to stick together in lumps.

    2 teaspoons olive oil
    ¾ cup finely chopped carrot
    ⅓ cup finely chopped celery
    2 tablespoons finely chopped shallots
    2½ cups fat-free, less-sodium chicken broth
    1 cup long-grain brown rice
    ¼ teaspoon freshly ground black pepper
    2 thyme sprigs

1. Heat oil in a medium saucepan over medium-high heat. Add carrot, celery, and shallots; cook 5 minutes or until vegetables are crisp-tender, stirring occasionally. 2. Add broth and next 3 ingredients. Bring to a boil; cover, reduce heat, and simmer 50 minutes or until rice is tender and liquid is absorbed. Discard thyme sprigs. YIELD: 8 SERVINGS (SERVING SIZE: ½ CUP).

PER SERVING: CAL 110 (16% from fat); FAT 1.9g (sat 0.3g); PRO 3.3g; CARB 20.2g; FIB 1.7g; CHOL 0mg; IRON 0.5mg; SOD 190mg; CALC 14mg

APRICOT AND PECAN CURRIED RICE

POINTS value: 3

PREP: 5 minutes ■ COOK: 1 hour and 4 minutes

Cooking spray
1½ cups finely chopped onion
1½ cups water
12 dried apricot halves, chopped
½ cup brown rice
1 teaspoon curry powder
¼ teaspoon salt
½ cup chopped pecans, toasted

1. Heat a medium saucepan over medium-high heat. Coat pan with cooking spray. Add onion; sauté 6 minutes or until tender. Add 1½ cups water; bring to a boil. Stir in apricots and next 3 ingredients. Cover, reduce heat, and simmer 55 minutes or until liquid is absorbed. Add pecans; fluff with a fork. YIELD: 6 SERVINGS (SERVING SIZE: ½ CUP).

PER SERVING: CAL 160 (43% from fat); FAT 7.7g (sat 0.7g); PRO 2.9g; CARB 21.6g; FIB 2.8g; CHOL 0mg; IRON 0.9mg; SOD 100mg; CALC 25mg

DRIED FRUITS

Dried fruit is a wonderful, healthy snack, but when you're counting your calories, it's important to remember that the dehydration process concentrates the nutrients. Bottom line: Dried fruits typically contain 4 or 5 times the number of calories by weight as that of their fresh counterparts, so use them in moderation.

MEXICAN RICE

POINTS value: 2

PREP: 5 minutes ■ COOK: 14 minutes

Frozen microwave brown rice makes this side dish superquick. The 40%-less-sodium taco seasoning mix is readily available at larger supermarkets. This mix is a convenient and easy way to add a lot of authentic Mexican flavor without overdoing it on sodium.

1 (10-ounce) package frozen microwave brown rice (such as Birds Eye Steamfresh)
Cooking spray
4½ teaspoons olive oil, divided
1½ cups chopped onion
1½ cups chopped red bell pepper
2 tablespoons 40%-less-sodium taco seasoning (such as Old El Paso)

1. Prepare rice according to package directions. 2. Heat a large nonstick skillet over medium-high heat; coat pan with cooking spray. Add 1 teaspoon oil to pan. Add onion and bell pepper; sauté 10 minutes or until tender and lightly browned. 3. Add taco seasoning and remaining 3½ teaspoons oil to pan; cook 30 seconds over medium-high heat. Add rice; cook 1 minute, stirring constantly. YIELD: 6 SERVINGS (SERVING SIZE: ½ CUP).

PER SERVING: CAL 117 (31% from fat); FAT 4g (sat 0.6g); PRO 2.2g; CARB 18.6g; FIB 2.1g; CHOL 0mg; IRON 0.2mg; SOD 203mg; CALC 19mg

POLENTA WITH ROSEMARY-ROASTED CHERRY TOMATOES

POINTS value: 2

PREP: 5 minutes ■ **COOK:** 15 minutes

Here is a great way to use a terrific convenience product. You won't be able to tell the difference between our creamy version of polenta and a fresh-from-scratch version.

> 1 bacon slice
> 2 pints cherry tomatoes
> ½ teaspoon chopped fresh rosemary
> 1 garlic clove, minced
> ½ teaspoon salt, divided
> ¼ teaspoon pepper
> 1 (17-ounce) tube of polenta
> 1¼ cups fat-free, less-sodium chicken broth

1. Preheat oven to 450°.
2. Place bacon in a large ovenproof skillet, and cook over medium heat 7 minutes or until crisp. Remove bacon from pan, reserving drippings in pan; crumble bacon, and set aside.
3. Add tomatoes, rosemary, garlic, ¼ teaspoon salt, and pepper to drippings in pan, stirring to combine. Bake at 450° for 8 minutes or until tomatoes begin to burst.
4. While tomatoes bake, mash polenta and broth in a medium saucepan. Cook over medium-low heat until hot and creamy, stirring occasionally with a whisk. Stir in remaining ¼ teaspoon salt. Spoon roasted tomatoes over polenta and top with crumbled bacon. **YIELD: 6 SERVINGS (SERVING SIZE: ABOUT ½ CUP POLENTA, ABOUT ½ CUP TOMATOES, AND 1 TEASPOON CRUMBLED BACON).**

PER SERVING: CAL 98 (18% from fat); FAT 2g (sat 0.7g); PRO 3.3g; CARB 16.4g; FIB 2.6g; CHOL 2mg; IRON 1mg; SOD 479mg; CALC 6mg

BULGUR, MUSHROOM, AND BROWNED ONION TOSS

POINTS value: 2

PREP: 6 minutes ■ **COOK:** 19 minutes

The rich caramelized flavor from browning the onions would make this side dish an ideal accompaniment to grilled steak or lamb.

> 1 tablespoon olive oil
> 1 cup chopped onion
> 2 garlic cloves, minced
> 1½ cups sliced fresh mushrooms
> ¼ teaspoon dried thyme
> 1⅓ cups water
> ⅔ cup bulgur
> ¼ teaspoon salt
> ¼ teaspoon freshly ground black pepper

1. Heat oil in a large saucepan over medium-high heat. Add onion and garlic; sauté 4 minutes or until onion is browned. Add mushrooms and thyme; sauté 4 minutes or until mushrooms are tender.
2. Stir in water, bulgur, salt, and pepper; bring to a boil. Cover, reduce heat, and simmer 7 minutes or until water evaporates. **YIELD: 5 SERVINGS (SERVING SIZE: ½ CUP).**

PER SERVING: CAL 109 (26% from fat); FAT 3.1g (sat 0.5g); PRO 3.2g; CARB 18.5g; FIB 4.1g; CHOL 0mg; IRON 0.7mg; SOD 123mg; CALC 21mg

SERVE YOURSELF

Portion control has become harder to gauge in the last few years because of the growth of serving sizes at restaurants and the increase in package sizes in grocery stores. Here are a few tips to help you watch how much food gets on your plate:

1. When eating out, split an entrée with a friend, or wrap up half the meal in a take-home container.

2. Instead of putting serving bowls on the table, serve up the amount you plan to eat on the plate before you sit down.

3. Don't eat directly from the package while watching TV—put the snacks in a bowl first.

4. Do some reorganizing of your cupboards and refrigerator. Fresh, healthy foods go front-and-center at eye-level; indulgences like ice cream, candy, and potato chips move to the back or up high where reaching for them takes a little effort.

Apricot and Wasabi–Sauced
Pork Tenderloin, *page 90*

Grilled Lamb Chops with
Gremolata, *page 91*

Picadillo,
page 86

Wild Rice–Stuffed Chicken Breasts,
page 95

Japanese One-Pot
Chicken, *page 94*

Turkey-Sausage
Meat Loaf, *page 98*

Lemon-Braised Chicken and Artichokes,
page 97

Asparagus Spear Salad with
Caesar-Style Dressing, *page 103*

Red Potato–Cauliflower Salad,
page 106

Sweet Lime Summer Fruits, *page 102*

Greek Steak Salad,
page 109

137

Salmon Burgers,
page 113

Thanksgiving Wraps,
page 116

Italian Steak Sandwiches,
page 114

Sautéed Summer Squash
with Basil and Tomatoes,
page 124

Artichokes with
Garlic Aïoli,
page 118

Chilled Mango
Soup, *page 146*

142

Poblano-Chicken Chowder, *page 153*

Blender Gazpacho, *page 146*

soups & stews

Blender Gazpacho, *page 146*

CHILLED MANGO SOUP

POINTS value: 2   *pictured on page 142*

PREP: 11 minutes ■ **OTHER:** 2 hours

Garnished with fresh raspberries and kiwi, this creamy milkshake of a soup is perfect for a ladies' luncheon, served alongside a tossed green salad with grilled chicken.

  1½ cups coarsely chopped peeled ripe mango
        (about 2 medium)
   1 cup pineapple-orange-banana juice (such as Dole)
  ½ cup half-and-half
  ½ teaspoon grated fresh lime rind
   2 tablespoons fresh lime juice
  ½ cup diced peeled kiwi
 15 raspberries

1. Place first 5 ingredients in a blender; process until smooth. Cover and chill 2 hours.

2. Ladle soup into bowls; top with kiwi and raspberries.

YIELD: 5 SERVINGS (SERVING SIZE: ½ CUP SOUP, ABOUT 1½ TABLE-SPOONS KIWI, AND 3 RASPBERRIES).

PER SERVING: CAL 130 (22% from fat); FAT 3.2g (sat 1.8g); PRO 1.9g; CARB 26.2g; FIB 2.8g; CHOL 9mg; IRON 0.4mg; SOD 17mg; CALC 54mg

BLENDER GAZPACHO

POINTS value: 2   *pictured on page 144*

PREP: 17 minutes ■ **OTHER:** 2 hours

This easy summer soup is a great way to add more veggies to your meal. For a great lunch, offer it with Mediterranean-Style Pitas, found on page 116.

   4 cups grape tomatoes
   1 cup chopped seeded peeled cucumber
  ½ cup chopped yellow bell pepper
 1½ cups low-sodium tomato juice
  ¼ cup chopped red onion
   3 tablespoons chopped fresh parsley
 1½ tablespoons olive oil
  ½ teaspoon grated fresh lemon rind
 1½ tablespoons fresh lemon juice
   1 tablespoon white balsamic vinegar
  ¼ teaspoon salt
  ¼ teaspoon freshly ground black pepper
   4 thin cucumber slices (optional)

1. Place tomatoes and cucumber in a blender; process until vegetables are finely chopped. Add remaining ingredients except cucumber slices; process until well blended. Chill 2 hours.

2. Ladle soup into bowls; top with cucumber slices, if desired. YIELD: 4 SERVINGS (SERVING SIZE: 1 CUP).

PER SERVING: CAL 117 (45% from fat); FAT 5.9g (sat 0.8g); PRO 2.6g; CARB 15.2g; FIB 2.9g; CHOL 0mg; IRON 1.2mg; SOD 215mg; CALC 37mg

CREAM OF CARAMELIZED VEGETABLE SOUP

POINTS value: 2

PREP: 16 minutes ■ **COOK:** 1 hour and 5 minutes

This filling, highly rated soup is comfort food at its best and has a ***POINTS*** value of only 2. Pureeing the roasted vegetables brings out a rich, deep, caramelized flavor.

- 4 large yellow bell peppers, halved and seeded
- Cooking spray
- 1 medium tomato, halved
- 1 medium yellow squash, quartered lengthwise
- 1 medium onion, cut into 8 wedges
- 2 (14-ounce) cans fat-free, less-sodium chicken broth
- 1 tablespoon dried oregano
- 2 teaspoons bottled minced roasted garlic
- ¾ teaspoon salt
- ⅛ teaspoon ground red pepper
- 1 cup half-and-half

1. Preheat broiler.
2. Place bell peppers, skin sides up, on a foil-lined baking sheet coated with cooking spray, and flatten with hand. Arrange tomato halves, squash, and onion on baking sheet. Broil 15 minutes; turn vegetables, and broil an additional 20 minutes or until vegetables are richly browned, rearranging as necessary to prevent overbrowning.
3. Combine broth and next 4 ingredients in a Dutch oven. Add roasted vegetables; bring to a boil. Cover, reduce heat, and simmer 20 minutes.
4. Place one-third of soup mixture in a blender; process until smooth. Pour pureed soup into a large bowl. Repeat procedure with remaining soup mixture. Return pureed soup to Dutch oven; stir in half-and-half. Cook 2 to 3 minutes or until thoroughly heated. YIELD: 6 SERVINGS (SERVING SIZE: 1 CUP).

PER SERVING: CAL 108 (43% from fat); FAT 5.2g (sat 3g); PRO 4.9g; CARB 12.2g; FIB 3.2g; CHOL 15mg; IRON 1.1mg; SOD 694mg; CALC 75mg

CURRIED EGGPLANT AND CHICKPEA STEW

POINTS value: 2

PREP: 16 minutes ■ **COOK:** 45 minutes

- 1 (1½-pound) eggplant, cut into 1-inch pieces
- Cooking spray
- 1 (16-ounce) can chickpeas (garbanzo beans), rinsed and drained
- 4 carrots, cut into 1-inch pieces
- 2 medium tomatoes, halved
- 6 garlic cloves
- 4 cups fat-free, less-sodium chicken broth, divided
- 2 teaspoons curry powder
- 2 teaspoons olive oil
- ½ teaspoon pepper
- ¼ teaspoon salt

1. Preheat oven to 425°.
2. Place eggplant on a large baking pan coated with cooking spray; coat eggplant with cooking spray. Place chickpeas, carrot, tomato halves, and garlic on another large baking pan coated with cooking spray; coat vegetables with cooking spray. Place both pans in oven, with pan of eggplant on rack above pan of chickpeas. Bake at 425° for 40 minutes or until vegetables are tender and browned.
3. Remove and discard skins from tomato halves. Place tomato halves, garlic, half of remaining roasted vegetables, half of chicken broth, and next 4 ingredients in a blender; process until smooth.
4. Combine pureed mixture, remaining roasted vegetables, and remaining chicken broth in a large saucepan. Bring to a boil; reduce heat, and simmer 3 minutes or until thoroughly heated, stirring frequently. YIELD: 6 SERVINGS (SERVING SIZE: 1⅓ CUPS).

PER SERVING: CAL 137 (20% from fat); FAT 3.1g (sat 0.3g); PRO 6g; CARB 23.9g; FIB 7g; CHOL 0mg; IRON 1.6mg; SOD 584mg; CALC 54mg

ITALIAN VEGETABLE-BEAN SOUP

POINTS value: 3

PREP: 6 minutes ■ **COOK:** 37 minutes

Canned tomatoes taste fresh from the garden with the addition of basil, oregano, and garlic during the canning process. Crushed red pepper adds a spicy kick to this soup. Increase or decrease the amount used according to your personal preference.

  Cooking spray
  1 cup chopped onion
  1 cup chopped green bell pepper
  3 garlic cloves, minced
  1 (15-ounce) can no-salt-added navy beans, rinsed and drained
  1 (14.5-ounce) can stewed tomatoes with basil, oregano, and garlic
  1 (14-ounce) can fat-free, less-sodium chicken broth
  ⅓ cup chopped bottled roasted red bell peppers
  1½ teaspoons dried Italian seasoning
  ¼ teaspoon crushed red pepper
  ½ cup chopped fresh basil
  1 tablespoon olive oil
  ¼ cup (1 ounce) grated fresh Parmesan cheese

1. Heat a Dutch oven over medium-high heat. Coat pan with cooking spray. Add onion and bell pepper; cook 6 minutes or until lightly browned, stirring frequently. Add garlic; cook 1 minute, stirring constantly. Add navy beans and next 5 ingredients; bring to a boil. Cover, reduce heat, and simmer 25 minutes.
2. Remove from heat; stir in basil and oil. Ladle soup into bowls, and sprinkle with cheese. **YIELD: 4 SERVINGS (SERVING SIZE: ABOUT 1¼ CUPS SOUP AND 1 TABLESPOON CHEESE).**

PER SERVING: CAL 184 (29% from fat); FAT 6g (sat 1.6g); PRO 10.2g; CARB 25g; FIB 7.1g; CHOL 5mg; IRON 2.2mg; SOD 808mg; CALC 187mg

GRATED FRESH PARMESAN CHEESE

When recipes call for "grated fresh Parmesan cheese," purchase a wedge or block of Parmesan cheese and grate it just before you plan to use it. This approach versus selecting pre-grated Parmesan cheese takes a little extra time, but the flavor is worth it. Also, it's best to grate fresh Parmesan after it has come to room temperature and grating only the amount needed. The remaining Parmesan will keep up to a month in the refrigerator, wrapped tightly in plastic wrap.

WILD MUSHROOM SOUP

POINTS value: 1

PREP: 13 minutes ■ **COOK:** 20 minutes
■ **OTHER:** 8 minutes

  ½ cup dried porcini mushrooms
  2 teaspoons olive oil
  ½ cup chopped celery
  ⅓ cup minced shallots
  2 garlic cloves, minced
  1 cup sliced button mushrooms
  1 cup chopped shiitake mushrooms
  1 cup sliced cremini mushrooms
  1 tablespoon minced fresh thyme
  1 tablespoon dry sherry
  1 (32-ounce) carton organic vegetable broth
  1 bay leaf
  1 tablespoon chopped fresh parsley
  ½ teaspoon salt
  ½ teaspoon freshly ground black pepper

1. Place porcini mushrooms in a medium bowl; cover with water. Let stand 8 minutes or until soft. Drain and chop porcini mushrooms, discarding water.
2. Heat oil in a large saucepan over medium-high heat. Add celery, shallots, and garlic; sauté 4 minutes or until tender. Add all mushrooms, thyme, and sherry; cook 5 minutes, stirring frequently. Add broth and bay leaf; bring to a boil. Cover, reduce heat, and simmer 8 minutes. Stir in parsley, salt, and pepper. Discard bay leaf. **YIELD: 4 SERVINGS (SERVING SIZE: ABOUT 1¼ CUPS).**

PER SERVING: CAL 83 (27% from fat); FAT 2.5g (sat 0.4g); PRO 2.9g; CARB 10.8g; FIB 1.9g; CHOL 0mg; IRON 1.5mg; SOD 881mg; CALC 23mg

MEXICAN SPINACH SOUP WITH LIME

POINTS value: 2

PREP: 5 minutes ■ **COOK:** 20 minutes
■ **OTHER:** 5 minutes

To prepare this soup as quickly as we did, chop the spinach, bell pepper, green onions, and cilantro while the onion cooks. Pair this fresh-tasting soup with cheese quesadilla wedges or a simple grilled cheese sandwich.

- 1 tablespoon olive oil
- 1 cup chopped onion
- 2 (14-ounce) cans fat-free, less-sodium chicken broth
- 1 (4.5-ounce) can chopped green chiles
- 1 teaspoon ground cumin
- ¼ teaspoon salt
- ¼ teaspoon crushed red pepper
- 1½ cups packed fresh baby spinach leaves, coarsely chopped
- 1 cup chopped red bell pepper
- ½ cup chopped green onions
- ¼ cup chopped fresh cilantro
- ¼ cup light sour cream
- 4 lime wedges

1. Heat oil in a large saucepan over medium-high heat. Add onion; sauté 6 minutes. Add broth and next 4 ingredients. Bring to a boil; cover, reduce heat, and simmer 10 minutes. Remove from heat. Stir in spinach and next 3 ingredients. Cover and let stand 5 minutes. **2.** Ladle soup into bowls, and top with sour cream. Serve with lime wedges. **YIELD: 4 SERVINGS (SERVING SIZE: 1¼ CUPS SOUP AND 1 TABLESPOON SOUR CREAM).**

PER SERVING: CAL 107 (41% from fat); FAT 5g (sat 1.3g); PRO 5.1g; CARB 13g; FIB 2.7g; CHOL 5mg; IRON 1.3mg; SOD 819mg; CALC 54mg

TUSCAN SQUASH AND BEAN SOUP

POINTS value: 3

PREP: 5 minutes ■ **COOK:** 37 minutes

Using grated hard cheese in combination with no-salt-added and regular beans keeps the sodium in check. In our testing, we used a 3-cheese Italian blend that includes Parmesan, Asiago, and Romano. If that's not available, Parmesan cheese works equally well.

- 2 teaspoons olive oil
- 2 cups chopped onion
- 1¼ cups chopped celery
- 4 small yellow squash, halved lengthwise and sliced
- 2 large garlic cloves, minced
- 1 (15-ounce) can no-salt-added Great Northern beans, undrained (such as Eden Organic)
- 1 (15-ounce) can Great Northern beans, rinsed and drained
- 1 (14-ounce) can roasted garlic–flavored chicken broth (such as Swanson)
- ¼ teaspoon black pepper
- 2 teaspoons chopped fresh rosemary
- ⅔ cup (2½ ounces) grated 3-cheese Italian blend cheese (such as Kraft)
- 2 tablespoons chopped fresh basil
- 2 tablespoons fresh lemon juice

1. Heat oil in a Dutch oven over medium-high heat. Add onion and celery; sauté until tender. Add squash; cook 7 minutes, stirring occasionally. Add garlic; sauté 30 seconds. **2.** Stir in beans, broth, and pepper; bring to a boil. Cover, reduce heat, and simmer 15 minutes. Stir in rosemary; simmer 5 minutes. Remove from heat; stir in cheese, basil, and lemon juice. **YIELD: 7 SERVINGS (SERVING SIZE: 1 CUP).**

PER SERVING: CAL 173 (29% from fat); FAT 5.7g (sat 2.5g); PRO 10.7g; CARB 23.8g; FIB 7.7g; CHOL 1mg; IRON 1.8mg; SOD 666mg; CALC 221mg

HARVEST POTATO-APPLE SOUP

POINTS value: 3

PREP: 15 minutes ■ **COOK:** 26 minutes

The ultimate fall comfort food, this soup marries a hearty potato soup with a pinch of apple pie.

- 1 bacon slice, diced
- ¼ cup chopped onion
- 2 garlic cloves, minced
- 3 cups fat-free, less-sodium chicken broth
- 2 cups cubed peeled baking potato
- 3 cups cubed peeled apple
- ½ teaspoon ground cinnamon
- ¼ teaspoon salt
- 1 (15.8-ounce) can Great Northern beans, rinsed, drained, and mashed

1. Cook bacon in a large Dutch oven over medium-high heat until crisp. Remove bacon from pan, reserving drippings in pan. Crumble bacon and set aside.

2. Add onion to pan; sauté until tender. Add garlic; cook 1 minute, stirring constantly. Add broth and potato; bring to a boil. Cover and cook 5 minutes or until potato is almost done. Add apple, cinnamon, and salt; cook, uncovered, 10 minutes or until apple is tender.

3. Stir in mashed beans; cook 1 minute or until thoroughly heated, stirring occasionally. Ladle soup into bowls, and sprinkle evenly with bacon. **YIELD: 4 SERVINGS (SERVING SIZE: 1½ CUPS SOUP AND ABOUT ½ TEASPOON BACON).**

PER SERVING: CAL 183 (4% from fat); FAT 0.9g (sat 0.3g); PRO 8.2g; CARB 40.4g; FIB 7.4g; CHOL 1mg; IRON 1.8mg; SOD 768mg; CALC 43mg

A LITTLE BIT OF BACON

The use of bacon in a recipe holds a two-part advantage: It has great flavor, and it's thrifty. Whatever the dish, bacon's rich, smoky taste has the ability to rise to the occasion and has been used to flavor everything from turnip greens to pasta. In addition to its knack for blending with various ingredients, bacon also delivers a wallop of flavor per slice, so a little goes a long way.

ROOT VEGETABLE SOUP WITH ROSEMARY

POINTS value: 2

PREP: 14 minutes ■ **COOK:** 45 minutes

You can make this soup as smooth as you like by mashing it to the desired consistency.

- 1 tablespoon canola oil
- 4 cups (1-inch) cubed peeled sweet potato
- 1⅓ cups (1-inch) cubed peeled turnip
- 1⅓ cups (1-inch) cubed carrot
- 1¼ cups (1-inch) cubed parsnip
- ¾ cup (1-inch) cubed cored peeled red pear
- 4½ cups fat-free, less-sodium chicken broth
- 4 garlic cloves, minced
- 1 tablespoon minced fresh rosemary
- 1 teaspoon kosher salt
- ⅛ teaspoon ground red pepper

1. Heat oil in a Dutch oven over medium-high heat. Add sweet potato and next 4 ingredients; cook 8 minutes, stirring occasionally. Stir in chicken broth and remaining 4 ingredients. Bring to a boil; cover, reduce heat, and simmer 30 minutes or until vegetables are tender.

2. Mash soup with a potato masher to desired consistency. Ladle soup into bowls. **YIELD: 7 SERVINGS (SERVING SIZE: 1 CUP).**

PER SERVING: CAL 121 (17% from fat); FAT 2.3g (sat 0.2g); PRO 3.9g; CARB 22.6g; FIB 4.4g; CHOL 0mg; IRON 0.7mg; SOD 696mg; CALC 48mg

SMOKY LENTIL SOUP WITH HAM

POINTS value: 4

PREP: 6 minutes ■ **COOK:** 37 minutes

- **2 teaspoons canola oil**
- **1½ cups chopped onion**
- **½ cup chopped carrot**
- **3¾ cups fat-free, less-sodium chicken broth**
- **¾ cup dried lentils**
- **¾ teaspoon dried thyme**
- **¼ teaspoon freshly ground black pepper**
- **1 cup chopped low-sodium deli ham (such as Boar's Head)**
- **¼ cup chopped fresh parsley**

1. Heat oil in a large saucepan over medium-high heat. Add onion and carrot; cook 5 minutes or until golden brown, stirring frequently.
2. Add broth and next 3 ingredients; bring to a boil. Cover, reduce heat, and simmer 20 minutes. Add ham; return mixture to a simmer, and cook, uncovered, 8 to 10 minutes or until lentils are tender. Ladle soup into bowls, and top with parsley. YIELD: 4 SERVINGS (SERVING SIZE: 1 CUP).

PER SERVING: CAL 234 (13% from fat); FAT 3.5g (sat 0.3g); PRO 18.1g; CARB 34g; FIB 6.7g; CHOL 13mg; IRON 4mg; SOD 777mg; CALC 38mg

YELLOW SPLIT PEA SOUP WITH SPICY SAUSAGE

POINTS value: 3

PREP: 10 minutes ■ **COOK:** 1 hour and 12 minutes

Split peas are simply dried peas that are mechanically cut in half so that they will cook faster.

- **4 ounces spicy turkey Italian sausage (such as Jennie-O)**
- **1½ cups chopped onion**
- **½ cup chopped celery**
- **½ cup chopped carrot**
- **1½ teaspoons olive oil**
- **⅛ teaspoon crushed red pepper**
- **2 garlic cloves, minced**
- **3 cups fat-free, less-sodium chicken broth**
- **3 cups water**
- **1½ cups yellow split peas**

1. Remove casings from sausage. Cook sausage in a large Dutch oven over medium-high heat until browned, stirring to crumble. Add onion and next 4 ingredients; sauté 10 minutes or until vegetables are tender. Add garlic; cook 1 minute, stirring frequently. Stir in broth, 3 cups water, and peas. Bring to a boil. Partially cover, reduce heat, and simmer 45 minutes or until peas are tender. YIELD: 7 SERVINGS (SERVING SIZE: ABOUT 1 CUP).

PER SERVING: CAL 200 (15% from fat); FAT 3.4g (sat 0.5g); PRO 13g; CARB 30g; FIB 13g; CHOL 10mg; IRON 1.2mg; SOD 356mg; CALC 27mg

CHEESE RAVIOLI
AND SAUSAGE STEW

POINTS value: 5

PREP: 5 minutes ■ **COOK:** 15 minutes

Canned broth selections continue to expand and occupy large portions of the soup aisle in stores. Be sure to study the labels carefully if you are watching your sodium intake.

Cooking spray
1 (7-ounce) link smoked turkey sausage, sliced
1½ cups organic chicken broth
½ cup water
1 teaspoon dried Italian seasoning
1 (14½-ounce) can no-salt-added diced tomatoes, undrained
1 (9-ounce) package fresh four-cheese ravioli (such as Buitoni)
4 cups packed fresh baby spinach

1. Heat a large saucepan over medium-high heat. Coat pan with cooking spray. Add smoked sausage; cook until lightly browned, stirring frequently. Add chicken broth, ½ cup water, and Italian seasoning; bring to a boil. Add tomatoes and ravioli. Cover, reduce heat, and simmer 6 to 8 minutes or until ravioli is tender. Stir in spinach, and cook 1 minute or until spinach wilts. **YIELD: 5 SERVINGS (SERVING SIZE: ABOUT 1 CUP PLUS 2 TABLESPOONS).**

PER SERVING: CAL 260 (33% from fat); FAT 9.4g (sat 4.4g); PRO 14.4g; CARB 30.2g; FIB 3.5g; CHOL 50mg; IRON 2mg; SOD 924mg; CALC 120mg

TORTILLA SOUP WITH CHICKEN, AVOCADO, AND LIME

POINTS value: 4

PREP: 7 minutes ■ **COOK:** 40 minutes

6 (6-inch) corn tortillas
Cooking spray
½ cup chopped onion
1 finely chopped seeded jalapeño pepper
4 cups fat-free, less-sodium chicken broth
1 (14.5-ounce) can diced tomatoes, undrained
1 teaspoon ground cumin
¼ teaspoon garlic salt
2 cups chopped cooked chicken
1 diced peeled avocado
¼ cup chopped fresh cilantro
¼ cup (1 ounce) shredded Monterey Jack cheese
7 lime wedges

1. Preheat oven to 425°.
2. Cut tortillas into ¼-inch-thick strips. Place strips on a jelly-roll pan coated with cooking spray. Coat strips with cooking spray. Bake at 425° for 12 minutes or until golden and crisp, stirring once. Set aside.
3. Heat a large Dutch oven over medium-high heat. Coat pan with cooking spray. Add onion and jalapeño; sauté 2 minutes or until browned. Stir in broth and next 3 ingredients; bring to a boil. Cover, reduce heat, and simmer 15 minutes.
4. Add chicken to soup; cook 5 minutes or until thoroughly heated. Ladle soup into bowls; top with avocado, cilantro, and cheese. Serve with lime wedges. **YIELD: 7 SERVINGS (SERVING SIZE: 1 CUP SOUP, ABOUT 2 TABLESPOONS AVOCADO, ABOUT 2 TEASPOONS CILANTRO, ABOUT 2 TEASPOONS CHEESE, AND ABOUT 6 TABLESPOONS TORTILLA STRIPS).**

PER SERVING: CAL 190 (36% from fat); FAT 7.6g (sat 1.9g); PRO 17.3g; CARB 15g; FIB 3.6g; CHOL 38mg; IRON 1.1mg; SOD 495mg; CALC 64mg

JALAPEÑO SEEDS

The extreme heat normally associated with jalapeños actually comes from the seeds and ribs, not so much the flesh. A compound called capsaicin is most intensely concentrated in those areas, so seeding the pepper cuts down on the spicy warmth. As jalapeños ripen, they turn redder in color; dried and smoked, they are identified as chipotle peppers and are used in many Mexican-inspired dishes.

POBLANO-CHICKEN CHOWDER

POINTS value: 5   *pictured on page 143*

PREP: 22 minutes ■ **COOK:** 1 hour and 24 minutes
■ **OTHER:** 10 minutes

Some like it hot; some don't. For more heat, increase the amount of poblano chile to ¾ cup. For little or no heat, substitute an Anaheim or green bell pepper for the poblano.

1½ pounds skinless, bone-in chicken thighs
  3 cups water
  2 teaspoons olive oil
  ¾ cup chopped onion
  ½ cup diced seeded poblano chile
  1 pound small red potatoes, chopped
  2 cups fresh corn kernels
  ¾ teaspoon salt
  ¼ teaspoon black pepper
  ¼ cup chopped fresh cilantro

1. Combine chicken and 3 cups water in a Dutch oven; bring to a boil. Cover, reduce heat, and simmer 45 minutes. Remove chicken from pan; cool 10 minutes. Remove chicken from bones; shred chicken. Discard bones. Reserve broth in pan.
2. Heat oil in a large nonstick skillet over medium-high heat. Add onion and poblano chile; sauté 5 minutes or until tender. Add onion mixture to broth; stir in chicken, potato, and next 3 ingredients. Bring to a boil; cover, reduce heat, and simmer 20 minutes or until potato is tender. Stir in cilantro. **YIELD: 6 SERVINGS (SERVING SIZE: 1⅓ CUPS).**

PER SERVING: CAL 256 (31% from fat); FAT 8.9g (sat 2.2g); PRO 19.3g; CARB 26.5g; FIB 3.3g; CHOL 57mg; IRON 1.8mg; SOD 361mg; CALC 29mg

TURKEY CHILI

POINTS value: 2

PREP: 17 minutes ■ **COOK:** 1 hour and 12 minutes

Chili is ideal for casual entertaining. Round out the menu with trustworthy sides like coleslaw, corn bread or cheese bread, and brownies.

  1 tablespoon olive oil
1¾ cups chopped onion
  1 cup chopped celery
  ½ cup chopped carrot
  2 tablespoons chopped jalapeño pepper
  2 cups water, divided
  ½ pound lean ground turkey
  2 (14.5-ounce) cans diced tomatoes, undrained
  1 (27-ounce) can red kidney beans, rinsed and drained
  3 tablespoons chili powder
  1 bay leaf
  ½ teaspoon ground cinnamon
  ¼ teaspoon salt
  ¼ teaspoon freshly ground black pepper
  3 tablespoons chopped fresh parsley (optional)

1. Heat oil in a large Dutch oven over medium-high heat. Add onion and next 3 ingredients; cook 16 minutes or until tender, stirring frequently. While vegetables cook, add ½ cup water, 1 tablespoon at a time, to prevent vegetables from sticking to pan.
2. Add turkey to pan; cook 6 minutes or until turkey is browned, stirring to crumble. Add remaining 1½ cups water, tomatoes, and next 6 ingredients; bring to a boil. Cover, reduce heat, and simmer 45 minutes. Discard bay leaf. Ladle into bowls; sprinkle with parsley, if desired. **YIELD: 8 SERVINGS (SERVING SIZE: 1 CUP).**

PER SERVING: CAL 149 (23% from fat); FAT 3.8g (sat 0.8g); PRO 10.4g; CARB 19.9g; FIB 7g; CHOL 16mg; IRON 1.8mg; SOD 466mg; CALC 50mg

CURRIED CHICKEN AND VEGETABLE STEW

POINTS value: 6

PREP: 5 minutes ■ **COOK:** 35 minutes

Curry lightly seasons this stew with exotic flavor. It is perfect to brighten up a gray winter day.

- 2 teaspoons canola oil
- ½ cup chopped onion
- 1 pound skinless, boneless chicken thighs, cut into 1-inch chunks
- 3 tablespoons all-purpose flour
- 2 teaspoons red curry powder (such as McCormick)
- 3 cups fat-free, less-sodium chicken broth
- 1 (12-ounce) package fresh stir-fry vegetables, coarsely chopped
- 1 (16-ounce) can chickpeas (garbanzo beans), drained
- 5 tablespoons plain low-fat Greek yogurt (such as Fage)
- 2½ tablespoons chopped fresh mint

1. Heat oil in a large saucepan over medium heat. Add onion; sauté 5 minutes or until tender. Add chicken; cook 10 minutes, stirring frequently. Add flour and curry powder, stirring until blended. Stir in broth and stir-fry vegetables. Bring to a boil; cover, reduce heat, and simmer 10 minutes or until chicken is done and vegetables are tender.
2. Stir in chickpeas; cook 2 minutes or until thoroughly heated. Ladle into bowls; top with yogurt, and sprinkle with mint. YIELD: 5 SERVINGS (SERVING SIZE: 1⅓ CUPS SOUP, 1 TABLESPOON YOGURT, AND 1½ TEASPOONS MINT).

PER SERVING: CAL 285 (31% from fat); FAT 9.9g (sat 2.4g); PRO 24.8g; CARB 25.2g; FIB 5g; CHOL 60mg; IRON 2.4mg; SOD 594mg; CALC 68mg

SZECHUAN NOODLE SOUP

POINTS value: 3

PREP: 5 minutes ■ **COOK:** 18 minutes

China's Szechuan region is well known for its spicy-hot dishes, and this soup lives up to its name. Use less crushed red pepper if you prefer a milder soup.

- 1 (3.5-oz) package shiitake mushrooms
- 2 teaspoons peanut oil
- 2 garlic cloves, minced
- 2 teaspoons grated peeled fresh ginger
- ¼ teaspoon crushed red pepper
- 3 cups chicken broth
- 1 cup water
- 2 tablespoons low-sodium soy sauce
- 1 cup uncooked fine egg noodles
- 2 ounces deli ham, cut into julienne strips
- ¼ cup diagonally cut green onions
- 2 teaspoons dark sesame oil

1. Thinly slice shiitake mushroom caps, and finely chop mushroom stems. Heat oil in a large saucepan over medium-high heat. Add mushrooms, garlic, ginger, and red pepper; sauté 2 minutes. Add broth, 1 cup water, and soy sauce. Bring to a boil; stir in noodles. Reduce heat; simmer 5 minutes, stirring occasionally.
2. Stir in ham and green onions; simmer 3 minutes or until noodles are done. Stir in sesame oil. YIELD: 4 SERVINGS (SERVING SIZE: 1¼ CUPS).

PER SERVING: CAL 138 (40% from fat); FAT 6.1g (sat 1g); PRO 6.3g; CARB 14g; FIB 1.2g; CHOL 23mg; IRON 1.3mg; SOD 869mg; CALC 14mg

seasonal menus

Chunky Tuscan Minestrone, page 160;
Mini Corn Bread Muffins, page 161

FALL MENU
Total POINTS   value per serving: 11

Favorite Meat Loaf, page 157
Mashed Cauliflower, page 157
Balsamic Sautéed Spinach, page 158
Stuffed Baked Apples, page 158

WINTER VEGETARIAN MENU
Total POINTS   value per serving: 9

Chunky Tuscan Minestrone, page 160
Mixed Greens Salad with Classic Vinaigrette, page 160
Mini Corn Bread Muffins, page 161
Spiced Oat Cookies, page 161

SPRING MENU
Total POINTS   value per serving: 10

Sautéed Pork with Chimichurri, page 163
Roasted Asparagus with Goat Cheese, page 163
Strawberry Salad with Greens and Berry Vinaigrette, page 163
whole wheat dinner rolls

SUMMER MENU 1
Total POINTS   value per serving: 11

Grilled Tuna with Mango-Avocado Salsa, page 165
Black Bean Cakes, page 165
Lime Green Beans, page 166
Pineapple Skewers with Tropical Yogurt Sauce, page 166

SUMMER MENU 2
Total POINTS   value per serving: 10

Teriyaki Strip Steaks, page 168
Buttered Grilled Corn, page 168
Marinated Cherry Tomato Salad, page 169
Watermelon Sorbet, page 169

Fall Menu

Serves 6

Total **POINTS** value per serving: 11

Favorite Meat Loaf

Mashed Cauliflower

Balsamic Sautéed Spinach

Stuffed Baked Apples

GAME PLAN:

1. One day in advance:
- Prepare **Mashed Cauliflower;** cover and chill.

2. About 1½ hours before the meal:
- Prepare **Favorite Meat Loaf.**

3. While meat loaf bakes:
- Assemble **Stuffed Baked Apples.**

4. While meat loaf stands:
- Warm **Mashed Cauliflower.**
- Prepare **Balsamic Sautéed Spinach.**

5. Bake Stuffed Baked Apples during dinner.

FAVORITE MEAT LOAF

POINTS value: 5

PREP: 17 minutes ■ **COOK:** 1 hour
■ **OTHER:** 5 minutes

Using three different types of ground meat may seem unusual in a homey meat loaf, but in this highly rated recipe it accentuates the flavor and ensures moistness. To get the same juicy results we did, purchase ground turkey, which is both white and dark meat and is more moist than ground turkey breast.

⅓ cup chopped fresh parsley
2 large egg whites
3 tablespoons fat-free milk
½ teaspoon kosher salt
½ teaspoon black pepper
½ pound ground round
½ pound ground pork
½ pound ground turkey
¾ cup Italian-seasoned breadcrumbs
½ cup finely chopped onion
Cooking spray
6 tablespoons ketchup
1 tablespoon brown sugar

1. Preheat oven to 350°.
2. Combine first 5 ingredients in a medium bowl, stirring with a whisk. Add ground round and next 4 ingredients, stirring well. Spoon meat mixture into a 9 x 5–inch loaf pan coated with cooking spray. Pack meat mixture evenly into loaf pan using the back of a spoon.
3. Combine ketchup and brown sugar, stirring well. Spread evenly on top of meat mixture. Bake at 350° for 1 hour or until a thermometer registers 160°. Let meat loaf stand in pan 5 minutes before cutting into 6 even slices. YIELD: 6 SERVINGS (SERVING SIZE: 1 SLICE).

PER SERVING: CAL 248 (29% from fat); FAT 7.9g (sat 2.8g); PRO 26.8g; CARB 18.1g; FIB 1g; CHOL 70mg; IRON 2.3mg; SOD 643mg; CALC 43mg

MASHED CAULIFLOWER

POINTS value: 1

PREP: 6 minutes ■ **COOK:** 12 minutes

3 pounds cauliflower
¾ cup water
1 large garlic clove
¾ cup light garlic-and-herbs spreadable cheese (such as Alouette light)
½ teaspoon freshly ground black pepper
¼ teaspoon salt

1. Trim and cut cauliflower into florets. Discard remaining cauliflower. Combine cauliflower florets, ¾ cup water, and garlic in a large microwave-safe bowl. Cover with plastic wrap, and vent. Microwave at HIGH 12 minutes or until cauliflower is tender. Drain well.
2. Place cauliflower, garlic, cheese, pepper, and salt in a food processor; process until smooth. YIELD: 6 SERVINGS (SERVING SIZE: ½ CUP).

PER SERVING: CAL 73 (51% from fat); FAT 4.1g (sat 3g); PRO 3.8g; CARB 6g; FIB 2.3g; CHOL 20mg; IRON 0.4mg; SOD 244mg; CALC 41mg

BALSAMIC SAUTÉED SPINACH

POINTS value: 1

PREP: 2 minutes ■ **COOK:** 10 minutes

Rich in iron and vitamins A and C, this quick side dish is a flavorful addition to any meal.

> 2 teaspoons olive oil
> 1 garlic clove, minced
> 4 (6-ounce) packages fresh baby spinach
> 1 tablespoon balsamic vinegar

1. Heat oil in a large nonstick skillet over medium-high heat. Add garlic; sauté 30 seconds. Add 1 package spinach; cook 2 minutes or until spinach begins to wilt, stirring frequently. Add remaining spinach, 1 package at a time, stirring frequently until spinach wilts and mixture is hot. Stir in vinegar; serve immediately. **YIELD: 6 SERVINGS (SERVING SIZE: ½ CUP).**

PER SERVING: CAL 43 (42% from fat); FAT 2g (sat 0.3g); PRO 3.3g; CARB 4.7g; FIB 2.5g; CHOL 0mg; IRON 3.1mg; SOD 90mg; CALC 114mg

STUFFED BAKED APPLES

POINTS value: 4

PREP: 14 minutes ■ **COOK:** 1 hour
■ **OTHER:** 10 minutes

A crispy brown sugar–oat topping crowns these yummy warm apples.

> 6 small Fuji apples
> Cooking spray
> ⅓ cup dried fruit bits (such as Sun-Maid)
> ¼ cup packed brown sugar, divided
> 2 tablespoons chopped almonds
> 1 teaspoon ground cinnamon, divided
> 2 tablespoons unsalted butter, cubed and divided
> ¼ cup apple juice
> ¼ cup regular oats
> ¼ teaspoon almond extract
> ¼ cup plus 2 tablespoons vanilla fat-free yogurt

1. Preheat oven to 350°.
2. Core apples, starting at stem end, cutting to, but not through, opposite end. Enlarge opening to about 2 inches. Place apples in an 11 x 7–inch baking dish coated with cooking spray.
3. Combine fruit bits, 2 tablespoons brown sugar, almonds, and ½ teaspoon cinnamon; pack mixture evenly into cored apples. Top apples with 1 tablespoon cubed butter; drizzle with apple juice.
4. Combine remaining 2 tablespoons brown sugar, remaining 1 tablespoon butter, remaining ½ teaspoon cinnamon, oats, and almond extract in a small bowl, stirring until crumbly. Top each apple with crumb mixture, pressing to pack.
5. Bake at 350° for 1 hour or until tender but not mushy. Let stand 10 minutes. Serve apples with yogurt. **YIELD: 6 SERVINGS (SERVING SIZE: 1 STUFFED APPLE AND 1 TABLESPOON YOGURT).**

PER SERVING: CAL 207 (22% from fat); FAT 5.1g (sat 2.5g); PRO 1.9g; CARB 41.2g; FIB 6.2g; CHOL 10mg; IRON 1.2mg; SOD 18mg; CALC 50mg

Winter Vegetarian Menu

Serves 8

Total **POINTS** value per serving: 9

Chunky Tuscan Minestrone

Mixed Greens Salad with Classic Vinaigrette

Mini Corn Bread Muffins

Spiced Oat Cookies

GAME PLAN:

1. **One day in advance:**
   - Prepare **Spiced Oat Cookies;** store in an airtight container.
   - Prepare **Classic Vinaigrette;** store in an airtight container in refrigerator.

2. **About 1 hour before the meal:**
   - Prepare **Chunky Tuscan Minestrone.**

3. **While soup cooks:**
   - Prepare **Mini Corn Bread Muffins.**

4. **Toss Mixed Greens Salad with Classic Vinaigrette just before serving.**

CHUNKY TUSCAN MINESTRONE

POINTS value: 2   *pictured on page 155*

PREP: 15 minutes ■ COOK: 39 minutes

  1 tablespoon olive oil, divided
Cooking spray
  2 cups chopped onion
  2 cups chopped fennel bulb
  1 cup chopped celery
  1 cup chopped carrot
  2 garlic cloves, minced
3¾ cups organic vegetable broth (such as Swanson
    Certified Organic)
  1 (14.5-ounce) can diced tomatoes with basil, garlic,
    and oregano
  4 cups fresh baby spinach
  1 cup chopped zucchini
  1 (15.5-ounce) can cannellini beans, rinsed and drained
  ½ teaspoon salt
  ¼ teaspoon crushed red pepper

1. Heat 2 teaspoons oil in a large Dutch oven coated with cooking spray over medium-high heat. Add onion and next 4 ingredients. Sauté 9 minutes or until tender. Add vegetable broth and tomatoes; bring to a boil. Cover, reduce heat, and simmer 20 minutes.
2. While broth mixture simmers, heat remaining 1 teaspoon oil in a large nonstick skillet coated with cooking spray. Add spinach and zucchini; cook 4 minutes or until spinach wilts and zucchini is lightly browned, stirring frequently. Add spinach mixture, beans, salt, and crushed red pepper to vegetable broth mixture. Cook 5 minutes or until thoroughly heated. YIELD: 8 SERVINGS (SERVING SIZE: ABOUT 1¼ CUPS).

PER SERVING: CAL 111 (18% from fat); FAT 2.2g (sat 0.3g); PRO 4g; CARB 19.9g; FIB 4.5g; CHOL 0mg; IRON 2.2mg; SOD 777mg; CALC 99mg

MIXED GREENS SALAD WITH CLASSIC VINAIGRETTE

POINTS value: 2

PREP: 8 minutes

Radishes are a great source of fiber, vitamin C, and potassium. They add extra crispness to this garden salad.

  ¼ cup red wine vinegar
  2 tablespoons olive oil
  1 tablespoon minced shallots
  1 tablespoon Dijon mustard
  1 teaspoon sugar
  ⅛ teaspoon freshly ground black pepper
  8 cups packed mixed salad greens
1½ cups matchstick-cut carrots
  ¾ cup thinly sliced radishes (about 4 small)
  2 tablespoons chopped fresh basil

1. Combine red wine vinegar and next 5 ingredients, stirring with a whisk.
2. Combine salad greens, carrots, radishes, and basil in a large bowl. Pour vinaigrette over salad greens; toss to coat. YIELD: 8 SERVINGS (SERVING SIZE: ABOUT 1 CUP).

PER SERVING: CAL 81 (66% from fat); FAT 5.9g (sat 1.8g); PRO 2.6g; CARB 5.1g; FIB 1.5g; CHOL 6mg; IRON 0.5mg; SOD 99mg; CALC 71mg

MINI CORN BREAD MUFFINS

POINTS value: 2   *pictured on page 155*

PREP: 9 minutes ■ **COOK:** 11 minutes
■ **OTHER:** 1 minute

Use any leftover canned cream-style corn for the Mahimahi Tostadas found on page 67.

  ½ cup all-purpose flour
  ½ cup yellow cornmeal
  ½ teaspoon baking powder
  ½ teaspoon salt
  ¼ teaspoon baking soda
  ½ cup fat-free buttermilk
  ½ cup canned cream-style corn
  1 large egg, lightly beaten
  1 large egg white, lightly beaten
  2 teaspoons vegetable oil
  ⅓ cup reduced-fat shredded sharp Cheddar cheese
  1 tablespoon minced seeded jalapeño pepper (optional)
Cooking spray

1. Preheat oven to 425°.

2. Lightly spoon flour into a dry measuring cup; level with a knife. Combine flour and next 4 ingredients in a large bowl. Combine buttermilk and next 4 ingredients, stirring with a whisk. Add buttermilk mixture to flour mixture, stirring just until moist. Fold in cheese and, if desired, jalapeño.

3. Spoon batter into 24 miniature muffin cups coated with cooking spray. Bake at 425° for 11 to 13 minutes or until muffins spring back when touched lightly in center. Let muffins cool in pan 1 minute before removing to wire racks to cool completely. **YIELD: 2 DOZEN (SERVING SIZE: 2 MUFFINS).**

PER SERVING: CAL 79 (25% from fat); FAT 2.2g (sat 0.7g); PRO 3.2g; CARB 12g; FIB 0.5g; CHOL 20mg; IRON 0.6mg; SOD 193mg; CALC 51mg

SPICED OAT COOKIES

POINTS value: 3

PREP: 13 minutes ■ **COOK:** 15 minutes per batch

These cookies remind us of old-fashioned tea cakes with a hint of sweet spices. They're soft and melt in your mouth.

  ½ cup unsalted butter, softened
  1 cup sugar
  1 large egg, lightly beaten
  1 large egg white
  2 tablespoons fat-free milk
  1 teaspoon vanilla extract
  2 cups all-purpose flour
  ¼ cup regular oats
  1½ teaspoons pumpkin pie spice
  1 teaspoon baking powder
  ½ teaspoon baking soda
  ¼ teaspoon salt

1. Preheat oven to 350°.

2. Place butter in a large bowl; beat with a mixer at medium speed until fluffy. Add sugar, beating until blended. Add egg and next 3 ingredients, beating until well blended.

3. Lightly spoon flour into dry measuring cups; level with a knife. Combine flour and next 5 ingredients in a bowl.

4. Gradually add flour mixture to sugar mixture, stirring just until combined.

5. Drop dough by 2 tablespoonfuls 2 inches apart onto baking sheets.

6. Bake at 350° for 15 to 17 minutes or until lightly browned. Remove from pans; cool completely on wire racks. **YIELD: 22 SERVINGS (SERVING SIZE: 1 COOKIE).**

PER SERVING: CAL 122 (34% from fat); FAT 4.6g (sat 2.7g); PRO 1.9g; CARB 18.7g; FIB 0.4g; CHOL 21mg; IRON 0.7mg; SOD 85mg; CALC 20mg

Spring Menu

Serves 4

Total **POINTS** value per serving: 10

Sautéed Pork with Chimichurri

Roasted Asparagus with Goat Cheese

Strawberry Salad with Greens and Berry Vinaigrette

whole wheat dinner rolls

GAME PLAN:

1. **One day in advance:**
   - Prepare **Berry Vinaigrette;** store in an airtight container in refrigerator.
   - Prepare **Chimichurri;** store in an airtight container in refrigerator.

2. **About 45 minutes before the meal:**
   - Prepare **Roasted Asparagus with Goat Cheese.**
   - Prepare Steps Two and Three of **Sautéed Pork with Chimichurri.**

3. **Toss Strawberry Salad with Greens and Berry Vinaigrette just before serving.**

SAUTÉED PORK WITH CHIMICHURRI

POINTS value: 5

PREP: 5 minutes ■ **COOK:** 6 minutes

Grilled pork chops are topped with a pungent emerald-colored sauce. Considered the barbecue sauce of Argentina, chimichurri is built on olive oil, parsley, vinegar, and garlic. It's a cross between a vinaigrette and pesto and is the perfect accompaniment to simply seasoned meats.

- 1¼ cups fresh flat-leaf parsley leaves
- ¼ cup white balsamic vinegar
- 4 teaspoons olive oil, divided
- 3 garlic cloves
- ¼ teaspoon crushed red pepper
- 4 (4-ounce) boneless center-cut loin pork chops
- 1 teaspoon lemon pepper
- ⅛ teaspoon salt
- Cooking spray

1. Combine parsley, vinegar, 2 teaspoons olive oil, garlic, and red pepper in a food processor; process until minced. Set chimichurri aside.
2. Sprinkle pork chops with lemon pepper and salt. Heat remaining 2 teaspoons oil in a large nonstick skillet coated with cooking spray over medium-high heat. Add pork chops to pan; cook 3 to 4 minutes on each side or until desired degree of doneness.
3. Serve pork chops with chimichurri. YIELD: 4 SERVINGS (SERVING SIZE: 1 PORK CHOP AND 1½ TABLESPOONS CHIMICHURRI).

PER SERVING: CAL 230 (44% from fat); FAT 11.2g (sat 3g); PRO 24.6g; CARB 7g; FIB 0.7g; CHOL 65mg; IRON 1.9mg; SOD 131mg; CALC 55mg

ROASTED ASPARAGUS WITH GOAT CHEESE

POINTS value: 1

PREP: 2 minutes ■ **COOK:** 10 minutes

This dish is great because it serves up so much flavor and is unbelievably fast and easy.

- 1 pound asparagus, trimmed
- Olive oil–flavored cooking spray
- ⅛ teaspoon salt
- ⅛ teaspoon freshly ground black pepper
- ¼ cup (1 ounce) crumbled goat cheese

1. Preheat oven to 450°.
2. Spread asparagus on a large rimmed baking sheet coated with cooking spray. Coat asparagus with cooking spray. Sprinkle evenly with salt and pepper.
3. Bake asparagus at 450° for 10 to 12 minutes or until crisp-tender. Sprinkle with goat cheese and serve immediately. YIELD: 4 SERVINGS (SERVING SIZE: ¼ OF ASPARAGUS AND 1 TABLESPOON GOAT CHEESE).

PER SERVING: CAL 43 (48% from fat); FAT 2.3g (sat 1.5g); PRO 3.1g; CARB 3.3g; FIB 1.5g; CHOL 6mg; IRON 0.4mg; SOD 109mg; CALC 37mg

STRAWBERRY SALAD WITH GREENS AND BERRY VINAIGRETTE

POINTS value: 3

PREP: 12 minutes ■ **COOK:** 2 minutes

Very little oil is needed in the homemade vinaigrette that dresses the popular mix of greens, fruit, and almonds. For the best results, select the freshest fruit available. Raspberries, blackberries, or seedless grapes are delicious replacements for strawberries and blueberries.

- ¼ cup raspberry vinegar
- 1 tablespoon honey
- 2 teaspoons olive oil
- ¼ teaspoon freshly ground black pepper
- ⅛ teaspoon salt
- 1 small garlic clove, minced
- 4 cups mixed baby greens
- 1 cup sliced strawberries
- ⅓ cup blueberries
- 2 tablespoons sliced almonds, toasted

1. Combine raspberry vinegar and next 5 ingredients, stirring with a whisk.
2. Combine mixed baby greens, strawberries, blueberries, and almonds in a large bowl. Pour Berry Vinaigrette over greens; toss to coat. YIELD: 4 SERVINGS (SERVING SIZE: ABOUT 1¼ CUPS).

PER SERVING: CAL 134 (43% from fat); FAT 6.4g (sat 1.7g); PRO 3.4g; CARB 17.8g; FIB 2.6g; CHOL 6mg; IRON 0.8mg; SOD 123mg; CALC 81mg

Summer Menu 1

Serves 4

Total **POINTS** value per serving: 11

Grilled Tuna with Mango-Avocado Salsa

Black Bean Cakes

Lime Green Beans

Pineapple Skewers with Tropical Yogurt Sauce

GAME PLAN:

1. **One day in advance:**
   - Prepare **Mango-Avocado Salsa;** store in an airtight container in refrigerator.
   - Prepare **Black Bean Cakes** through Step Two; cover and store in an airtight container in refrigerator.

2. **About 1 hour before the meal:**
   - Prepare grill.
   - Prepare **Lime Green Beans** through Step One; set aside.
   - Combine **Tropical Yogurt Sauce** and assemble **Pineapple Skewers;** cover and set aside.

3. **About 30 minutes before the meal:**
   - Prepare Steps Three and Four of **Black Bean Cakes;** keep warm.
   - Prepare Step Two of **Lime Green Beans;** keep warm.

4. **Grill tuna steaks.**

5. **Grill Pineapple Skewers just before serving.**

GRILLED TUNA WITH MANGO-AVOCADO SALSA

POINTS value: 7

PREP: 11 minutes ■ **COOK:** 6 minutes

Usher in the fresh flavors of summer with a dish that plates grilled fresh tuna steaks with a bright, fruity salsa. The jalapeño pepper gives the salsa a nice kick.

- 1 large mango, peeled and chopped
- 1 avocado, peeled and chopped
- 1 jalapeño pepper, seeded and minced
- ½ cup finely chopped red onion
- 2 tablespoons chopped fresh cilantro
- 4 tablespoons fresh lime juice, divided
- 3 teaspoons olive oil, divided
- ¼ teaspoon salt, divided
- 4 (6-ounce) tuna steaks
- Cooking spray

1. Prepare grill.
2. Combine mango, avocado, jalapeño pepper, red onion, cilantro, 2 tablespoons lime juice, 1 teaspoon oil, and ⅛ teaspoon salt in a medium bowl; cover surface of mixture with plastic wrap. Chill.
3. Sprinkle fish with remaining ⅛ teaspoon salt and drizzle with remaining 2 tablespoons lime juice and remaining 2 teaspoons oil. Place fish on grill rack coated with cooking spray; grill 3 to 4 minutes on each side or until fish flakes easily when tested with a fork. Serve with Mango-Avocado Salsa. YIELD: 4 SERVINGS (SERVING SIZE: 1 STEAK AND ABOUT ⅓ CUP SALSA).

PER SERVING: CAL 341 (34% from fat); FAT 13g (sat 2.2g); PRO 41.4g; CARB 15.9g; FIB 4g; CHOL 77mg; IRON 1.9mg; SOD 216mg; CALC 45mg

BLACK BEAN CAKES

POINTS value: 2

PREP: 5 minutes ■ **COOK:** 15 minutes
■ **OTHER:** 1 hour

- Cooking spray
- ⅓ cup chopped red bell pepper
- ¼ cup chopped onion
- 2 garlic cloves, minced
- 2 (15-ounce) cans black beans, rinsed and drained
- 2 large egg whites, lightly beaten
- ⅓ cup dry breadcrumbs
- 1 teaspoon ground cumin
- ½ teaspoon crushed red pepper
- ½ teaspoon salt
- 2 tablespoons dry breadcrumbs
- 2 teaspoons olive oil

1. Heat a large nonstick skillet over medium-high heat. Coat pan with cooking spray. Add bell pepper, onion, and garlic; sauté 4 minutes. Cool slightly.
2. Place black beans in a large bowl; partially mash beans with a fork. Add vegetable mixture, egg whites, and next 4 ingredients, stirring until combined. Divide mixture into 8 equal portions, shaping each into a ½-inch-thick patty. Cover and chill 1 hour.
3. Place remaining 2 tablespoons breadcrumbs in a shallow dish. Dredge patties in breadcrumbs.
4. Heat oil in a large nonstick skillet over medium heat. Add patties and cook 3 minutes on each side or until browned. YIELD: 4 SERVINGS (SERVING SIZE: 2 BLACK BEAN CAKES).

PER SERVING: CAL 204 (17% from fat); FAT 3.8g (sat 0.6g); PRO 12g; CARB 34.4g; FIB 9g; CHOL 0mg; IRON 2.4mg; SOD 724mg; CALC 56mg

LIME GREEN BEANS

POINTS value: 0

PREP: 4 minutes ■ **COOK:** 10 minutes

Brighten microwave-ready green beans with the flavor
of fresh lime.

    1 (12-ounce) package trimmed green beans
    Cooking spray
    1 shallot, thinly sliced
    1 teaspoon grated fresh lime rind
    2 tablespoons fresh lime juice
    ⅛ teaspoon salt
    ⅛ teaspoon freshly ground black pepper

1. Cook green beans in microwave according to package directions.
2. Heat a large nonstick skillet over medium–high heat.
Coat pan with cooking spray. Add shallot; cook 2 minutes or until tender, stirring frequently. Add green
beans, lime rind, lime juice, salt, and pepper; toss gently to coat. Cook 2 minutes or until thoroughly
heated. **YIELD: 4 SERVINGS (SERVING SIZE: ¾ CUP).**

PER SERVING: CAL 33 (4% from fat); FAT 0.1g (sat 0g); PRO 1.7g;
CARB 8.1g; FIB 3.2g; CHOL 0mg; IRON 1mg; SOD 78mg; CALC 37mg

PINEAPPLE SKEWERS WITH TROPICAL YOGURT SAUCE

POINTS value: 2

PREP: 7 minutes ■ **COOK:** 8 minutes

If you use wooden skewers, be sure to soak them in water
30 minutes before grilling so they don't burn.

    1 (6-ounce) carton vanilla fat-free yogurt
    1 teaspoon grated fresh lime rind
    3 tablespoons fresh lime juice, divided
    1 cored fresh pineapple, cut into chunks
    Cooking spray
    2 tablespoons flaked sweetened coconut, toasted

1. Prepare grill.
2. Combine yogurt, lime rind, and 1 tablespoon lime
juice in a small bowl; cover and chill.
3. Thread pineapple onto 8 (6-inch) skewers, and place
in a shallow dish; drizzle with remaining 2 tablespoons
lime juice.
4. Place skewers on grill rack coated with cooking
spray. Grill 6 to 8 minutes or until browned, turning
occasionally. Sprinkle pineapple with coconut, and
serve with yogurt mixture. **YIELD: 4 SERVINGS (SERVING
SIZE: 2 SKEWERS AND ABOUT 2 TABLESPOONS SAUCE).**

PER SERVING: CAL 111 (8% from fat); FAT 1g (sat 0.7g); PRO 3g;
CARB 25.2g; FIB 2g; CHOL 1mg; IRON 0.5mg; SOD 31mg; CALC 96mg

Summer Menu 2

Serves 4

Total **POINTS** value per serving: 10

Teriyaki Strip Steaks

Buttered Grilled Corn

Marinated Cherry Tomato Salad

Watermelon Sorbet

GAME PLAN:

1. **One day in advance:**
   - Prepare **Watermelon Sorbet;** store in an airtight container in freezer.

2. **About 2 hours before the meal:**
   - Prepare **Marinated Cherry Tomato Salad** through Step One.

3. **About 1 hour before the meal:**
   - Prepare grill.
   - Marinate steaks.

4. **While steaks marinate:**
   - Prepare Step Two of both **Buttered Grilled Corn** and **Marinated Cherry Tomato Salad.**

5. **Prepare Step Three of both Teriyaki Strip Steaks and Buttered Grilled Corn.**

TERIYAKI STRIP STEAKS

POINTS value: 4

PREP: 8 minutes ■ **COOK:** 10 minutes
■ **OTHER:** 30 minutes

No need to add extra salt to the steaks before grilling. The marinade has a double dose of garlic that provides plenty of flavor.

- ¼ cup low-sodium soy sauce
- 2 tablespoons honey
- 1 tablespoon minced peeled fresh ginger
- 1 garlic clove, pressed
- ½ teaspoon garlic powder
- ½ teaspoon crushed red pepper
- ¼ teaspoon freshly ground black pepper
- 2 (8-ounce) strip steaks, trimmed
- Cooking spray

1. Prepare grill.
2. Combine first 7 ingredients in a large zip-top plastic bag. Add steaks, and seal bag. Marinate in refrigerator 30 minutes.
3. Remove steaks from bag, reserving marinade. Place steaks on grill rack coated with cooking spray; brush with all of reserved marinade. Grill 5 minutes on each side or until desired degree of doneness. Slice steak into thin slices. **YIELD: 4 SERVINGS (SERVING SIZE: 3 OUNCES).**

PER SERVING: CAL 196 (24% from fat); FAT 5.2g (sat 2g); PRO 25.5g; CARB 11.1g; FIB 0.3g; CHOL 67mg; IRON 2.4mg; SOD 601mg; CALC 12mg

BUTTERED GRILLED CORN

POINTS value: 3

PREP: 6 minutes ■ **COOK:** 9 minutes

Grilling and topping with lime-flavored butter elevates common corn on the cob to a summertime treat.

- 2 tablespoons butter, melted
- 2 tablespoons fresh lime juice
- ½ teaspoon salt
- ½ teaspoon pepper
- 4 medium ears shucked corn
- Cooking spray

1. Prepare grill.
2. Combine first 4 ingredients in a small bowl. Brush corn with butter mixture.
3. Place corn on grill rack coated with cooking spray. Grill 9 minutes or until slightly charred, turning occasionally. **YIELD: 4 SERVINGS (SERVING SIZE: 1 EAR OF CORN).**

PER SERVING: CAL 136 (44% from fat); FAT 6.7g (sat 3.8g); PRO 2.7g; CARB 20.2g; FIB 2.2g; CHOL 15mg; IRON 0.5mg; SOD 344mg; CALC 5mg

MARINATED CHERRY TOMATO SALAD

POINTS value: 1

PREP: 12 minutes

- ⅓ cup cider vinegar
- 2 teaspoons olive oil
- 1 garlic clove, minced
- ¼ teaspoon salt
- ¼ teaspoon Italian seasoning
- ¼ teaspoon freshly ground black pepper
- 1 thinly sliced English cucumber
- 3 cups halved cherry tomatoes
- 2 tablespoons chopped red onion
- ¼ cup diced peeled avocado
- 2 tablespoons chopped fresh basil

1. Combine cider vinegar and next 5 ingredients in a large bowl, stirring with a whisk. Add cucumber, tomatoes, and red onion; toss gently to coat.

2. Stir in avocado and basil; chill up to 30 minutes.

YIELD: 4 SERVINGS (SERVING SIZE: 1½ CUPS).

PER SERVING: CAL 76 (53% from fat); FAT 4.5g (sat 0.7g); PRO 1.6g; CARB 8.2g; FIB 2.3g; CHOL 0mg; IRON 0.9mg; SOD 159mg; CALC 20mg

WATERMELON SORBET

POINTS value: 2

PREP: 3 minutes ■ COOK: 8 minutes
■ OTHER: 1 hour and 30 minutes

- ¾ cup sugar
- ¾ cup water
- 3 cups cubed seeded watermelon
- ½ cup white grape juice
- ¼ cup fresh lemon juice

1. Combine sugar and water in a saucepan; bring to a boil. Reduce heat; simmer 6 minutes, stirring constantly until sugar dissolves. Cool sugar syrup completely.

2. Place watermelon in a food processor, and process until smooth. Strain watermelon mixture through a sieve into a bowl. Discard solids.

3. Combine cooled sugar syrup, watermelon, and remaining ingredients. Pour mixture into the freezer can of an ice-cream freezer; freeze according to manufacturer's instructions. Serve immediately, or cover and place in freezer until ready to serve. YIELD: 10 SERVINGS (SERVING SIZE: ½ CUP).

PER SERVING: CAL 79 (0% from fat); FAT 0g (sat 0g); PRO 0.2g; CARB 21.4g; FIB 0.3g; CHOL 0mg; IRON 0.1mg; SOD 3mg; CALC 4mg

One day's menu provides at least two servings of dairy and at least five servings of fruits and/or vegetables.

	MONDAY	TUESDAY	WEDNESDAY	THURSDAY
BREAKFAST	**low-fat granola,** ½ cup **fat-free milk,** 1 cup	**Weight Watchers bagel,** 1 toasted **peanut butter,** 1 tablespoon **banana,** 1 small **fat-free milk,** 1 cup	**Orange Biscuits, page 29,** 1 serving **honey,** 1 tablespoon **fat-free milk,** 1 cup	**Weight Watchers bagel,** 1 toasted **light cream cheese,** 2 tablespoons **peach fat-free yogurt,** 1 (6-ounce) carton
LUNCH	**Roast Beef and Cheddar Bagel Melt** (Split and lightly toast a Weight Watchers bagel. Spread 1 teaspoon each light mayonnaise and Dijon mustard over each cut side of bagel. Top 1 bagel half with 2 ounces lean deli roast beef and 1 ounce reduced-fat Cheddar cheese. Broil until melted; top with tomato slice, lettuce, and remaining toasted bagel half - **POINTS value: 7.)** **plum,** 1 medium **mixture of raw vegetables** (celery, carrots, broccoli florets), 1 cup **light ranch dressing,** 2 tablespoons	**grilled chicken sandwich,** 1 fast-food without mayonnaise **lettuce leaf and tomato slice,** 1 each **mixed fruit salad,** 1 cup	**Wheat Berry, Spinach, and Sweet Potato Salad, page 107,** 1 serving **blueberries,** 1 cup	**Balsamic Tuna Salad** (Combine 4 ounces chunk light tuna, ¼ cup chopped tomato, 2 tablespoons each light balsamic vinaigrette and chopped fresh basil, and a dash each of salt and pepper; mix well. Gently spoon over 2 large lettuce leaves - **POINTS value: 3.)** **whole wheat crackers,** 6 **raspberries,** 1 cup
DINNER	**Turkey Cutlets with Lemon-Caper Sauce, page 97,** 1 serving **brown rice,** 1 cup **steamed carrots,** 1 cup	**Lasagna-Stuffed Peppers, page 80,** 1 serving **fat-free milk,** 1 cup	**grilled or baked salmon,** 6 ounces cooked **Parmesan couscous,** ½ cup **Raspberry-Walnut Salad** (Top 2 cups mixed salad greens with ¼ cup raspberries, 2 tablespoons each feta cheese and light balsamic dressing, and 1 tablespoon chopped walnuts; toss gently - **POINTS value: 3.)**	**Wild Rice–Stuffed Chicken Breasts, page 95,** 1 serving **steamed green beans,** 1 cup **watermelon,** 1 cup
SNACK	**amaretto cheesecake fat-free yogurt,** 1 (6-ounce) carton	**Blueberry-Pomegranate Sorbet, page 48,** 2 servings	**strawberry fat-free yogurt,** 1 (6-ounce) carton **grapes,** 1 cup	**Banana Cream Pie, page 44,** 1 serving **fat-free milk,** 1 cup
POINTS VALUE	**POINTS** value for the day: 27	**POINTS** value for the day: 26	**POINTS** value for the day: 28	**POINTS** value for the day: 24

	FRIDAY	SATURDAY	SUNDAY
BREAKFAST	**Granola Breakfast Parfait** (Spoon half of 1 [6-ounce] carton mixed berry fat-free yogurt into a parfait glass; top with ½ cup blueberries and ¼ cup low-fat granola. Repeat layers - **POINTS** value: 5.)	**Weight Watchers bagel,** 1 toasted **light cream cheese,** 2 tablespoons **fat-free milk,** 1 cup **orange sections,** 1 cup	**low-fat granola,** ½ cup **fat-free milk,** 1 cup **raspberries,** 1 cup
LUNCH	**sweet and sour chicken,** 1 light frozen entrée **baby carrots,** 10 **plum,** 1 medium	**Ham and Vegetable Frittata** (Saute ¼ cup each onion and mushrooms in 1 teaspoon olive oil in a small skillet. Whisk together 1 large egg, 3 large egg whites, and a dash each of salt and pepper; stir in 1 ounce chopped lean deli ham and 3 tablespoons reduced-fat Cheddar cheese. Pour egg mixture into pan; cook until set - **POINTS** value: 7.) **mixed salad greens,** 2 cups **light balsamic vinaigrette,** 2 tablespoons	**canned tomato soup,** 1 cup **Cheese Bagel** (Place 1 slice reduced-fat Cheddar cheese on each cut side of a Weight Watchers bagel; toast until melted - **POINTS** value: 4.) **black cherry fat-free yogurt,** 1 (6-ounce) carton
DINNER	**pork tenderloin,** 4 ounces cooked **Roasted Sweet Potatoes** (Cut a small sweet potato into 6 wedges. Toss with 1 teaspoon olive oil, ¼ teaspoon finely chopped fresh rosemary, and ⅛ teaspoon salt. Roast potato at 450° for 30 minutes or until crisp, stirring occasionally - **POINTS** value: 3.) **steamed sugar snap peas,** 1 cup	**Grilled Barbecue Shrimp, page 73,** 1 serving **whole wheat French bread,** 1 ounce **Sweet and Spicy Slaw, page 102,** 1 serving	**Marsala Beef Tenderloin Steaks with Mushrooms, page 87,** 1 serving **mashed potatoes,** ½ cup **Blue Cheese Spinach Salad** (Combine 2 cups baby spinach leaves, 6 cherry tomatoes, and 1 tablespoon each of chopped walnuts and blue cheese. Top with 2 tablespoons light raspberry-walnut vinaigrette - **POINTS** value: 3.)
SNACK	**low-fat graham crackers,** 2 full sheets **peanut butter,** 1 tablespoon **fat-free milk,** 1 cup	**black cherry fat-free yogurt,** 1 (6-ounce) carton **grapes,** 1 cup **almonds,** ¼ cup	**Roasted Red Pepper and Sun-Dried Tomato Dip, page 18,** 2 servings **carrot and celery sticks,** 1 cup
POINTS VALUE	**POINTS** value for the day: 24	**POINTS** value for the day: 27	**POINTS** value for the day: 25

WEEK 1

One day's menu provides at least two servings of dairy and at least five servings of fruits and/or vegetables.

	MONDAY	TUESDAY	WEDNESDAY	THURSDAY
BREAKFAST	**Peach-Maple Waffles** (Top 2 toasted low-fat multigrain waffles with ½ cup diced peaches; drizzle with 2 tablespoons light maple syrup - **POINTS** value: 5.) **fat-free milk**, 1 cup	**wheat bran flakes cereal with raisins**, 1 cup **fat-free milk**, 1 cup **cantaloupe**, 1 cup	**whole wheat English muffin**, 1 **fruit spread**, 2 tablespoons **light butter**, 2 teaspoons **raspberry fat-free yogurt**, 1 (6-ounce) carton	**wheat bran flakes cereal with raisins**, 1 cup **fat-free milk**, 1 cup **peach**, 1 medium
LUNCH	**deluxe pizza**, 1 light frozen entrée **pineapple chunks**, 1 cup **fat-free milk**, 1 cup **carrot and celery sticks**, 1 cup	**Greek Steak Salad, page 109**, 1 serving **warm pita bread**, ½ of a round **plum**, 1 medium	**Spicy Black Bean Soup** (Warm 1 cup canned black bean soup; gently stir in 3 tablespoons salsa and a dash of red pepper. Top with 2 tablespoons each reduced-fat shredded Cheddar cheese and fat-free sour cream - **POINTS** value: 4.) **whole wheat French bread**, 1 ounce **grapes**, 1 cup **deli coleslaw**, ½ cup	**Chicken, Cheddar, and Broccoli Spud** (Cut a large baked potato [7 ounces cooked] in half; top with 2 ounces shredded cooked skinless chicken breast, 1 cup steamed broccoli florets, and ⅓ cup reduced-fat sharp Cheddar cheese. Dollop with 2 tablespoons fat-free sour cream - **POINTS** value: 7.) **strawberry fat-free yogurt**, 1 (6-ounce) carton
DINNER	**Fresh Lemon and Basil Pork Chops, page 90**, 1 serving **wild rice**, ½ cup **mixed salad greens**, 2 cups **light balsamic vinaigrette**, 2 tablespoons	**rotisserie chicken breast**, 4 ounces breast meat with skin removed **roasted garlic rice pilaf**, ½ cup **Marinated Green Bean and Red Onion Salad, page 104**, 1 serving	**Grouper with Pan-Roasted Tomatoes, page 66**, 1 serving **Pesto Fettuccine** (Toss 1 cup hot cooked whole wheat fettuccine with 1 tablespoon refrigerated pesto and ⅛ teaspoon salt - **POINTS** value: 5.) **steamed asparagus**, 12 spears	**Steak Fajitas with Fresh Pico de Gallo, page 87**, 1 serving **pineapple chunks**, 1 cup
SNACK	**Brownie Sundae** (Heat 1 Weight Watchers brownie in the microwave for 10 seconds; place in bowl, and top with ½ cup vanilla low-fat, no sugar added ice cream. Drizzle with 1 tablespoon chocolate syrup - **POINTS** value: 5.)	**PB and Honey Dip, page 18**, 1 serving **apple**, 1 medium, cut into wedges **fat-free milk**, 1 cup	**mixed berry fat-free yogurt**, 1 (6-ounce) carton **blueberries**, 1 cup	**pretzels**, 15 small twists **part-skim mozzarella string cheese**, 1 **orange sections**, 1 cup
POINTS VALUE	**POINTS** value for the day: 28	**POINTS** value for the day: 24	**POINTS** value for the day: 28	**POINTS** value for the day: 25

	FRIDAY	SATURDAY	SUNDAY	
BREAKFAST	low-fat multigrain waffles, 2 frozen low-calorie syrup, 2 tablespoons fat-free milk, 1 cup blueberries, 1 cup	egg, 1 hard-cooked large whole wheat English muffin, 1 light butter, 2 teaspoons	whole wheat English muffin, 1 fruit spread, 2 tablespoons turkey bacon, 3 slices cantaloupe, 1 cup	
LUNCH	chicken carbonara, 1 light frozen entrée tomato slices, 2 large apple, 1 medium fat-free milk, 1 cup	Tomato-Basil Salad (Top 2 cups torn romaine lettuce leaves with 2 [1-ounce] slices fresh mozzarella cheese and 3 large tomato slices. Sprinkle with 2 tablespoons chopped fresh basil; drizzle with 2 tablespoons light balsamic vinaigrette - *POINTS* value: 5.) warm pita bread, ½ round	Roasted Chicken Sandwich (Combine 2 teaspoons fat-free mayonnaise with 1 tablespoon refrigerated pesto; spread over 1 slice reduced-calorie bread. Top with 3 ounces skinless rotisserie chicken breast, 1 large lettuce leaf, 1 large tomato slice, and additional bread slice - *POINTS* value: 6.) cucumber slices, 1 cup vanilla fat-free yogurt, 1 (6-ounce) carton	
DINNER	grilled vegetable burger, 1 patty lite wheat hamburger bun, 1 tomato slice and lettuce leaf, 1 each baked potato chips, 11	Chicken-Vegetable Stir-Fry, page 96, 1 serving fat-free milk, 1 cup	steamed shrimp, 6 ounces cooked and shelled steamed small red potatoes, 5 ounces light butter, 2 teaspoons Coleslaw with Feta, page 101, 1 serving	
SNACK	hummus, ¼ cup baby carrots, 1 cup vanilla fat-free pudding cup, 1	Weight Watchers brownie, 1 fat-free milk, 1 cup	apple, 1 medium peanut butter, 1 tablespoon fat-free milk, 1 cup	
POINTS VALUE	*POINTS* value for the day: 24	*POINTS* value for the day: 25	*POINTS* value for the day: 27	

WEEK 2

One day's menu provides at least two servings of dairy and at least five servings of fruits and/or vegetables.

	MONDAY	TUESDAY	WEDNESDAY	THURSDAY
BREAKFAST	**Weight Watchers low-fat banana-nut muffin,** 1 **light orange juice,** 1 cup	**Strawberry-Orange Breakfast Smoothie** (Combine 1 cup strawberries, 1 cup light orange juice, 1 [6-ounce] carton vanilla fat-free yogurt, and 1 cup ice cubes in a blender; process until smooth - **POINTS** value: 3.)	**whole-grain puffed cereal,** 1 cup **fat-free milk,** 1 cup **strawberries,** 1 cup sliced **light orange juice,** 1 cup	**reduced-calorie toast,** 2 slices **peanut butter,** 1 tablespoon **banana,** 1 small
LUNCH	**Ham and Cheddar Wrap** (Combine 2 teaspoons fat-free mayonnaise with 1 teaspoon spicy mustard; spread over 1 [8-inch] low-fat whole wheat tortilla. Top with 2 ounces lean deli ham, ¾ cup lettuce, and ¼ cup each reduced-fat shredded Cheddar cheese and diced tomato; roll up tightly - **POINTS** value: 6.) **baked potato chips,** 11 **baby carrots,** 10 **fat-free milk,** 1 cup	**Panzanella,** page 101, 1 serving **grapes,** 1 cup **fat-free milk,** 1 cup	**New England clam chowder,** 1 cup canned, made with fat-free milk **saltine crackers,** 6 **mixed salad greens,** 2 cups **light balsamic vinaigrette,** 2 tablespoons	**hamburger,** 1 small fast-food **lettuce leaf and tomato slice,** 1 each **pear,** 1 medium **fat-free milk,** 1 cup
DINNER	**Seared Scallops with Soy-Ginger Sauce,** page 72, 1 serving **brown rice,** ½ cup **Roasted Asparagus** (Coat 12 asparagus spears with olive oil–flavored cooking spray; toss with ¼ teaspoon garlic salt. Place on a baking sheets, and bake at 450° for 8 minutes - **POINTS** value: 0.)	**grilled or broiled flank steak,** 4 ounces trimmed and cooked **baked sweet potato,** 1 medium (4 ounces cooked) **light butter,** 2 teaspoons **steamed broccoli,** 1 cup	**Spinach Quesadillas with Mango-Avocado Salsa,** page 78, 1 serving **grapefruit sections,** 1 cup **fat-free milk,** 1 cup	**Roasted Grouper with Herbed Breadcrumbs,** page 66, 1 serving **whole wheat couscous,** 1 cup **sautéed summer squash and zucchini,** 1 cup
SNACK	**Coconut-Oat Cookies,** page 42, 1 serving **fat-free milk,** 1 cup	**baked tortilla chips,** 18 **guacamole,** ¼ cup **salsa,** ¼ cup	**Chocolate Chip Ice-Cream Sandwich** (Unwrap 2 Weight Watchers chocolate chip cookies; place ⅓ cup vanilla low-fat, no sugar added ice cream in the center of bottom side of 1 cookie. Top with remaining cookie; press gently together. Wrap in plastic wrap and freeze until ready to eat - **POINTS** value: 4.)	**Soft Pretzels,** page 34, 1 serving **strawberry fat-free yogurt,** 1 (6-ounce) carton
POINTS VALUE	**POINTS** value for the day: 25	**POINTS** value for the day: 23	**POINTS** value for the day: 25	**POINTS** value for the day: 25

	FRIDAY	SATURDAY	SUNDAY
BREAKFAST	Weight Watchers low-fat **banana-nut muffin,** 1 **grapefruit sections,** 1 cup **fat-free milk,** 1 cup	**Garden Omelet with Goat Cheese, page 83,** 1 serving **light orange juice,** 1 cup	whole-grain puffed cereal, 1 cup **fat-free milk,** 1 cup **banana,** 1 small
LUNCH	**Greek Chicken Wrap** (Toss together 2 cups salad greens with 2 tablespoons light balsamic vinaigrette; spoon onto 1 [8-inch] low-fat whole wheat tortilla. Top with 2 ounces cooked chicken breast, ¼ cup chopped tomato, and 2 tablespoons feta cheese; roll up to serve - ***POINTS*** value: 6.) **baked potato chips,** 11 **strawberries,** 1 cup	**four-cheese pizza,** 1 light frozen entrée **mixed salad greens,** 2 cups **light ranch dressing,** 2 tablespoons **fat-free milk,** 1 cup	**cheese tortellini,** 1 cup refrigerated **low-fat pasta sauce,** ½ cup **parmesan cheese,** 2 tablespoons grated **watermelon,** 1 cup
DINNER	**Southwestern Salad, page 107,** 1 serving **grapes,** 1 cup	grilled chicken breast tenders, 3 ounces cooked **Buttery Rosemary New Potatoes** (Steam 2 to 3 small red potatoes [5 ounces]; toss with 2 teaspoons light butter, 1 teaspoon chopped fresh rosemary, and a dash of salt - ***POINTS*** value: 3.) **Sweet-Hot Cucumber Salad, page 105,** 1 serving	**Braised Lamb Shanks with Roasted Butternut Squash, page 92,** 1 serving **whole wheat French bread,** 1 ounce **steamed green beans,** 1 cup
SNACK	Weight Watchers low-fat **chocolate chip cookie,** 1 **fat-free milk,** 1 cup	cherry cheesecake fat-free **yogurt,** 1 (6-ounce) carton	pear, 1 medium **fat-free cottage cheese,** 1 cup
POINTS VALUE	***POINTS*** value for the day: 26	***POINTS*** value for the day: 28	***POINTS*** value for the day: 26

WEEK 3

One day's menu provides at least two servings of dairy and at least five servings of fruits and/or vegetables.

	MONDAY	TUESDAY	WEDNESDAY	THURSDAY
BREAKFAST	**Tomato-Basil Omelet** (Whisk together 1 large egg and 3 large egg whites, 1 tablespoon water, and a dash each of salt and pepper. Pour into a small skillet coated with cooking spray, and cook over medium heat 1 minute or until almost set. Top with ⅓ cup diced tomato, ¼ cup reduced-fat sharp Cheddar cheese, and 1 tablespoon finely chopped fresh basil; fold in half - **POINTS** value: 5.) **honeydew**, 1 cup	**oatmeal**, 1 cup cooked **blueberries**, 1 cup **fat-free milk**, 1 cup	**poached egg**, 1 large **turkey bacon**, 3 slices **reduced-calorie toast**, 2 slices	**Maple-Pecan Oatmeal** (Stir 2 tablespoons light maple syrup and 2 teaspoons chopped pecans into 1 cup hot cooked oatmeal - **POINTS** value: 4.) **fat-free milk**, 1 cup
LUNCH	**canned minestrone soup**, 1 cup **saltine crackers**, 6 **orange sections**, 1 cup **fat-free milk**, 1 cup	**lasagna**, 1 light frozen entrée **cucumber slices**, 1 cup **light ranch dressing**, 2 tablespoons **grapes**, 1 cup	**Lean and Green Pasta Salad, page 103**, 1 serving **apple**, 1 medium **fat-free milk**, 1 cup	**Turkey Club Sandwich** (Spread 2 teaspoons each of fat-free mayonnaise and Dijon mustard over 2 slices reduced-calorie bread. Place 2 ounces sliced deli turkey, 1 [¾-ounce] reduced-fat Swiss cheese slice, 2 lettuce leaves, 2 tomato slices, and 2 slices cooked turkey bacon, halved, on 1 bread slice; top with remaining bread slice - **POINTS** value: 6.) **honeydew**, 1 cup **cherry cheesecake fat-free yogurt**, 1 (6-ounce) carton
DINNER	**Turkey-Sausage Meat Loaf, page 98**, 1 serving **mashed potatoes**, ½ cup **Balsamic Sautéed Spinach, page 158**, 1 serving	**Salmon Burgers, page 113**, 1 serving **lettuce leaf and tomato slice**, 1 each **deli coleslaw**, ½ cup **baked potato chips**, 11	**baked pork loin**, 3 ounces cooked and trimmed **Buttered Grilled Corn, page 168**, 1 serving **steamed broccoli and carrots**, 1 cup	**Butternut Squash and Leek Risotto, page 82**, 1 serving **mixed salad greens**, 2 cups **light balsamic vinaigrette**, 2 tablespoons
SNACK	**Strawberry-Banana Smoothie** (Combine 1 small banana, 1 cup frozen strawberries, and 1 [6-ounce] carton strawberry fat-free yogurt; process until smooth - **POINTS** value: 3.)	**peach fat-free yogurt**, 1 (6-ounce) carton	**Currant Scones, page 30**, 1 serving **fat-free milk**, 1 cup	**raspberries**, 1 cup **pretzels**, 15 small twists
POINTS VALUE	**POINTS** value for the day: 25	**POINTS** value for the day: 28	**POINTS** value for the day: 24	**POINTS** value for the day: 25

	FRIDAY	SATURDAY	SUNDAY	
BREAKFAST	**Honey-Blueberry Yogurt** (Gently stir 1 cup blueberries into 1 [6-ounce] carton vanilla fat-free yogurt; drizzle with 1 tablespoon honey - **POINTS value: 3.**)	**oatmeal,** 1 cup cooked **turkey bacon,** 3 slices **grapefruit sections,** 1 cup	**Banana-Honey Bread, page 30,** 1 serving **light butter,** 2 teaspoons **honeydew,** 1 cup **fat-free milk,** 1 cup	
LUNCH	**Italian Steak Sandwiches, page 114,** 1 serving **orange sections,** 1 cup **cucumber slices,** 1 cup **light ranch dressing,** 2 tablespoons	**bean burrito,** 1 fast-food **apple,** 1 medium **fat-free milk,** 1 cup **baby carrots,** 10 **light ranch dressing,** 2 tablespoons	**reduced-calorie bread,** 2 slices **peanut butter,** 1 tablespoon **fruit spread,** 2 tablespoons **fat-free milk,** 1 cup **pear,** 1 medium	
DINNER	**Red Snapper with White Beans over Spinach, page 71,** 1 serving **Honey-Lime Fruit Salad** (Whisk together 1 tablespoon honey and 1 teaspoon lime juice in a small bowl; stir in 1 cup mixed fresh fruit. Sprinkle with 2 teaspoons chopped fresh mint - **POINTS value: 2.**)	**Grilled Sirloin with Adobo Aïoli, page 88,** 1 serving **saffron rice,** ½ cup **Wedge Salad with Avocado-Cilantro Dressing, page 100,** 1 serving	**Teriyaki Chicken and Orange Kebabs, page 94,** 1 serving **couscous,** ½ cup **steamed green beans,** 1 cup	
SNACK	**Chocolate–Caramel Crunch Roulade, page 39,** 1 serving **fat-free milk,** 1 cup	**Lemon Cream Pie Parfait** (Spoon half of 1 [6-ounce] carton lemon cream pie fat-free yogurt into a parfait glass. Top with ½ sheet low-fat graham cracker, crumbled; repeat layers. Dollop with ¼ cup light whipped topping - **POINTS value: 3.**)	**whole wheat crackers,** 6 **extrasharp Cheddar cheese slices,** 1 ounce	
POINTS VALUE	**POINTS** value for the day: 27	**POINTS** value for the day: 28	**POINTS** value for the day: 26	

7-Day Menu Planner

WEEK 4

GENERAL RECIPE INDEX

SUBJECT INDEX

POINTS® Value Index

0 POINTS value

1 POINTS value

2 POINTS value

About Our Recipes

Weight Watchers® *Annual Recipes for Success 2010* gives you the nutrition facts you need to stay on track. Every recipe in this book includes a **POINTS**® value per serving. For more information on Weight Watchers, see page 6.

Each recipe has a list of nutrients—including calories
(CAL), percent of calories from fat, fat, saturated fat (sat), protein (PRO), carbohydrates (CARB), dietary fiber (FIB), cholesterol (CHOL), iron, sodium (SOD), and calcium (CALC)—as well as a serving size and the number of servings. This information makes it easy for you to use the recipes for any weight-loss program that you may choose to follow. Measurements are abbreviated g (grams) and mg (milligrams). Nutritional values used in our calculations come from either The Food Processor, Version 8.9 (ESHA Research), or are provided by food manufacturers.

Numbers are based on these assumptions:

- Unless otherwise indicated, meat, poultry, and fish always refer to skinned, boned, and cooked servings.
- When we give a range for an ingredient (3 to 3½ cups flour, for instance), we calculate using the lesser amount.
- Some alcohol calories evaporate during heating; the analysis reflects this.
- Only the amount of marinade absorbed by the food is used in calculations.
- Garnishes and optional ingredients are not included in an analysis.

Safety Note: Cooking spray should never be used near direct heat. Always remove a pan from heat before spraying it with cooking spray.

A Note on Diabetic Exchanges: You may notice that the nutrient analysis for each recipe does not include Diabetic Exchanges. Most dietitians and diabetes educators are now teaching people with diabetes to count total carbohydrates at each meal and snack, rather than counting exchanges.

Almost all of our recipes can be incorporated into a diabetic diet by using the carbohydrate amount in the nutrient analysis and incorporating that into the carbohydrate amount recommended by your physician.

10 SIMPLE SIDE DISHES

Vegetable	Servings	Preparation	Cooking Instructions
Asparagus	3 to 4 per pound	Snap off tough ends. Remove scales, if desired.	To steam: Cook, covered, on a rack above boiling water 2 to 3 minutes. To boil: Cook, covered, in a small amount of boiling water 2 to 3 minutes or until crisp-tender.
Broccoli	3 to 4 per pound	Remove outer leaves and tough ends of lower stalks. Wash; cut into spears.	To steam: Cook, covered, on a rack above boiling water 5 to 7 minutes or until crisp-tender.
Carrots	4 per pound	Scrape; remove ends, and rinse. Leave tiny carrots whole; slice large carrots.	To steam: Cook, covered, on a rack above boiling water 8 to 10 minutes or until crisp-tender. To boil: Cook, covered, in a small amount of boiling water 8 to 10 minutes or until crisp-tender.
Cauliflower	4 per medium head	Remove outer leaves and stalk. Wash. Break into florets.	To steam: Cook, covered, on a rack above boiling water 5 to 7 minutes or until crisp-tender.
Corn	4 per 4 large ears	Remove husks and silks. Leave corn on the cob, or cut off kernels.	To boil: Cook, covered, in boiling water to cover 8 to 10 minutes (on cob) or in a small amount of boiling water 4 to 6 minutes (kernels).
Green beans	4 per pound	Wash; trim ends, and remove strings. Cut into 1½-inch pieces.	To steam: Cook, covered, on a rack above boiling water 5 to 7 minutes. To boil: Cook, covered, in a small amount of boiling water 5 to 7 minutes or until crisp-tender.
Potatoes	3 to 4 per pound	Scrub; peel, if desired. Leave whole, slice, or cut into chunks.	To boil: Cook, covered, in boiling water to cover 30 to 40 minutes (whole) or 15 to 20 minutes (slices or chunks). To bake: Bake at 400° for 1 hour or until done.
Snow peas	4 per pound	Wash; trim ends, and remove tough strings.	To steam: Cook, covered, on a rack above boiling water 2 to 3 minutes. Or sauté in cooking spray or 1 teaspoon oil over medium-high heat 3 to 4 minutes or until crisp-tender.
Squash, summer	3 to 4 per pound	Wash; trim ends, and slice or chop.	To steam: Cook, covered, on a rack above boiling water 6 to 8 minutes. To boil: Cook, covered, in a small amount of boiling water 6 to 8 minutes or until crisp-tender.
Squash, winter (including acorn, butternut, and buttercup)	2 per pound	Rinse; cut in half, and remove all seeds. Leave in halves to bake, or peel and cube to boil.	To boil: Cook cubes, covered, in boiling water 20 to 25 minutes. To bake: Place halves, cut sides down, in a shallow baking dish; add ½ inch water. Bake, uncovered, at 375° for 30 minutes. Turn and season, or fill; bake an additional 20 to 30 minutes or until tender.